DOCUMENTING CITYSCAPES

Nonfictions is dedicated to expanding and deepening
the range of contemporary documentary studies.
It aims to engage in the theoretical conversation
about documentaries, open new areas of scholarship,
and recover lost or marginalised histories.

Other titles in the **Nonfictions** series:

IVÁN VILLARMEA ÁLVAREZ

DOCUMENTING CITYSCAPES

Urban Change in Contemporary Non-Fiction Film

WALLFLOWER PRESS
LONDON & NEW YORK

A Wallflower Press Book
Published by
Columbia University Press
Publishers Since 1893
New York • Chichester, West Sussex
cup.columbia.edu

Cover image: *Of Time and the City* (2008) © Hurricane Films

A complete CIP record is available from the Library of Congress

ISBN 978-0-231-17452-7 (cloth : alk. paper)
ISBN 978-0-231-17453-4 (pbk. : alk. paper)
ISBN 978-0-231-85078-0 (e-book)

Columbia University Press books are printed on permanent
and durable acid-free paper.
This book is printed on paper with recycled content.
Printed in the United States of America

c 10 9 8 7 6 5 4 3 2 1
p 10 9 8 7 6 5 4 3 2 1

TABLE OF CONTENTS

ACKNOWLEDGEMENTS

The entire research and writing process of this book lasted six long years, from 2008 to 2014, during which I met many people who have helped me in many ways. The starting point of this story was my arrival at the English Department of the Universidad de Zaragoza with a FPI grant from the Spanish Ministry of Science and Research (BES-2008-007953) associated to the Research Project HUM2007-61183. There I had the pleasure of meeting the members of the research group 'Cinema, Culture and Society', as well as other postgraduate students, who soon became friends and colleagues. I would like to thank all of them for supporting me during these years, especially my supervisor Luis Miguel García Mainar, who has been an excellent editor of all the texts that make up this book.

There have been many other people who have somehow contributed to bringing this research to a successful conclusion: some have invited me to give lectures, take part in conferences or publish in academic books and journals; while others have given me access to archives, libraries and schools, have read and corrected my papers, have lent me films, or simply have given me ideas. For all these reasons, I would like to mention Sorin Alexandrescu, Marta Álvarez, Ana Maria Amaro, Thom Andersen, Steve Anker, Elvira Antón Carrillo, Tiago Baptista, María Soliña Barreiro, Charlotte Brunsdon, Josep María Caparrós Lera, Josetxo Cerdán Los Arcos, Michael Chanan, Efrén Cuevas, Paulo Cunha, Eva Darias Beautell, Max Doppelbauer, Susana Duarte, Justin D. Edwards, Dino Everett, Angelica Fenner, Georges Fournier, Paulo Granja, Hanna Hatzmann, Ángel Luis Hueso, Óscar Iglesias Álvarez, Alisa Lebow, Margarita Ledo Andión, Delphine Letort, Asunción López-Varela, Laura Montero Plata, Mariana Net, Martin Pawley, Laura Rascaroli, Michael Renov, Daniel Ribas, Jesús Rodrigo, Filipa Rosário, Inmaculada Sánchez Alarcón, José Manuel Sande, Isabel Santaolalla, Kathrin Sartingen, Ana Soares, Juan A. Suárez, Luis Urbano and Susana Viegas.

I would also like to express my infinite gratitude to all my comrades in the Cineclube de Compostela, the Tertulia Perdiguer and the film magazine *A Cuarta Parede*, because our endless debates on cinema have probably been the most important part of my film education. I am tempted to mention many other people, basically all my friends in Galicia, Zaragoza, Barcelona, Portugal, Colombia, London and Los Angeles for having accompanied me during different periods of my life and remained friends despite my absence in recent times, but that list would certainly be too long for this section. Let me then finish with a few words of thanks to my parents, who have taken me to the movies since I was a child, and are still now funding my life as an unemployed researcher; to my sister Cristina, who has taught me almost everything I know; and to my partner Teresa, who has had to endure too many cold nights alone in bed while I was writing this book.

Places, Images and Meanings

A Short Spatial Autobiography

As a child, I used to spend a few weeks every summer at my grandparents' home in Ferrol, in northern Galicia. Most times, I travelled there by car with my whole family; my father drove through the meandering roads, my mother talked for most of the trip, and my sister and I simply got bored or, at worst, felt sick. An important part of this family ritual took place when we entered the town, after crossing As Pías Bridge. In that particular spot, my mother almost always made the same comment: 'this area was full of fields before'. Then, I looked through the car window and invariably saw the same tower blocks to the left and the same warehouses to the right: everything pretty ugly, to be honest. I systematically tried to imagine those fields, but they clearly belonged to another town, a previous and missing town that I could never meet. Unconsciously, I have hitherto retained my mother's words, and now, wherever I go, I cannot help but wonder what those places would have been like in the past.

It did not take me too long to realise that space is constantly changing. One Saturday morning in the early 1990s, when I was about ten years old, a giant bulldozer began clearing the empty plot that had been in front of my house for my whole life. In the course of a decade, my childhood playground became first a construction site and then a residential area, which I never liked despite the architect's efforts to create a friendly urban environment. At the time, that empty plot was an important part of my life, although it was nothing special: a hillside full of weeds and rubbish with a narrow path that climbed up to the top, which was already another neighbourhood. The place was not particularly beautiful, but it was there, it was my everyday horizon each time I left my house. Unwittingly, I grew fond of that wasteland, and I still remember it today, when it is long gone. To me, like the fields on the outskirts of Ferrol to my mother, that empty plot is a place of memory, and I would say that my fascination with changing cityscapes comes from the awareness that everything that stands today may disappear tomorrow.

Places of Memory

Subjective spatial history depends on the feelings, emotions and experiences that we associate with certain places, which may ultimately become our places of memory. This term was coined by French historian Pierre Nora, who defined a *lieu de mémoire* as 'any significant entity, whether material or non-material in nature, which by dint of human will or the work of time has become a symbolic element of the memorial heritage of any community' (1996: xvii). Originally, Nora used this concept to refer to the places and objects in which French national memory is incarnated, meaning that places of memory should be regarded as a collective heritage. Nevertheless, the same term can also be applied to those places that have a personal significance by simply shifting perspective: once grand narratives have been overshadowed – for better or for worse – by local and short-term concerns, what was formerly understood as 'individual' and 'subjective' has recently acquired as much importance as what was formerly understood as 'collective' and 'objective', at least in its capacity to address existential issues. Therefore, our respective places of memory help us explain to ourselves who we are, where we come from and, sometimes, even where we are going.

Everything can be a place of memory, because this status only depends on the affective meaning that we project on a given space. It is an unconscious activity: we are constantly imbuing our everyday environment and the places we have visited just once with positive or negative connotations. We may feel topophilia or topophobia for them, but we have to feel something, because otherwise they would not be our places of memory. We can even consider them as 'sacred places' for each of us, at least from a Durkheimian perspective, inasmuch as they follow a similar dynamic to that observed by Jennifer Jordan in Berlin memorials:

> Many of these sites seem to have a sacred quality about them in the sense of their having been set apart from the mundane and infused with unusual powers of instruction and remembrance. The term *sacred* is perhaps problematic in this setting, but it captures the sense that these sites are literally out of the ordinary, infused with mourning and warning, with messages about right and wrong. Using the term in the Durkheimian sense also reminds us that 'by sacred things one must not understand simply those personal beings which are called gods or spirits; a rack, a tree, a spring,

a pebble, a piece of wood, a house, in a word, anything can be sacred'
(Durkheim 1965: 52). Similarly, a parking lot, a vacant building, or a
playground may also become invested with powerful meanings of mourning, atonement, and warning. (2003: 44)

Places of memory are thereby our anchors in time and space, the points of reference
from which we can shape our personality, establish our identity and counteract
the alienation resulting from contemporary processes of globalisation. They are as
real as imaginary, because they are located in both landscape and mindscape: if
they are long-standing places, we can ritually visit them, but if not, which is usually more common, we have to remember or imagine them. Their volatile nature
prevents our eternal return to these places, but there are a few tools that make
our way back easier: a picture, a postcard, a film, a gift, a souvenir, a melody, a
smell, a flavour ... in short, anything that can trigger our memory. Since moving
images occupy a prominent place on this list, we must wonder how they manage
to shape, document, recreate and even reinterpret our places of memory, wherever
they are.

A Matter of Approach

The relationship between cinema and the city has been one of the favourite subjects of film researchers in recent decades. I have been working on this issue for a
decade, in which time I have written many papers about the representation of the
city in the work of certain filmmakers and national cinemas, or simply about the
representation of a given city (2006, 2008, 2009, 2010a, 2010b, 2014a). As I pro-
gressed in my research, I realised that there already are dozens of books that deal
with the same subject (see, for example, Althabe & Comolli 1994; Barrios 1997;
Clarke 1997; Shield & Fitzmaurice 2001, 2003; Barber 2002; Jousse & Paquot
2005; AlSayyad 2006; Mennell 2008; Webber & Wilson 2008; Koeck & Roberts
2010). This bibliography has explored the possibilities of auterist, national, transnational, geographical and even architectural approaches better than I could ever
do, so I took my time to find out what else I could say about this subject. Another
book on the different ways a particular city has been depicted? No, because I
would be neither the first nor the last scholar in undertaking a similar research
(see, for example, Costa e Silva 1994; Sanders 2001; Brunsdon 2007; Wrigley
2008; Solomons 2011). Should I extend the scope of my study to all the cities in
a given country and a given national cinema? Or, better still, to all the cities in a
whole continent and its respective national cinemas? Again, I think I am too late
to do that (see Niney 1994; Mazierska & Rascaroli 2003; Everett & Goodbody

2005). Should I embrace a sociological approach to address a theoretical abstraction like the global city, the transnational city, the cosmopolitan city, or whatever else that sounds up-to-date? Well, sincerely, I have to admit that my research profile is not the most appropriate to undertake that job, which anyway has also already been done (see Krause & Petro 2003; Rodríguez Ortega 2012).

If I have learnt anything in the past few years is that the way we perceive the city in film has more to do with the evolution of cinema than with that of urbanism (see Sorlin 2005: 34–5). The meaning of an image of a place of memory will always be mediated by the formal device chosen by the filmmaker to show that particular spot. Accordingly, instead of directly interpreting the content of images, I have decided to search for their meaning in their formal features, that is, their *dispositif*, a key term that originated in French theory and has been defined by Australian critic Adrian Martin as 'a way of filming according to certain pre-established rules and concepts' (2010: 382). That is to say that I will try to decode images through forms, focusing first on the 'how' in order to then explain the 'what' and 'why'. How has the cinematic city been depicted on film? What modes of representation have been employed by filmmakers? And, above all, what do these devices mean? What are their connotations?

These preliminary questions have obviously conditioned the structure of this book, which is based on style, although this will not be the only aspect analysed. In fact, I would like to locate my discourse within several fields of study; namely, film studies, urban studies, history, aesthetics, geography, sociology and, last but not least, documentary studies. Since non-fiction film has a privileged relationship with the real, it would clearly be of special interest to know how documentary makers have depicted the city, because they create a cinematic space that, unlike fiction, never ceases to represent a real space. Of course, I am not the first researcher interested in this issue. French critic and filmmaker Jean-Louis Comolli wrote an excellent article on the representation of the city in non-fiction film for the encyclopaedia *La ville au cinéma* (2005). In that text, he analysed ten selected moments in film history associated with different periods of urban history. The following table seeks to summarise his main ideas and categories.

Concept	English Translation	Main Examples
La ville-temps	The Time-City	actuality films of the 1890s
La ville érotisée / héroïsée	The Eroticised / Heroised City	urban symphonies of the 1920s
La ville des masses	The City of Masses	*Triumph des Willens* (Leni Riefensthal, 1935)

La ville ruinée	The Ruined City	post-war documentaries
La ville coloniale	The Colonial City	*Moi, un noir* (Jean Rouch, 1958)
La ville en lutte: Mai 1968	The Struggling City: May 1968	*Grands soirs & petit matins* (William Klein, 1978)
La ville quadrillée	The Gridded City	*Faits divers* (Raymond Depardon, 1983)
La ville-souvenir	The Memory-City	*Les vivants et les morts de Sarajevo* (Radovan Tadic, 1993)
La ville-cinéma	The Film-City	*Berlin 10/90* (Robert Kramer, 1991)
La ville jouée	The Played City	*Site specific - Roma 04* (Olivo Barbieri, 2004)

In each case, Comolli describes and interprets the formal features of certain documentaries, which he uses to link significant historical periods with a type of city and a type of film device. Sometimes, he chooses his examples from the milestones of non-fiction film, but his article is actually more attentive to historical events than to cinematic forms. On the contrary, I intend to develop an analysis that starts from formal issues to later reach historical concerns. It is the opposite approach, but my aims are almost the same as Comolli's: to examine those non-fiction practices that have shaped the cinematic city in order to understand their influence on our perception of past and present cities, whether they are real or imaginary. This job has already been extensively developed regarding the urban symphonies of the 1920s (see, for example, Barrios 1997; Weihsmann 1997; Gaughan 2001; Jelavich 2001; Strathausen 2001; Barber 2002; AlSayyad 2006; Mennell 2008), but there is still some room for manoeuvre to discuss later films, as suggested by Patrick Sjöberg:

> The re-evaluation and re-contextualization of the theory and history of the city film as they relate to new technologies, new stylistic modes of presentation and new touristic sensibilities of space is well on the way – when it comes to *fiction film*. The same, however, cannot be said when it comes to my own field – the study of documentary media and, in this case, how it relates to the depiction of the city. [...] The ambition of finding new ways of articulating how these contemporary city films work in relation to the social, cultural and technological conditions of our own time is hard to find. (2011: 45, 46)

The lack of reference works devoted to exploring the representation of the current urban experience in non-fiction film opens a wide field of study, inasmuch as it allows me to fill a gap in academic criticism without leaving my main research interests: contemporary history, urban geography and non-fiction film. It is time, therefore, to accurately define the scope and topics of this book.

An Economic and Aesthetic Cycle

The whole of twentieth century documentary is too extensive for me to consider its modes of representation, as scholars such as Eric Barnouw (1993) or Bill Nichols (1991, 2001) have done. It seems more appropriate to focus on a specific period of time in order to establish a manageable corpus of films. In this sense, I have chosen the industrial and urban crisis that followed the 1973 oil shock as a starting point for this book, the time frame of which will last until the beginning of the current economic crisis in the late 2000s. Throughout this period, economic changes have left an irreversible imprint on the territory, first due to the depletion of the previous production model and then to the fleeting success of the new paradigm: the first stage, which covered the 1970s and 1980s, was characterised by urban decay and the subsequent abandonment of modernity's project; while the second stage, which spanned from the late 1980s to the late 2000s, resorted to the creative destruction of the city by private developers in order to clean up rundown areas and replace obsolete infrastructures. These renewal processes reshaped urban space from an economic perspective, causing the privatisation of public spaces, the eviction of former residents from renewed areas, the destruction of their places of memory and, overall, the loss of urban identity.

Such transition from the industrial to the post-industrial city has become a historical narrative that lies behind many films. Cinema, however, not only reflects this discourse but also contributes to its development by providing images, settings and stories that have rendered this historical process visible and have spread the socio-economic theories associated with it. The main goal of this book is therefore to identify those film devices able to explain the everyday experience of the post-industrial city, especially regarding the affective relationship established between its residents and their respective places of memory. Obviously, the reading of these films is never literal or transparent, because they are always part of a cultural discourse constructed in aesthetic terms that must be carefully decoded.

In the late 1970s, cinema in general and non-fiction in particular replaced the totalising logic of the great narratives of modernity by the particular logic of smaller narratives – such as the urban crisis or the disappearance of countless places of memory – which addressed abstract and global issues from a material and local perspective (see, for example, Ang 1992: 28; Mazierska & Rascaroli 2003: 238). In order to develop a formal analysis of these local narratives, I have arranged my case studies in three groups according to their filmic device and degree of subjectivity. Thus, the first part of this book will be devoted to documentary landscaping, a style that has updated Comolli's concept of the time-city by means of three variations that I name observational, psychogeographical and autobiographical landscaping. The films analysed in this section share a minimalist *mise-en-scène* that establishes a distancing effect with regard to the filmed space, thereby conveying both the feeling and meaning of being there. This device combines the objective observation of urban space with the simultaneous expression of its subjective experience, a dimension that will be further explored in the second part of the book, which will be focused on urban self-portraits. This subgenre pays particular attention to Comolli's memory-city, that is, a lost city made up of missing places to which we can only return through moving images. Finally, the third and last section of the book explores the subjective resonances of metafilmic strategies, which are ultimately responsible for the emergence of Comolli's film-city.

This explanation may seem a bit abstract, if not directly cryptic, because it leaves too many questions unanswered: What exactly are these three parts about? What are their case studies? Where have they been filmed? What type of cities do they depict? A small table may solve these doubts by providing a conceptual map of the formal, urban and geographic coordinates of this book.

Film Device	Case Study	City	Type of City
Observational Landscaping	*One Way Boogie Woogie / 27 Years Later* (James Benning, 2004)	Milwaukee, Wisconsin	Rust Belt City
Observational Landscaping	*Los* (James Benning, 2000)	Los Angeles, California	Global City Port City Post-Industrial City Multicultural City
Psychogeographical Landscaping	*L.A.X.* (Fabrice Ziolkowski, 1980)	Los Angeles, California	Multicultural City
Psychogeographical Landscaping	*Thames Film* (William Raban, 1986)	London, UK	Port City Post-Industrial City
Psychogeographical Landscaping	*London* (Patrick Keiller, 1994)	London, UK	Global City Multicultural City Post-Industrial City
Autobiographical Landscaping	*News from Home* (Chantal Akerman, 1977)	New York, NY	Global City Port City Post-Industrial City Multicultural City

Autobiographical Landscaping	*Lost Book Found* (Jem Cohen, 1996)	New York, NY	Global City Multicultural City
Urban Self-Portrait	*Lightning Over Braddock* (Tony Buba, 1988)	Braddock, Pennsylvania	Rust Belt Town
Urban Self-Portrait	*Roger & Me* (Michael Moore, 1989)	Flint, Michigan	Rust Belt City
Urban Self-Portrait	*Les hommes du port* (Alain Tanner, 1995)	Genoa, Italy	Port City
Urban Self-Portrait	*Of Time and the City* (Terence Davies, 2008)	Liverpool, UK	Port City Post-Industrial City
Urban Self-Portrait	*Porto da Minha Infância (Porto of My Childhood,* Manoel de Oliveira, 2001)	Porto, Portugal	Port City
Urban Self-Portrait	*My Winnipeg* (Guy Maddin, 2007)	Winnipeg, Canada	Post-Industrial City
Metafilmic Strategies	*The Decay of Fiction* (Pat O'Neill, 2002)	Los Angeles, California	Cinematic City
Metafilmic Strategies	*Los Angeles Plays Itself* (Thom Andersen, 2003)	Los Angeles, California	Global City Cinematic City Post-Industrial City Multicultural City

The two main subjects of these films are the need to document endangered cityscapes before they vanish and the memory of those that have already disappeared. In both cases, filmmakers explore the urban surface in search of their places of memory, contrasting their current appearance with their own personal memories. This narrative usually takes place in two kinds of cities: those most affected by the socio-economic paradigm shift, especially industrial and port cities, such as Milwaukee, Winnipeg, Flint, Genoa, Liverpool, Porto or the tiny Braddock; and those most favoured by the rise of the service economy, such as global, multicultural and cinematic cities, which are here represented by New York, Los Angeles and London. Any reader will note that these cities are scattered all over the Northern Hemisphere, spread across two continents and six countries. At first sight, these cities are too far from each other to establish a direct comparison among them, but the problem with this selection is just the opposite: they are not enough to cover the whole world, which nevertheless would be an overly ambitious task for this particular work.

A World-Systems Approach

In 2007, American filmmaker Travis Wilkerson wrote a film manifesto entitled 'Incomplete Notes on the Character of the New Cinema' in which he criticised what he called 'a set of anachronistic conventions dictated by the agents of commerce' (2007: n.p.). Among many other limitations that prevent a new cinema practice, he drew attention to the control role of national and generic borders: 'The new cinema refuses to recognize national borders. It identifies itself neither as fiction nor as documentary. Likewise, it is unconcerned with genre, which is useful only to the agents of commerce' (ibid.). Beyond his concern with 'the agents of commerce', Wilkerson's manifesto reveals the mentality of many independent filmmakers who work outside the traditional film industry and do not feel any attachment to national or genre traditions. These filmmakers, who are precisely those that will be studied here, often meet more fellow travellers in the international film festival circuit than in their own national cinema, as Laura Rascaroli has pointed out regarding the essay film:

> It is transnational ... because it is the cinema of international filmmakers who programmatically experiment and explore new territories, not only spatial, but existential, affective, aesthetic, communicative, political. The absence of rules in this field means that essayistic directors are in conversation with one another, rather than with established national and generic practices. (2009: 190)

A possible solution to understand the main tendencies in contemporary non-fiction film beyond national borders may be to adopt what Dudley Andrew has termed 'a "world systems" approach', which is basically interested in mapping the transnational network of mutual influences in terms of approach, narrative and visual style that has always existed in filmmaking: 'You can't study a single film, nor even a national cinema,' Andrew says, 'without understanding the interdependence of images, entertainment, and people all of which move with increasing regularity around the world' (2006: 22). From this notion, Deborah Shaw has recently argued that 'every film made has been consciously or unconsciously shaped by pre-existing cultural products from all over the world' (2013: 58), meaning that every film made is part of a global mediascape that can no longer be addressed solely from a single national perspective. After all, Arjun Appadurai's original definition of the term 'mediascape' already drew attention to the increasingly rapid circulation of all kinds of images beyond geographical, national, cultural and linguistic borders:

Mediascapes refer both to the distribution of the electronic capabilities to produce and disseminate information (newspapers, magazines, television stations, and film-production studios), which are now available to a growing number of private and public interests throughout the world, and to the images of the world created by these media. [...] What is most important about these mediascapes is that they provide (especially in their television, film, and cassette forms) large and complex repertoires of images, narratives, and ethnoscapes to viewers throughout the world, in which the world of commodities and the world of news and politics are profoundly mixed. (1996: 35)

By using a world-systems approach, my aim is to avoid those theoretical frameworks that lock researchers in a sole field of study. Why then analyse a Belgian film together with an American one, a Swiss with a British or a Portuguese with a Canadian? Because these international pairs show how the same device may be used similarly anywhere in the Western world, whether as a result of acknowledged influences or due to what Jonathan Rosenbaum has termed 'global synchronicity', that is, 'the simultaneous appearance of the same apparent taste, styles and/or themes in separate parts of the world, without any signs of these common and synchronous traits having influenced one another' (2003a: 61). Consequently, as this book is focused on style, it seems logical to analyse the evolution of a *dispositif* from one film to another, regardless of the national cinema they belong to. This choice, moreover, tries to be consistent with the global nature of the aforementioned economic cycle, which has developed at different paces in different countries since the 1970s. As we shall see in the pages that follow, the slow decline and further renewal of industrial urban areas is a global process depicted from many geographic and cinematic perspectives, whose temporal and aesthetic links will allow us to understand the way urban change has been perceived and experienced in North American and European cities.

CHAPTER ONE

On City and Cinema

From Post-Industrial City to Postmetropolis

The concept of post-industrialism refers to the transition of Western societies from an economy based on production and manufactured goods to another based on consumption and signs (see Touraine 1969; Bell 1973). The most profitable activities in this new paradigm no longer belong to the manufacturing sector but to the service one, and more specifically to the finance, insurance and real estate sectors. From the 1980s, revolutions in transport and communications have made it possible to relocate both labour and production away from urban centres, which have been abandoned or renewed according to the economic success of their respective cities: old industrial and port cities have lost their former dominant position to become urban wastelands replete with derelict factories and useless docks, while so-called global cities have been able to create spectacular cityscapes – whether simulated or restored ones – in order to attract capital and people.

The dichotomy between old and new spaces has affected every city in the world, although some have been more responsive than others, especially global cities. This term, coined by Saskia Sassen (1991), along with others such as 'the overexposed city' (Virilio 1984), 'the informational city' (Castells 1989), 'the generic city' (Koolhaas & Mau 1995) or 'the banal city' (Muñoz 2010), seek to synthesise the shifts in urban space at the end of the twentieth century. All these concepts describe an increasingly fragmented and illusory cityscape in which the old social and urban fabric has been destroyed to make way for another type of city. Its main features, according to American architectural critic Michael Sorkin, would be as follows:

> The first is the dissipation of all stable relations to local physical and cultural geography, the loosening of ties to any specific space. [...] The new city replaces the anomaly and delight of such places with a universal

11

particular, a generic urbanism inflected only by appliqué. [...] A second characteristic of this new city is its obsession with 'security', with rising levels of manipulation and surveillance over its citizenry and with a proliferation of new modes of segregation. [...] City planning has largely ceased its historic role as the integrator of communities in favor of managing selective development and enforcing distinction. [...] Finally this new realm is a city of simulations, television city, the city as theme park. This is nowhere more visible than in its architecture, in buildings that rely for their authority on images drawn from history, from a spuriously appropriated past that substitutes for a more exigent and examined present. (1992: xiii–xiv)

Sorkin's themed city leaves no room for places of memory, which seem to have disappeared as a result of what Spanish geographer Francesc Muñoz has named a process of urbanalisation: 'a system of landscape production that aims to generate simulated or cloned urban morphologies, atmospheres and environments without real temporality and spatiality' (2010: 50; my translation). By means of this concept, Muñoz specifically refers to the gradual replacement of local places shaped by a particular *zeitgeist* and *genius loci* with global spaces serially reproduced from a model which is not exactly an original but an idealised image of an original. Accordingly, cities no longer resemble each other: they rather look like an abstract ideal that exists only as an image. This means that postmodern urban planning also tends toward homogenisation: places may be different, but their appearance is increasingly similar.

Another factor to consider is the growing cinematisation of social life, a tendency by which, according to French sociologists Gilles Lipovetsky and Jean Serroy, everything – including urban centres – seems to imitate the cinematic universe (2009: 322–4). Oksana Bulgakowa (2013) has found evidence that this effect dates back to the 1920s and 1930s, at least, when cinema began to be consciously used to influence the motor behaviour of the audience. Lately, however, the cinematisation of social life has become part of a broader process in which the real is merging with its own representation: nowadays, most cityscapes are both real and imaginary, as American geographer Edward Soja has pointed out regarding the postmetropolis, a 'metaphysical reality' characterised by its regional scale and imaginary dimension (2000: 147). Soja's own definition of this key term introduces it as 'a distinctive variation on the themes of crisis-generated restructuring and geohistorically uneven development that have been shaping (and reshaping) cityscapes since the origins of urban-industrial capitalism' (2000: 148). For him, the postmetropolis is a new stage of urban evolution that arises as a consequence of the interplay between the combined processes of deterritorialisation and re-territorialisation:

> Deterritorialization involves the breaking down of Fordist worlds of pro-duction and related spatial divisions of labor, the long-standing politi-cal and discursive hegemony of the modern nation-state and traditional forms of nationalism and internationalism, and established patterns of real-and-imagined cultural and spatial identity at every scale from the lo-cal to the global. Reterritorialization is the critical response to globaliza-tion and postfordist restructuring, generating new efforts by individuals and collectivities, cities and regions, business firms and industrial sectors, cultures and nations, to reconstitute their territorial behavior, their funda-mental spatiality and lived spaces, as a means of resisting and/or adapting to the contemporary condition. (2000: 212)

Within the postmetropolis, any lived space, understood as a place of memory, may be as important for its residents as the simulated cityscapes that have extended the boundaries of the city beyond its traditional sphere of influence, because it pro-vides both individuals and collectivities with an emotional landmark that coun-teracts the loss of urban identity in an ever-changing environment. The transition from post-industrial city to postmetropolis is therefore a process marked by both objective changes and subjective perceptions, in which the physical disappearance of lived spaces and places of memory does not necessarily entail their immediate forgetting. In this regard, it is no coincidence that in recent decades social sciences and humanities have undergone a spatial turn that has put the spotlight on the role of places in shaping our worldview.

The Social Production of Space

The genealogy of the spatial turn began with a few groundbreaking works in the 1970s, among which stands out Henri Lefebvre's *The Production of Space* (1974), and later developed in the 1980s and 1990s through titles such as Michel de Cer-teau's *The Practice of Everyday Life* (1980), David Harvey's *The Condition of Postmodernity* (1989), Edward Soja's *Postmodern Geographies: The Reassertion of Space in Critical Social Theory* (1989), Mike Davis's *City of Quartz: Exca-vating the Future in Los Angeles* (1990) and Fredric Jameson's *Postmodernism, or, the Cultural Logic of Late Capitalism* (1991). All these authors coincided in highlighting space and spatiality as socially constructed concepts that condition our individual and collective identities, our social and cultural practices, and, in short, our way of being in the world.

More than a century ago, German sociologist Georg Simmel was probably the first scholar in realising that the social production of space was particularly advanced in urban environments: 'the city is not a spatial entity which entails sociological characteristics', he said, 'but a sociological entity that is formed spatially' (1971: 324). Later on, throughout the second half of the twentieth century, the perceiving subject gradually gained prominence in the process of creating space, and today we know that space is objectively and subjectively produced as a result of an endless chain of mutual influences: the territory determines the living conditions of its inhabitants, who in turn shape and reshape the territory, only to be influenced again by the forms and features that they have contributed to creating. This ontological interdependence between subject and territory was theorised by Henri Lefebvre in the 1970s by means of a 'spatial triad' that would later be used by Michel de Certeau (1980), Edward Soja (1996) or Marta Traquino (2010), among other scholars. The following excerpt contains Lefebvre's original definition of the three elements that form this triad:

> 1. *Spatial practice*: the spatial practice of a society secretes that society's space; it propounds and presupposes it, in a dialectical interaction; it produces slowly and surely as it masters and appropriates it. From the analytic standpoint, the spatial practice of a society is revealed through the deciphering of its space. What is spatial practice under neocapitalism? It embodies a close association, within perceived space, between daily reality (daily routine) and urban reality (the routes and networks which link up the places set aside for work, 'private' life and leisure). This association is a paradoxical one, because it includes the most extreme separation between the places it links together. The specific spatial competence and performance of every society member can only be evaluated empirically. 'Modern' spatial practice might thus be defined – to take an extreme but significant case – by the daily life of a tenant in a government-subsidized high-rise housing project. Which should not be taken to mean that motorways or the politics of air transport can be left out of the picture. A spatial practice must have a certain cohesiveness, but this does not imply that it is coherent (in the sense of intellectually worked out or logically conceived).
>
> 2. *Representations of space*: conceptualized space, the space of scientists, planners, urbanists, technocratic subdividers and social engineers, as of a certain type of artist with a scientific bent – all of whom identify what is lived and what is perceived with what is conceived. [...] This is the dominant space in any society (or mode of production). Conceptions

of space tend ... towards a system of verbal (and therefore intellectually worked out) signs.

    3. *Representational spaces*: space as directly *lived* through its associated images and symbols, and hence the space of 'inhabitants' and 'users', but also of some artists and perhaps of those, such as a few writers and philosophers, who *describe* and aspire to do no more than describe. This is the dominated – and hence passively experienced – space which the imagination seeks to change and appropriate. It overlays physical space, making symbolic use of its objects. Thus representational spaces may be said, though again with certain exceptions, to tend towards more or less coherent systems of non-verbal symbols and signs. (1991: 38–9)

The last of these three elements – which respectively correspond to the act of perceiving, conceiving and experiencing space – would be the main subject of this book, because it is precisely in representational spaces that cityscapes and memoryscapes merge into a subjective mindscape that includes both the experience and the expression of any lived space. It is important to note that Lefebvre explicitly wrote that representational spaces must be experienced through images, symbols and signs, that is, through different visual means of expressing those mindscapes. In theory, cinema should be one of them, but nonetheless Lefebvre disparaged its ability to depict space:

The claim is that space can be shown by means of space itself. Such a procedure (also known as tautology) uses and abuses a familiar technique that is indeed as easy to abuse as it is to use – namely, a shift from the part to the whole: metonymy. Take images, for example: photographs, advertisements, films. Can images of this kind really be expected to expose errors concerning space? Hardly. Where there is error or illusion the image is more likely to secrete it and reinforce it than to reveal it. No matter how 'beautiful' they may be, such images belong to an incriminated 'medium'. Where the error consists in a segmentation of space, moreover – and where the illusion consists in the failure to perceive this dismemberment – there is simply no possibility of any image rectifying the mistake. On the contrary, images fragment; they are themselves fragments of space. Cutting things up and rearranging them, *découpage* and *montage* – these are the alpha and omega of the art of image-making. As for error and illusion, they reside already in the artist's eye and gaze, in the photographer's lens, in the draftsman's pencil and on his blank sheet of paper. Error insinuates itself into the very objects that the artist discerns, as into the sets of objects that he selects. Wherever there is illusion, the optical and visual world plays an integral and integrative, active and passive, part in it. It fetishizes abstraction and imposes it as the norm. It detaches the pure form from its impure content – from lived time, everyday time, and from bodies with their opacity and solidity, their warmth, their life and their death. After its fashion, the image kills. In this it is like all signs. Occasionally, however, an artist's tenderness or cruelty transgresses the limits of the image. Something else altogether may then emerge, a truth and a reality answering to criteria quite different from those of exactitude, clarity, readability and plasticity. If this is true of images, moreover, it must apply equally well to sounds, to words, to bricks and mortar, and indeed to signs in general. (1991: 96–7)

This passage has been widely discussed because it denies film the possibility of generating representational spaces. In order to overcome this contradiction, some film scholars have turned this argument around, whether developing another reasoning to state exactly the opposite, as Michael Chanan does, or using this critique to claim a film aesthetics more committed to the material spatialities of actual cities, as Richard Koeck and Les Roberts suggest:

Just because the shot is indeed an abstraction, it becomes possible, through the recombinations of montage, to transgress and transcend its limits by conjoining images. Film thus becomes a way of reconstituting and reconstructing space. (Chanan 2007: 79)

Rather than reading this as a dismissal of film *per se* (where the valorization of lived space negates any possibility of a critical geography of film and urbanism), it is more instructive to look upon this critique in terms of its capacity to incite and problematize further the explicit nature of the relationship between the city and the moving image, as well as to explore the potential for an *anti-spectacular* aesthetic of the city in film: a strategy which, as argued above, demands a process of re-engagement with the constitutive and material spatialities from which these and other forms of urban projection are abstracted. (Koeck & Roberts 2010: 3)

Chanan and Koeck and Roberts politely disagree with Lefebvre because they do not want to refute his whole theory, but only dissent regarding the potential of cinema to produce representational spaces. Indeed, Koeck and Roberts imply that some aesthetics could be more appropriate than others to depict space. Nobody knows what kind of film Lefebvre had in mind when he wrote his controversial passage, but it had necessarily to be prior to the mid-1970s, that is, prior to the spatial turn and to the case studies of this book. Accordingly, we can interpret his critique as a challenge and try to find those film devices that aspire to do more than simply describe space.

Space and Place

Before going any further, it is necessary to clarify the difference between space and place from a theoretical point of view. To begin with, Michel de Certeau has provided us with an abstract definition inspired by geometry:

> A place is an instantaneous configuration of positions. It implies an indication of stability. A space exists when one takes into consideration vectors of direction, velocities, and time variables. Thus space is composed of intersections of mobile elements. It is in a sense actuated by the ensemble of movements deployed within it. (1984: 117)

De Certeau seems to say that a place is a fixed, defined and stable point in the territory, while a space is a wider area whose size may vary depending on which variables are considered. Nevertheless, this definition does not resolve all doubts: for example, how is it possible to configure the positions that give rise to a place? According to Marta Traquino, 'a place emerges from space due to its inscribed experience and memory' (2010: 57; my translation). In her book *A Construção do Lugar pela Arte Contemporânea* (*The Construction of Place in Contemporary Art*) she later explains that 'any inhabited place is associated with relationships and experiences that produce memories, which ultimately singularise that particular location when they are shared' (Traquino 2010: 65; my translation). Place is thereby distinguished from space by its meaning, as French anthropologist Marc Augé has pointed out: 'place – anthropological place – is a principle of meaning for the people who live in it, and also a principle of intelligibility for the person who observes it' (1995: 52). Thus, it is the perceiving subject, the anonymous individual, that creates meaning from his/her own everyday experience, as Soja has argued:

> This process of producing spatiality or 'making geographies' begins with the body, with the construction and performance of the self, the human subject, as a distinctively spatial entity involved in a complex relation with our surroundings. On the one hand, our actions and thoughts shape the

spaces around us, but at the same time the larger collectively or socially produced spaces and places within which we live also shape our actions and thoughts in ways that we are only beginning to understand. (2000: 6)

The issue of how we relate to our everyday environment was first addressed by American urban planner Kevin Lynch in *The Image of the City* (1960), a work in which he aimed to explain the way people give meaning to urban surroundings. In that book, Lynch coined the term 'environmental image', which would later become a key concept for behavioural geography:

> Environmental images are the result of a two-way process between the observer and his environment. The environment suggests distinctions and relations, and the observer – with great adaptability and in the light of his own purposes – selects, organizes, and endows with meaning what he sees. The image so developed now limits and emphasizes what is seen, while the image itself is being tested against the filtered perceptual input in a constant interacting process. Thus the image of a given reality may vary significantly between different observers. (1960: 6)

Lynch gave an active role to the observer, who is responsible for creating his/her own environmental images. This process, known as cognitive mapping, enables people to establish their everyday itineraries through the city by combining individual and social perceptions. It should be taken into account, however, that these environmental images are basically individual, inasmuch as there are as many of them as there are observers. What happens then when we try to share our subjective perceptions?

Cinema can help to establish a common perception because it first expresses the filmmaker's environmental images and then offers them to the audience, who may interpret them literally (as if they were the only possible way to represent a given place), differently (changing their original meaning) or complementarily (contrasting the filmmaker's images with their own). This is the way cinema individualises space and creates place: if a particular spot was not a place of memory before having been filmed, it may become one if preserved as a moving image. In conclusion, while space changes over time, a place – any place – may remain in memory after having disappeared, especially when it has been recorded by a film camera. Once the differences between these two concepts have been clarified, the next step would be to know what film devices are more appropriate to simultaneously express the subjective and collective perception of places of memory.

The City in Film

Film studies has traditionally addressed the presence of the city in film in terms of representation: overall, the city is understood as an urban text inside a cinematic text (see Shiel 2001: 3; Mazierska & Rascaroli 2003: 2). Beyond this approach, cinema has recently begun to be studied as 'a technology of place', that is, as a medium able to produce spatiality through the set of its creative tasks – namely, location filming, *mise-en-scène*, framing, lightning and editing (see Brunsdon 2010: 94). Edward Dimendberg, for instance, wrote a highly influential book entitled *Film Noir and the Spaces of Modernity* (2004), in which he analysed the evolution of American urban planning from 1939 to 1959 in parallel with the development of the film noir cycle. This work, among others, has inspired a new method of reading films summarised by Richard Koeck and Les Roberts as follows: 'one that moves towards seeing film not only as a genre-dependent *text*, but also as a rich *map* of socio-cultural, political, economic and, of course, architectural discourses' (2010: 10).

The map metaphor has led Teresa Castro to compare 'cinema's exploration of urban space' with a 'form of visual mapping' (2010: 144). According to her, 'the coupling of eye and instrument that distinguishes cartography's observation of space is not so distant from the one that determines cinema's careful coding and scaling of the world' (2010: 145). She has distinguished three different formal strategies through which urban space may be mapped:

> The first is linked to a certain topographic fascination, if not a real *topophilia*, in the sense of 'love of place'. In this sense, the notion of mapping refers less to a disciplinary instrument of visual domination than to a means of self-discovery. [...] Such a topographic appeal often goes hand in hand with a second formal procedure, concerning the seemingly *descriptive* motivation of the images in question, made evident by such camera movements as the panning shot or the travelling shot. In this second case, the notion of mapping evoked is certainly more conventional, since mapping as a cultural technology often worked as a way of cataloguing the important features of the earth's surface. [...] Finally, a third formal strategy would be *surveying,* either by means of walking – a pre-eminent spatial practice – or by looking from above. (Ibid.)

Each of these strategies is first and foremost 'an act of discourse production', as Colin McArthur has said, because they ultimately express the filmmaker's position regarding the filmed space (1997: 40). Consequently, the resulting images may have a historical, identity or simply expressive value according to the filmmaker's agenda. Since the meaning of a city usually shifts from one film to another – and from an observer to another – the meaning of a film device will always depend on the context in which it is used and, above all, on the purposes it serves.

The Historical Value of Film

When considering the historiographical value of fiction and documentary film, several theorists have denied the ontological differences between them. Bill Nichols, for example, has stated that 'even the most whimsical of fictions gives evidence of the culture that produced it and reproduces the likenesses of the people who perform within it' (2001: 1). For this reason, he distinguishes between 'documentaries of wish-fulfillment', which would be what everyone calls fiction, and 'documentaries of social representation', which would correspond to non-fiction (2001: 1, 2). Drawing on the permeability between both domains, a few historians began to interpret film works as signs of the collective representations and manipulations through which societies imagine and stage themselves (see, for example, Sorlin 1980, 1991; Lagny 1992; Hueso 1998; Sand 2002; Bulgakowa 2013). Among them was Marc Ferro, who in the late 1970s explicitly suggested studying film as 'source and agent of history' in order to undertake 'the historical reading of a film and the cinematographic reading of history' (1988: 14, 19). His main aim was to develop 'a counteranalysis of society' that challenged 'the assertions of rulers', 'the schemas of theorists' and 'the analysis of the [political] opposition' (1988: 28, 29). He invited researchers to 'go back to the images' and pay attention to 'the choice of themes, the tastes of an era, production necessities, the strength of the writing, and the creator's omissions', because he thought that the true historical reality of a film can be found in that kind of detail (1988: 29, 47–8). He thereby reminded us that films whose action is contemporaneous with their filming process are able to record, preserve and reproduce 'the real image of the past' (1988: 48).

If we apply this historical approach to urban documentaries, we will have an extensive archive of old spaces and spatialities; that is, a repository of authentic visual traces of the past and of their contemporary perception. It must be taken into account that any image, as Nichols has said, is 'a document of what once stood before the camera as well as of how the camera represented them' (2001: 36), which means that cinema is able to simultaneously preserve an objective and a subjective record of urban spaces. The device chosen to film a given place can therefore indicate the way it was perceived in the past, what its collective or subjective meaning was, and what the filmmaker wanted to express by filming it through that specific device.

Among the historians who have further developed these ideas, Robert Rosenstone stands out by having claimed the filmmakers' right to write history through images: 'History need not be done on the page. It can be a mode of thinking that utilizes elements other than the written word: sound, vision, feeling, montage' (1995: 11). Contrary to Ferro, Rosenstone was not as interested in films set in the present as in those that offer a creative reworking of the past:

> The limitations of the standard film became obvious as I encountered a far more interesting kind of historical work, one which uses the medium to revision, even reinvent History. This is what I call the postmodern history film, a work that, refusing the pretense that the screen can be an unmediated window onto the past, foregrounds itself as a construction. Standing somewhere between dramatic history and documentary, traditional history and personal essay, the postmodern film utilizes the unique capabilities of the media to create multiple meanings. Such works do not, like the dramatic feature or the documentary, attempt to recreate the past realistically. Instead they point to it and play with it, raising questions about the very evidence on which our knowledge of the past depends, creatively interacting with its traces. (1995: 12)

Symptomatically, many of the postmodern history films mentioned by Rosenstone belong to the non-fiction field, such as *Sans soleil* (Chris Marker, 1982), *Far from Poland* (Jill Godmilow, 1984), *Shoah* (Claude Lanzmann, 1985), *Surname Viet Given Name Nam* (Trinh T. Minh-ha, 1989) or *History and Memory: For Akiko and Takashige* (Rea Tajiri, 1991). The most remarkable feature of these works is that their directors share a subjective impulse to take part in the process of writing history as witnesses, narrators and even demiurges: they do not believe in the existence of a single official account and a single *mise-en-scène* to tell it, so they are willing to explore the formal possibilities of film to search and reflect on historical truth. Again, if we export this attitude to urban documentaries, we will realise that many filmmakers not only intend to document contemporary cityscapes or recover those that have already disappeared, but also aim to produce them as images in order to understand their historical significance. The audience, meanwhile, can also use its own subjectivity to appropriate, extend and even transform the meaning of these cinematic cityscapes to the point of turning them into symbolic places within the historical imaginary. In this regard, the act of visually documenting a space is not so far from the act of producing spatiality.

The Identity Value of Film

Many urban documentaries also address the creation of place and spatiality through the combined action of memory and identity. In these films, places are filmed for what they mean to a specific community, and that will to meaning is it-self historical for what it expresses about our time. Gilles Lipovetsky and Jean Ser-roy have pointed out that, despite being dominated by a presentist logic, our time is mainly characterised by the revitalisation of the past and the claim of identities based on collective memory: 'within societies in which futuristic systems are no longer credible, roots, poles of particularist identification and those community links that serve to counteract the dispersion, confusion and isolation of individuals have gained priority' (2009: 179; my translation). Two decades earlier, David Har-vey had already explained that this 'preoccupation with identity, with personal and collective roots' was related to the 'widespread insecurity in labour markets, technological mixes [and] credit systems' of the 1980s (1989: 87). Arguably, the social answer to the speeding of economic and technological shifts was the search for an anchor in time and space that gave some certainty to the subject.

Identity is usually rooted in class, gender, ethnic, cultural, national, linguistic or religious criteria. However, as Stuart Hall has warned, cultural identities are not 'eternally fixed in some essentialised past ... they are subject to the continuous "play" of history, culture and power' (1989: 70). This lack of historical stability forces people to adapt their identity to the evolution of the *zeitgeist* in an endless process in which memory, whether collective or individual, helps to take a stand regarding dominant social criteria: on the one hand, it serves to recover the knowl-edge gained in past experiences, and on the other hand, it offers a wide range of previous models that we can follow or reject. Memory itself, moreover, can be spatialised in places of memory, in which the visible signs of historical becoming are combined with the subjective perception of the passage of time. The latter can be visually expressed by simultaneously depicting a place as it is and as it has been, merging its current appearance with its former avatars. In these cases, cinema documents both the place and its historical heritage, which can be subsequently used for identity purposes. A place is thereby much more than what it is or what it has been, because it can symbolise something – whatever – that refers to the identity-building process of a given individual or community.

The Expressive Value of Film

In the first half of the twentieth century, most urban documentaries depicted the industrial city from the outside, beginning with those titles that turned trains entering urban space into an icon of modernity, from *L'arrivée d'un train à La Ciotat* (*Arrival of a Train at La Ciotat*, Auguste and Louis Lumière, 1896) to *Berlin: Die Sinfonie der Grosstadt* (*Berlin, Symphony of a Great City*, Walter Ruttmann, 1927). This mode of representation ceased to be dominant in the second half of the century, when modernist filmmakers chose to show the city from the inside, as Eulàlia Iglesias has explained:

> It is in modern contemporary cinema, however, that many directors convert a city, their city, into a protagonist that is not only objective or artistic but above all emotional, the space where they can build fictions with autobiographical echoes. Tsai Ming-liang – Taipei, Woody Allen – New York, Federico Fellini – Rimini and Roma, Yasujiro Ozu – Tokyo, and almost all the *nouvelle vague* with Paris create indissoluble alliances between life, emotions and the urban domain. (2008: 280)

Despite being the dominant trend, there is a slight lag between the subjective turn in fiction and in non-fiction film: while the former began in the 1950s and 1960s, once the classical and neorealist paradigms were exhausted, the latter could not develop until the 1980s, because the neorealist paradigm could only be fully achieved in documentary film after the emergence of lighter cameras and synchronised tape recorders in the early 1960s. Accordingly, the representation of the city as a subjective, lived space, in which the experience of place is physical, tactile and almost corporeal, is relatively recent in non-fiction film. Nowadays, urban documentary makers usually introduce themselves as residents, visitors, tourists or travellers in order to emphasise their personal ties to the depicted space, whether they are more or less intense. The resulting works are thus marked by the filmmaker's position regarding the cityscape, inasmuch as they express a series of environmental images and the feelings associated with them.

The subjective turn in non-fiction film has been fuelled by the growing interest in subjectivity among social scholars since the early 1980s. At that time, Michel Foucault coined the concept of 'technologies of the self', which encompasses a wide range of practices that 'permit individuals to effect by their own means or with the help of others a certain number of operations on their own bodies and souls, thoughts, conduct, and way of being, so as to transform themselves in order to attain a certain state of happiness, purity, wisdom, perfection, or immortality' (1988: 18). 'The care of the self' became the main topic of Foucault's latest works, in which he dated back to the ancient Greece and the origins of Christianity in the search for historical examples of these technologies, from Stoic correspondence to Christian confession (1984, 1988). These practices have been adopted by many filmmakers in their autobiographical works, giving rise to non-fiction subgenres such as the film correspondence, the video confession or the self-portrait film. This interest in the filmmaker's privacy was also fuelled by 'the culture of narcissism', a new stage of individualism that American historian Christopher Lasch (1979) regarded as a negative effect of the social evolution of the United States. Despite the opposition between his interpretation and Foucault's, which praised the care of the self as a human being's achievement, both actually addressed similar phenomena that emerged from the same historical turning point: the breakdown of the master narratives of modernity.

Already in 1983 the French philosopher Gilles Lipovetsky had noticed that the rise of narcissism entailed a series of features that were then also spreading in documentary film: 'the predominance of the individual over the universal, the psychological over the ideological, communication over politicisation, diversity over homogeneity [and] permissiveness over coercion' (1986: 115; my translation). In his book *L'ère du vide. Essais sur l'individualisme contemporain (The Age of Emptiness: Essays on Contemporary Individualism)*, he described postmodern Western societies as 'hungry for identity, difference, conservation, peace [and] personal fulfilment' because 'the trust and faith in the future are dissolved' and, consequently, 'people want to live right away, here and now, and stay young instead of forging a new man' (1986: 9; my translation). The crisis of the old systems of meaning based on egalitarianism and confidence in progress involved, according to him, 'a massive abandonment of the *res publica* and particularly of political ideologies', which finally resulted in the current hegemony of individualist discourses (1986: 217; my translation). This eclipse of the collective project of modernity was later explained by Polish sociologist Zygmunt Bauman through the metaphor of 'the melting of solids':

> The task of constructing a new and better order to replace the old and defective one is not presently on the agenda – at least not on the agenda of that realm where political action is supposed to reside. The 'melting of solids', the permanent feature of modernity, has therefore acquired a new meaning, and above all has been redirected to a new target – one of the paramount effects of that redirection being the dissolution of forces which could keep the question of order and system on the political agenda. The solids whose turn has come to be thrown into the melting pot and which are in the process of being melted at the present time, the time of fluid modernity, are the bonds which interlock individual choices in collective projects and actions. (2000: 5–6)

In this context, the subjective turn of documentary film can be considered an adaptation of contemporary non-fiction filmmakers to the postmodern *zeitgeist*. Laura Rascaroli, for instance, has interpreted it as 'a reflection and a consequence of the increased fragmentation of the human experience in the postmodern, globalised world, and of our need and desire to find ways to represent such fragmentation, and to cope with it' (2009: 4). Beyond these concerns, however, filmmakers continue to be interested in exploring new ways of achieving authenticity, as well as in taking part in public debates, two aims that have significantly benefited from the spread of the autobiographical approach. Thus, since the 1980s, subjectivity has become a guarantee of accuracy because it seems more credible than any attempt at objectivity: 'once the other side of the camera is exposed and the filmmaker implicated,' Jim Lane has written, 'the documentary can more truthfully depict reality' (2002: 35). This means that 'faithfulness to the facts in the camera images' has been replaced by 'honesty about what happens behind the camera', as stated by Josep María Catalá and Josetxo Cerdán (2007/8: 25). The categorical statements of expository documentaries, embodied by what Bill Nichols called the 'Voice-of-God' or 'voice-of-authority' (2001: 105), have given way to 'an awareness that one cannot encapsulate everything, and that the little that can be said should be done from the humility (in some cases) of someone who knows his/her limitations' (De Pedro 2010: 402). Hence postmodern cinematic representations of the historical world primarily focus on our perception of it, that is, on the subject and not on the object, or more exactly on the object (the historical world) through the subject (the filmmaker).

Voyeurs, Walkers and Drivers

Of all the possible roles adopted by urban documentary makers, there are three that will be of special interest for this book: the *voyeur*, the walker and the driver. Their respective gazes at the city entail a series of socio-cultural connotations that automatically condition the meaning of any image taken from their point of view, that is, from above, from below and from a moving car. As these concepts are a bit slippery, it seems appropriate to end this first chapter with Michel de Certeau's and Pablo Ocampo Failla's analysis of their main features.

De Certeau places the *voyeur* in an elevated position relative to street level, from which it 'makes the complexity of the city readable, and immobilizes its opaque mobility in a transparent text' (1984: 92). Up there, and despite being physically away from the city, the *voyeur* has the feeling of seeing it in its entirety and being able to read on its surface. On the contrary, the walker remains at street level, in a position that is 'below the thresholds at which visibility begins' (1984:

93). This means that those who walk are unable to see the spaces they inhabit and to read the text they write with their everyday itineraries. Nevertheless, walkers have a knowledge of the city based on experience that complements and counter-acts that of the *voyeur*. In fact, their physical immersion in the urban fabric allows them to transform 'each spatial signifier into something else' (1984: 98). Such an opposition between *voyeurs* and walkers is even political, because the former clearly hold a position of power: they can rule the city from the distance, with-out actually experiencing it, while walkers can only claim their right to the city by temporarily appropriating the places through which they walk every day. For this reason, the walker's gaze is usually associated with democratic values, while the *voyeur*'s gaze rather suggests the authoritarian mentality of demiurges and dictators. Furthermore, these two perspectives also refer to the concepts of 'hard city' and 'soft city', which respectively correspond to Lefevbre's representations of space and representational spaces: as explained by François Penz and Andong Lu, 'aerial shots of cities offer a God's eye perspective belonging to the "hard city" … associated with a world of urban planning, density and statistics. By contrast, the on-the-ground shots allow for the "soft city" to reveal the city of illusions and nightmares' (2011: 15).

For its part, the driver's gaze shares some features with the walker's and the *voyeur*'s, although it actually produces a completely different urban experience: on the one hand, drivers, like walkers, are located at street level, where they also create a moving text; but on the other hand, drivers are as far away from the city as *voyeurs*, because they are isolated inside their vehicle. From that position, driv-ers develop an unconscious indifference to the urban environment that ultimately causes their gradual distancing from the city, as Ocampo Failla has described: firstly, drivers experience a decrease in their ability to look at their surroundings; secondly, they lose their tactile perception; and finally, they become unable to rec-ognise identities because they end up perceiving everything as a two-dimensional image (see Traquino 2010: 18–19).[1]

At first sight, there seems to be a kind of gradation between the *voyeur*'s, the driver's and the walker's gazes: the first should be the more abstract, objective and manipulative, while the last should be the more specific, subjective and reliable, but this dichotomy is a fallacy. Urban documentary makers have indistinctly ad-opted these three roles with a wide variety of results, although it is true that the driver's and the walker's gazes have been more frequently used in the last decades, because both allow cinema to depict the city from the inside – indeed, the walker's gaze is the one that best conveys the physical, tactile and corporeal experience of the contemporary city. Anyway, these three viewpoints have been freely com-bined by non-fiction filmmakers to document the transition from post-industrial city to postmetropolis, taking advantage of their implicit meanings to produce a visual discourse about the effects of new spatialities on places of memory. As we shall see below, the way film devices incorporate these viewpoints can strengthen the historical, identity and/or expressive value of images, thereby offering a more complex insight of urban change in the last decades.

NOTE

1   Ocampo Failla's analysis was originally published in his book *Periferias: La Heterotopia del No-Lugar* (2002).

CHAPTER TWO

Documentary Film at the Turn of the Century

One of the most surprising and unexpected film tendencies at the beginning of the twenty-first century was the return of documentaries to movie theatres after a couple of decades dominated by hyperbolic fiction. A quick look at the list of the hundred highest-grossing documentaries in the US between 1982 and 2013 reveals that more than half belong to the twenty-first century, including the first block-buster documentary in history, *Fahrenheit 9/11* (Michael Moore, 2004), whose box-office profits surpassed the symbolic barrier of $100 million.[1] The other titles on the list grossed between one and ten million dollars, which is not too much for a fiction film, but it is certainly much more than a filmmaker expects to earn with a project of this kind. In fact, before the 1990s, documentaries hardly made much money in movie theatres, basically because their distribution seemed restricted to television. Let us take the five most-watched documentaries in the 1980s. They were: an oddity in movie listings, *Koyaanisqatsi: Life Out of Balance* (Godfrey Reggio, 1982); two biographies of celebrities, *Vincent: The Life and Death of Vincent van Gogh* (Paul Cox, 1987) and *Imagine: John Lennon* (Andrew Solt, 1988); and two documentaries that became film events due to their unusual prof-its, *That's Dancing* (Jack Haley Jr., 1985) and *Roger & Me* (Michael Moore, 1989). Since then, there have been other milestones in the recent economic his-tory of documentary film in the US – *Paris is Burning* (Jennie Livingston, 1990), *Madonna: Truth or Dare* (Alek Keshishian, 1991), *Hoop Dreams* (Steve James, Frederick Marx & Peter Gilbert, 1994), *Bowling for Columbine* (Michael Moore, 2002), *La marche de l'empereur* (*March of the Penguins*, Luc Jacquet, 2005), etc. – but these box office successes are just the tip of the iceberg, a brief sample of the global increase of non-fiction in the big screen.

The return of documentary film to movie theatres is, according to Michael Chanan, a reaction to 'the inadequacies of mainstream cinema', 'the inanities of

100 Highest Grossing Documentaries in the US (1982–2013)
Distribution by Decade

Decade	Number of Films	Percent Increase
1980s	5	-
1990s	16	320%
2000s	47	294%
2010–2013	32	-

Source: Box Office Mojo, March 8, 2014.

100 Highest Grossing Documentaries in the US (1982-2013)
Distribution by Year

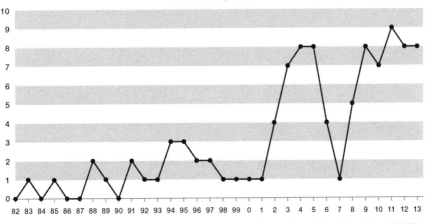

Source: Box Office Mojo, March 8, 2014.

television' and the lowering of production costs after the emergence of digital video (2007: 7). This first explanation has been extended by Lipovetsky and Serroy, who have related the rise of documentary to the disappearance of 'major collective references' and 'the main visions of historical future' (2009: 147; my translation). In this context, according to them, non-fiction film would serve to demystify the power discourse and to satisfy our need to feel free in – and be critical of – a system that forces us to consume everything (2009: 150). For this reason, documentary arguably fulfils a social function within the contemporary mediascape, as Chanan has highlighted: it 'speaks to the viewer as citizen, as a member of the social collective, [and] as putative participant in the public sphere' (2007: 16). It seems, therefore, that documentary film is here to stay as long as there are movie theatres, although these could disappear overnight without anyone noticing it, like silent cinema, drive-in theatres or videotapes before them. Anyway, let us leave this issue to researchers specialised in the exhibition sector and focus instead on contemporary documentary theory.

Aesthetic Functions and Modes of Representation

Just as the cinematic city has traditionally been understood as a simple representation of its real counterpart, non-fiction film has also been regarded as a reflection of reality. This approach, however, has shifted in the last decades to the extent that nowadays most film theorists address documentary as a discourse on the real, a line of argument constructed from visual materials that ultimately expresses a point of view on the historical world (see, for example, Nichols 1991: 111; Plantinga 1997: 83–6; Weinrichter 2004: 21–2, 2010: 270–1). In this sense, documentary film has developed several ways to fulfil its social function, as Nichols has pointed out:

> Some documentaries set out to *explain* aspects of the world to us. They analyze problems and propose solutions. They try to account for aspects of the historical world by means of their representations. They seek to mobilize our support for one position instead of another. Other documentaries *invite* us to *understand* aspects of the world more fully. They *observe,* describe, or poetically *evoke* situations and interactions. They try to enrich our understanding of aspects of the historical world by means of their representations. They complicate our adherence to positions by undercutting certainty with complexity or doubt. (2001: 165)

This passage indirectly echoes the four tendencies or aesthetic functions attributed to documentary film by Michael Renov: 'to record, reveal or preserve', 'to persuade or promote', 'to analyze or interrogate' and 'to express' (1993: 21; 2004: 74). With the sole exception of the second one, the other three lead to what has been named the historical, identity and expressive value of film. In principle, the correspondence between the first tendency – to record, reveal or preserve – and the historical value is quite clear, as well as between the fourth one – to express – and the expressive value: regarding the former, Renov has explained that 'the emphasis here is on the replication of the historical real, the creation of a second-order reality cut to the measure of our desire – to cheat death, stop time, restore loss'; while regarding the latter, he has stressed the importance of 'the ability to evoke emotional response or induce pleasure in the spectator by formal means' (1993: 25, 35) to establish any argument about the historical world. On the contrary, the relation between the third aesthetic function – to analyse or interrogate – and the identity value is a bit more complicated: Renov understands analysis 'as the cerebral reflex of the record/reveal/preserve modality' (1993: 30), which suggests that documentary film usually invites viewers to think and create meaning beyond what it shows. From this perspective, a place, an object, an event or even a manner of speaking may have an identity value in certain contexts, depending on the filmmaker's aims and the audience's sensibility.

These four aesthetic functions are not exclusive of a single type of documentary, and indeed they usually overlap each other. Nevertheless, some modes of representation are more appropriate than others to develop them: for instance, observational documentaries appear particularly suited to record live events, expository documentaries to persuade the audience, reflexive documentaries to analyse representational issues, and performative documentaries to express the filmmaker's subjectivity. These pairings are actually an attempt to link Renov's four aesthetic functions with Nichols' six documentary modes of representation, which have become the best-known typology of non-fiction film since they were first defined more than two decades ago.

Initially, Nichols only distinguished four documentary modes: the expository, the observational, the interactive and the reflexive (1991: 32–75). Later on, however, he had to increase those four modes to six in order to identify more precisely the new subjective strategies that emerged at the end of the twentieth century: while the expository and observational modes remained the same, the interactive changed its name to participatory, the reflexive was divided into two different categories – the poetic and the reflexive – and finally the performative mode was added to the list (2001: 99–138). Both the original typology and its renewed version established a historical succession of modes in which the new coexist with the old without replacing them, as Nichols has always said (1991: 23; 2001: 33–4). His own table is still today the best way to summarise this evolution:

Documentary Modes
Chief Characteristics
(Deficiencies)

Hollywood fiction [1910s]:
fictional narratives of imaginary worlds
(absence of 'reality')

Poetic documentary [1920s]:
reassemble fragments of the world poetically
(lack of specificity, too abstract)

Expository documentary [1920s]:
directly address issues in the historical world
(overly didactic)

Observational documentary [1960s]:
eschew commentary and reenactment; observe things as they happen.
(lack of history, context)

Participatory documentary [1960s]:
interview or interact with subjects; use archival film to retrieve history
(excessive faith in witnesses, naïve history, too intrusive)

Reflexive documentary [1980s]:
question documentary form, defamiliarize the other modes
(too abstract, lose sight of actual issues)

Performative documentary [1980s]:
stress subjective aspects of a classically objective discourse
(loss of emphasis on objectivity may relegate such films to the avant-garde; 'excessive' use of style)

(Nichols 2001: 138)

This typology has somehow inspired this book's division in three parts: just as these documentary modes represent 'different concepts of historical representation' (1991: 23), the formal devices discussed below represent, in turn, different ways of addressing a given historical process, the aforementioned transition from post-industrial city to postmetropolis. This time, there is no point in making a table to show the ascription of each case study to a documentary mode or another, because this information is not essential to understand the way these film devices depict urban space and create spatiality. Furthermore, almost no case study fits into one single category. The only exception would be *Los* (James Benning, 2000), whose *mise-in-scène* is clearly observational. In contrast, the rest of the case studies belong to several modes of representation at the same time: *London* (Patrick Keiller, 1994) combines expository, observational and reflexive strategies; *News from Home* (Chantal Akerman, 1977) and *Lost Book Found* (Jem Cohen, 1996) are simultaneously observational and performative works, *Roger & Me* has been regarded as an expository, participatory, reflexive and even performative documentary, *Porto da Minha Infância* (*Porto of My Childhood*, Manoel de Oliveira, 2001) and *My Winnipeg* (Guy Maddin, 2007) are themselves hybrids of documentary and fiction, and so on, to name but a few examples. Knowing to which documentary mode a film belongs is certainly useful to analyse it, but there is a more important reason to take into account Nichols' typology in this book: the evolution from expository to performative mode entails a shift from objectivity to subjectivity that also appears in the sequence formed by documentary landscaping, urban self-portraits and metafilm essays. In fact, the inherent tensions between objectivity and subjectivity have left a deep imprint on most case studies, which have been heavily influenced by the objectivity crisis and the subsequent subjective turn that non-fiction film has undergone over the last few decades.

The Objectivity Crisis

The idea of truth in documentary film has recently evolved beyond the concept of visible evidence, to the point that the strict authenticity of images no longer ensures the consistency of non-fiction discourse. Nowadays, the audience knows that truthfulness can be formally constructed through old rhetorical tricks: nobody believes that the omniscient voice of the classical expository mode is fully impartial and reliable, not even that the observational *mise-en-scène* is completely transparent. Since the 1970s, no expert or authority can guarantee anything anymore, because now any statement must come from personal, subjective experience. This is the reason why the concepts to which documentary film has historically been related – 'fullness and completion, knowledge and fact, explanations of the social world and its motivating mechanisms' – have been replaced by their opposites: 'incompleteness and uncertainty, recollection and impression, images of personal worlds and their subjective construction' (Nichols 1993: 174).

The so-called objectivity crisis has caused a sea change in the way contemporary documentary makers strive to produce a truthful discourse. Overall, they have resorted to three main strategies: the on-camera presence of the film apparatus, the use of the first-person singular and the systematic subjectification of discourse. The first strategy is directly related to the ethics of the gaze, which is currently based on the honesty and transparency with which filmmakers show the encounter between the real, the film apparatus and themselves (see Andreu 2009: 146). The second, in turn, involves a change of narrative position: 'the filmmaker comes to the fore,' Laura Rascaroli says, 'uses the pronoun "I", admits to his or her partiality and purposefully weakens her or his authority by embracing a contingent, personal viewpoint' (2009: 5). Finally, the third strategy establishes a new argumentative logic: the more subjective a statement is, the more reliable it seems, because it is the truth according to the speaker; and the more the audience knows about the speaker, the easier it is to know if the speaker is trustworthy. This reasoning may border on tautology and even fallacy, but at least it warns that truth is never universal, but rather biased. Consequently, 'subjectivity itself compels belief', as Nichols has argued: 'instead of an aura of detached truthfulness we have the honest admission of a partial but highly significant, situated but impassioned view' (2001: 51).

By dispensing with its pretensions of objectivity, documentary film has simultaneously evolved into avant-garde and fiction, becoming a hybrid domain in which a wide range of devices coexist. The social perception of terminology itself reflects this expansive tendency: both the nominal and adjectival forms of the terms 'documentary' and 'non-fiction' have hitherto been used as synonyms, but 'documentary' is actually a much more specific genre, which traditionally entails some kind of narrative and an illusion of transparency, of realness; while 'non-fiction' is a much broader category open to non-narrative practices and all kinds of manipulations. One of the side effects of the objectivity crisis has been the confusion of both terms, because postmodern documentaries have thoroughly explored the legacy of ethnography, autobiography, self-portrait, self-fiction, diary films, essay films, travelogues, actualities, rockumentaries, mockumentaries, metafilmic practices and the entire experimental film and video tradition, including found footage film and video art among many other subgenres of non-fiction. This evolution is partly due to a change in the theoretical background of many documentary makers, who have studied in film and art schools instead of journalism ones: in their effort to differentiate documentary film from audiovisual report, they have borrowed some features from other non-fiction genres previously considered beyond the boundaries of documentary film. At this point, the more innovative works have developed a new relationship with the historical world, as suggested by Spanish theorist Josep María Catalá: 'the proposals of contemporary non-fiction film go beyond the aesthetics of post-modernity, since they are not satisfied with the simple aesthetic expression of an idea on the world, as postmodern art usually does, but rather use aesthetics as a hermeneutic tool' (2010: 290–1). Therefore, the postmodern challenge to the concept of truth has made way for a new process of sense-making in documentary film in which creativity and subjectivity play a major role.

Subjectivity in Documentary Film

The expression of subjectivity has been historically repressed in documentary film, but its exploration, according to Renov, has never contradicted 'the elemental documentary impulse, the will to preservation' (2004: 81). From the origins of cinema, the camera has always recorded images that are objective and subjective at the same time, because the act of filming involves two overlapping operations, as explained by Nichols:

> To speak about the camera's gaze is ... to mingle two distinct operations: the literal, mechanical operation of a device to reproduce images and the metaphorical, human process of gazing upon the world. As a machine the camera produces an indexical record of what falls within its visual field.

As an anthropomorphic extension of the human sensorium the camera reveals not only the world but its operator's preoccupations, subjectivity, and values. The photographic (and aural) record provides an imprint of its user's ethical, political, and ideological stance as well as an imprint of the visible surface of things. (1991: 79)

Postmodern documentaries have strengthened the subjective dimension of images, inverting the social perception of which component is considered more important: thus, after decades of debate on the scientific value of documentary film (see Winston 1993), the current paradigm suggests that the filmmaker's subjective gaze usually precedes the camera's objective gaze, at least in terms of sense-making. That is to say that the reasons to record an image always influence both the content and sense of that particular image, inasmuch as every camera – even surveillance cameras – operate according to a purpose previously established by a human being. The lowest level of subjectivity would then arise from the decision to film or not to film, to place the camera here or there, to cut the shot now or later, and so on up to replacing the third person with the first one. Once this step has been taken, the desire to preserve and to analyse remain the same, but the will to persuade is less common than the will to express 'the filmmaker's own personal perspective and unique view of things' (Nichols 2001: 14).

In the last quarter of the twentieth century, subjectivity came to the fore in a series of minority cinemas made by women and men of diverse cultural backgrounds – mainly feminists, gays and lesbians, members of a particular ethnic minority and Third World citizens (see Nichols 2001: 133, 153; Renov 2004: xvii; Chanan 2007: 7). For all these people, subjectivity was, above all, a means to claim their otherness and counteract their usual misrepresentations in mainstream cinema: in their films, the filmmaker's explicit presence was a basic strategy to deal with the historical world from a gender, ethnic or national perspective. Later on, many other documentary makers have embraced this approach – even white heterosexual men living in a First World country – because subjectivity has become 'the filter through which the real enters discourse' (Renov 2004: 176). As a result, everything has been subjectivised, including space itself, which is currently perceived and depicted according to filmmakers' and filmed subjects' personal ties with film locations.

Space in Documentary Film

After the commercial release of *London*, British filmmaker Patrick Keiller stated in an article published in *Sight & Sound* that 'filmmaking on location offers the possibility of the transformation of the world we live in' (1994: 35). In this regard, François Penz and Andong Lu have praised the ability of cinema to turn 'even the most anonymous and banal city location [into] a consciously recorded space that becomes an expressive space' (2011: 9). Nevertheless, the relationship between the audience and profilmic space – the space that is shown on the screen – varies from fiction to documentary film. The space of fiction, according to Michael Chanan, is always beyond our reach, even if it is a real place, given that 'we cannot physically enter it and any connection with it is imaginary' (2007: 79). In fiction, film locations may play themselves, stand for other places or simply symbolise certain kinds of places. We can visit them, but even so we will never be in their cinematic doubles, because they do not exist outside fiction. On the contrary, the space of documentary is 'isomorphic with the physical reality in which we live our everyday lives', that is, it does belong to the afilmic reality ('the world that exists independently of the camera') and consequently we can enter it whenever possible, because we are already within it (Chanan 2007: 79, 13).

Let us take as example the Dietrichson House in *Double Indemnity* (Billy Wilder, 1944), which also appears in Thom Andersen's *Los Angeles Plays Itself*. In the first film, the façade was filmed on location and the interiors on studio sets, although their design remained fairly close to that of the original house. By juxtaposing both spaces, Wilder created a place that only exists on screen insofar as he shows it: the real house looks different indoors and the studio set lacks a real façade. In the second film, however, the house has lost its name – it must be remembered that the Dietrichsons were fictional characters – to simply become the house located at 6301 Quebec Drive, Los Angeles. Andersen shows it through a few architectural shots that recall the surveillance strategy described by Teresa Castro (2010: 145), thereby offering a synecdoche of the real place that invites the audience to visit it. This time, anyone can go there, adopt Andersen's gaze and check that the off-screen space actually exists, because the house belongs to the same reality as the audience.

When filming buildings, Spanish architect Jorge Gorostiza has distinguished two main attitudes that insist on the differences between the space of fiction and the space of documentary: 'the first attitude uses the cinematic apparatus in order to create new architectures or transform existing ones, usually as a space for developing fictions; while the second one places the filmmaker as a mere spectator who only describes the buildings without intervening in them, almost always through a documentary style' (2011: xviii; my translation). These two ways of filming architecture can be extended to the whole urban space, giving rise to 'creative geographies' or, conversely, maintaining a 'topographical coherence' (see Penz & Lu 2011: 14). In the former case, the usual result is what I will term a 'city-character';

while in the latter, the cinematic city remains faithful to a 'city-referent'. These categories are not necessary anchored in the concepts of fiction and documentary, because they may indistinctly refer to both: on the one hand, a fiction film can depict the city-referent as faithfully as a documentary, even though its profilmic space remains a cinematic double of the original referent; on the other, many documentaries usually resort to the city-character in order to convey a particular perception of urban space and thus create spatiality.

The city-referent basically appears in those films whose profilmic space ex-plicitly establishes a relation of continuity with real environments, regardless of whether the audience may enter it or not. Their images document urban space in past and present, preserving a visual record of its external appearance. The city-character, in turn, has more to do with both the city-text – 'the product of countless and intermingled instances of representation' – and the lived city – 'the experience of urban life and of its representations that an inhabitant or a visitor may have' – because it presents urban space as a subjective projection of the film-maker's or characters' mood (see Mazierska & Rascaroli 2003: 237). These two categories are therefore complementary: the city-referent describes a place and the city-character interprets it. Considering that 'cities in discourse have no absolute and fixed meaning', as Colin McArthur has warned (1997: 20), their combined presence in the same work allows filmmakers to develop a subjective discourse on urban space – that is, to give it a particular meaning – without ever losing the sense of place. In the case of documentary film, in which profilmic space extends into afilmic reality, the union of the city-referent and the city-character is even more desirable than in fiction, because it provides the audience with a window to the historical world that is simultaneously an entrance to its inhabitants' mind. This would be precisely the major virtue of most documentaries discussed below: they take us to a given time and place and make us understand its contemporary perception and socio-cultural connotations.

NOTE

1   The lifetime gross income of this documentary was exactly $119,194,771. These data, as well as the whole list, are available at http://www.boxofficemojo.com/genres/chart/?id=documentary.htm. Accessed 8 March 2014.

LANDSCAPING

The term 'landscaping' usually refers to any activity that modifies the visible features of the territory, but also identifies a genre of painting, photography or film devoted to the representation of landscape. In fact, landscape film is an aesthetic tradition that depicts the natural or built environment through attentive observation. Its *mise-en-scène* depends on three basic choices: finding the most appropriate camera position to show a given landscape; deciding the mobility of the camera, which can remain still, pan to left or right, or move in a tracking shot; and establishing the exact length of each shot.

Landscape film prefers long and static shots because they are able to stimulate the optical unconscious: images that are lengthier than necessary according to the narrative conventions of mainstream storytelling actually invite the audience to look at those details that might pass unnoticed at first sight. Moreover, the length of a shot is a key feature to distinguish landscape film from landscape photography, because the communicative possibilities of the moving image can change, expand or clarify the meaning of a freeze frame. In these cases, the inevitable question is 'why and for what reason does this image last that long?', and the answer, when this device succeeds, is that lengthy shots can give new or different meanings to the landscape in political, economic, social, cultural or ideological terms.

At the beginning of the twenty-first century, according to Elena Oroz and Iván G. Ambruñeiras, American landscape film set out 'a kind of critical geography of the political and cultural significance of places (and non-places), tracing the footsteps of the past and following them to the present' (2010: 334). In work such as James Benning's California Trilogy – a triptych formed by *El Valley Centro*, *Los* and *Sogobi* (1999, 2000, 2001), *An Injury to One* (Travis Wilkerson, 2002), *Chain* (Jem Cohen, 2004), *Profit Motive and the Whispering Wind* (John Gianvito, 2007), *California Company Town* (Lee Anne Schmitt, 2008) or *Blue Meridian* (Sofie Benoot, 2010), the signs of the passage of time are interpreted as presences or absences, or even as the subsequent overlap of both, producing a palimpsest in which the accumulation of socio-historical meanings and subjective experiences establishes a link between collective stories and personal memory. This is to say that landscape itself has become a repository of events and emotions, and consequently plays 'a social role', as explained by American urban planner Kevin Lynch in *The Image of the City*:

> The named environment, familiar to all, furnishes material for common memories and symbols which bind the group together and allow them to communicate with one another. The landscape serves as a vast mnemonic system for the retention of group history and ideals. (1960: 126)

Lynch studied the perception of urban space by its own inhabitants, because he considered that understanding the relationship between human being and built environment was essential to improve this environment. According to him, urban renewal did not have to change 'the physical shape itself but the quality of an image in the mind' (1960: 117), inasmuch as cognitive mapping is organised through a set of environmental images that come from both the external characteristics of a place and the subjective gaze of an observer. Therefore, if landscape can be condensed into a mental image, landscape films could be a record and a product of those images, or more exactly, of the filmmaker's environmental images. Considering that this record would also include the socio-historical meanings and subjective experiences associated with a given landscape, the subsequent analysis of these films will retrieve the cognitive mappings of the past in order to explain the relationship of individuals and communities with built environment over time. Indeed, landscape films offer, at their best, the possibility of time travelling through space, 'as if the gaze of the camera were able to penetrate opaque landscapes, digging them as if they were archaeological sites, delving into their forgotten memories' (Castro 2010: 151).

Depending on the degree of subjectivity, it is possible to distinguish three different types of landscaping. The most objective one would be 'observational landscaping', whose minimalist *mise-en-scène* is exclusively limited to looking at and listening to landscape. The filmmaker who has best used this device is probably James Benning, the director of *One Way Boogie Woogie / 27 Years Later* (1977/2004) – a diptych that depicts the impact of urban crisis on Milwaukee – and the aforementioned California Trilogy that establishes a circular dialectic between the rural, urban and natural landscape.

The second type entails a greater degree of subjectivity on the part of the filmmaker, who intends to relate the current look of landscape to its former incarnations, whether the buildings or structures that formerly stood in the same spot, or the events that took place right there years or centuries ago. I term this device 'psychogeographical landscaping' because it refers to works that simultaneously depict landscape as a historical location and a lived space, paying particular attention to the emotional effects of the territory in the subject, who may be both the viewer and the filmmaker. A few examples of this device would be *L.A.X.* (Fabrice Ziolkowski, 1980), *Thames Film* (William Raban, 1986) or Patrick Keiller's Robinson Trilogy, formed by *London*, *Robinson in Space* and *Robinson in Ruins* (1994, 1997, 2010). All of them combine the objective record of landscape with its historical and sociological interpretation, thereby offering a series of counter-narratives of urban change in cities such as Los Angeles or London.

Finally, the third type of landscaping is the most subjective one, because it develops a personal reading of the territory based on the filmmaker's own experiences of it. In principle, there are not too many differences in the way of filming space between this strategy and the previous two, but the images are this time accompanied by a first-person commentary that makes explicit the link between the filmmaker and the landscape. For this reason, as this commentary usually has a clear autobiographical component, I have decided to name this strategy 'autobiographical landscaping'. In these films, such as *News from Home* (Chantal Akerman, 1977) or *Lost Book Found* (Jem Cohen, 1996), the depicted space is always a lived space, whose current appearance allows filmmakers to return to the cities they knew at a particular time of their life. The ultimate purpose of this type of landscaping is the same as that of urban self-portraits, the device discussed in the second part of this book, but its main formal strategy is still the direct record of the cityscape. Accordingly, autobiographical landscape films never include reenactments, archival footage or the filmmaker's on-camera presence, because their main subject is space itself rather than urban change, the passage of time or the filmmaker's memory.

Overall, landscaping is concerned with the shape of space, its historical evolution, its current appearance and especially its visual perception, because any cinematic space is always perceived doubly: first by the filmmaker and then by the audience. The next three chapters will describe and discuss the formal features and possible meanings of these three variations, from the most objective to the most subjective one in a prearranged sequence that shows the gradual evolution of observational documentaries towards the performative mode.

CHAPTER THREE

Observational Landscaping*

The zero degree of *mise-en-scène* consists merely in establishing camera position and shot length, a simple matter of framing and duration. As early film pioneers were the first filmmakers to deal with these issues, all those works whose *mise-en-scène* choices are limited to these variables are usually described as 'primitivist'. The origins of this aesthetic have been theorised by Noël Burch, who has developed the concept of the 'Primitive Mode of Representation' in order to group a set of early film styles characterised by 'the autarchy of the tableau ... horizontal and frontal camera placement, maintenance of long shot and "centrifugality"' (1990: 188). Burch identifies these features with the ideal of 'pure cinema', a perception so widespread that all those film movements and formal devices attempting to recover the essence of cinema return one way or another to the conventions of early film. In this regard, observational landscaping is no exception to the rule, although its main influences are actually more recent: the avant-garde tradition of structural film and the modernist aesthetics of disappearance.

Structural film emerged in the US in the 1960s and was later developed in the UK. Its main representatives were American filmmakers Michael Snow, Hollis Frampton, Paul Sharits, Joyce Wieland, Tony Conrad, George Landow and Ernie Gehr, as well as British filmmaker-theoreticians Peter Gidal and Malcolm Le Grice. They all were primarily concerned with formal issues, to the point that the content of their works had to be 'minimal and subsidiary to the outline', as stated by P. Adams Sitney (2000: 327). According to this critic, the four main characteristics of structural film were 'fixed camera position (fixed from the viewer's perspective), the flicker effect, loop printing and rephotography off the screen' (ibid.), but they seldom appeared together in a single film. The temporal logic of these works sought to achieve a real-time aesthetic, in which the screen time should be equal to the time of shooting, a formal choice that would later influence James

Benning's and Chantal Akerman's works.

The aesthetics of disappearance, in turn, began with Michelangelo Antonioni's early 1960s films, especially *L'Avventura* (1960), in which a character leaves the frame to never re-enter, and *L'Eclisse* (1962), in which the story itself dissolves into the cityscape. In this title, the closing sequence shows a few places where the two main characters had previously been and should have met again, but neither of them finally appears. Their absence is emphasised by a series of inanimate objects – a roller shutter, a hose, a zebra crossing, a house under construction or a small piece of wood floating in a bucket of water – which actually depict the eclipse of their feelings. According to Domènec Font, this way of filming the landscape establishes 'a contiguity between characters and environments' that relies on the correspondence between 'cinematic, architectural and inner psychic space' (2002: 311; my translation). Thus, in *L'Eclisse*, a house under construction on the outskirts of Rome symbolises both the new suburban landscape and the emotional emptiness of Italian bourgeoisie.

Antonioni's aesthetics of disappearance has been taken up by a large number of filmmakers, including Wim Wenders, Théo Angelopoulos, Béla Tarr, Tsai Mingliang, Nuri Bilge Ceylan and Apitchapong Weerasethakul, among many others. The last one has even rewritten the closing sequence of *L'Eclisse* in *Syndromes and a Century* (2006), just as Richard Linklater and Lee Chang-dong had previously done in *Before Sunrise* (1995) and *Poetry* (2010), respectively, to show the absence or disappearance of the characters. Weerasethakul, however, quotes Antonioni to express an ontological emptiness that has recently been explored by Slow Cinema, which has been described by Jonathan Romney as 'a cinema that downplays event in favour of mood, evocativeness and an intensified sense of temporality' (2010: 43). In titles such as *Sátántangó* (Béla Tarr, 1994), *La libertad* (*Freedom*, Lisandro Alonso, 2001), *Gerry* (Gus Van Sant, 2002), *Goodbye Dragon Inn* (Tsai Mingliang, 2003) or *El cant dels ocells* (*Birdsongs*, Albert Serra, 2008), the aesthetics of disappearance has evolved into an aesthetics of emptiness in which there is no longer a story, but traces of a story. The narrative structure has been deprived of what we previously understood as beginning and end to focus instead on the middle, from which we have to deduce everything. Under these circumstances, the landscape often plays a key role as character, symbol or aesthetic motive, to the point that many of these films, despite being fictions, are also landscape films.

The ability of Slow Cinema – and by extension of observational landscaping – to depict the present time has been challenged by many critics who find these works a bit outdated. For example, Horacio Muñoz Fernández has said that 'many landscape films are aesthetically romantic, topically anti-modern and theoretically wrong' (2013; my translation). Previously, Antonio Weinrichter had already wondered what the point was of representing our experience in a world oversatu-rated with images by 'replacing the zapping paradigm with pan or fixed shots at geological pace' (2007: 72; my translation). Slowness, however, usually pursues an ideological agenda: to counteract the logic of spectacle, even at the risk of literally sending most contemporary viewers to sleep. For all those able to stay awake, the laconic *mise-en-scène* of observational landscaping can document a place, convey its subjective experience and draw attention to the uses and abuses of the territory where it is located.

In these films, the frame is always the mediator between landscape, filmmaker and audience: its composition determines the audience's experience of the land-scape and also echoes the filmmaker's experience while filming it. Hence, obser-vational landscaping offers a blend of explicit objectivity – because the audience directly looks at the landscape – and implicit subjectivity – because the audience is placed in the filmmaker's position. This double reading of landscape films ulti-mately explains why many white male structural filmmakers began to seek them-selves in the landscape after the subjective turn in documentary film, as David E. James has explained:

> The self-exploration and self-production of multicultural collectivities precipitated a crisis that was specifically acute for one group of filmmak-ers: white, heterosexual males. Excluded by definition from minority cin-emas and damagingly associated with the putative hyperrationalism of structural film, for them neither the psyche of the individual protagonist nor its social projection as an expansive political movement was available as the basis of a counter-cinema. Since the story of heterosexual white men appeared to have been already told over and over again in the main-stream media – in fact, other groups agreed that it was the *only* story that patriarchal capitalist culture had ever told – they no longer had a socially viable counterstory to tell. Bereft of a history or recourse to a functional subjectivity, white heterosexual men typically turned from the inside to the outside and from time to space; if they found themselves, it was often in geography and films about landscape. (2005: 413)

James Benning is one of these filmmakers who have rediscovered themselves as 'a perceptive being in space', as Nils Plath has pointed out (2007: 201). In the 1970s, his main aesthetic referents were Andy Warhol, Michael Snow and Hollis Frampton (see Yáñez Murillo 2009: 81; Bradshaw 2013: 46), although his work later evolved into a *mise-en-paysage* highly influenced by Land Art.[1] Like most landscape films, Benning's work is based on the choice of the proper frame, within which he introduces 'elements of plot intrigue, through marginal actions, and especially through soundtrack overlays' (Martin 2010: 386). The resulting shots establish a constant play with offscreen space while showing a recurring iconography composed of 'groups of cows, passing trains, emitting smokestacks, farmland being plowed, billboards, gunshots, oil wells (and) highways' (Ault 2007: 106). Wherever Benning has been, he manages to convey the sense of place by extending the length of each shot: according to him, 'place is always a function of time so one has to sit and look and listen over a period of time to get the feel of that place and see how that place can be represented' (in Ault 2007: 91–2). Duration is then the key factor 'to give you time to think about the image while you're watching it (because) the way you think about the image will change over the course of its duration' (Benning in Ault 2007: 88). In fact, looking at and listening to Benning's films, they can be read in both personal and historical terms, as Julie Ault has suggested:

> Benning's work is as much a record of his consciousness in time and place, and therefore memory and how he incorporates time and place within himself, as it is concerned with society, industry, race, history, landscape, the Midwest, the American West, and America at large. (2007: 111–12)

This polysemy has to do with the open nature of the best landscape films, which can be as boring or significant as the audience wants. In Benning's case, his habit of frequently filming his places of memory creates a cinematic geography endowed with multiple meanings: for instance, the Milwaukee neighbourhood where he was born and grew up has been depicted as 'story, location, memory, history, imagery and metaphor' (Ault 2007: 108) in five different films: *Grand Opera: An Historical Romance* (1978), *Him and Me* (1982), *Four Corners* (1997) and *One Way Boogie Woogie / 27 Years Later.* The last two – which are actually the same, as we will see – chronicle the impact of the urban crisis on Milwaukee and also express Benning's affection for the depicted people and locations. Consequently, they are a prime example of how observational landscaping can simultaneously document place and mood, architecture and feeling, and, ultimately, urban change and passing time.

One Way Boogie Woogie / 27 Years Later: Documenting Time and Space

Milwaukee was once one of the great industrial metropolises in the United States, ranked the 11th most populous city in the mid-twentieth century. According to the

1960 Census, there were 741,324 people living in its urban area, but this figure has kept falling since then: 717,099 in 1970; 636,212 in 1980; 628,088 in 1990; 596,974 in 2000; and finally 594,833 in 2010. The 1970s seem to have been the worst time, when the population experienced a decline of 11.3% due to the industrial crisis and white flight, the same reasons that also affected other Rust Belt cities. This is precisely the period depicted in *One Way Boogie Woogie* (1977), in which Benning documented 'a specific social space at a specific moment in time', as Barbara Pichler has highlighted (2007: 34).

This film was shot in Milwaukee's industrial valley, an area where the filmmaker used to play as a kid, 'hopping freight trains and fishing in the Menomenee River' (Pichler & Slanar 2007: 248). By the late 1970s, however, the valley had been hit by the crisis, becoming a ruinscape that Benning decided to film: thus, in March 1977, he recorded images of factories, workshops, smokestacks, warehouses, quarries, storefronts, streets, roads and several street signs – especially the one-way sign – in order to capture and convey the sense of the place. These locations belong to work space instead of residential or leisure space, but they are deliberately filmed as haunted places: Benning shot them on Sunday mornings, 'when no one was there' (in MacDonald 1992: 235), because he did not want to idealise what was actually a romantic place for him.

Essentially, *One Way Boogie Woogie* consists of sixty one-minute fixed shots that show sixty self-conclusive sequences without any clear narrative link between them. Some are purely contemplative, but most have a kind of internal microaction that increases or decreases the tension generated by the shot's length. The dynamics are very simple, as Scott MacDonald has described: 'the film allows us to become accustomed to a particular composition, then supplies an event that forces us to see the composition in a new way' (1992: 221). Sometimes, these micronarratives have an explanatory function, as when Benning's daughter – filmmaker Sadie Benning, who was then four years old – rapidly crosses the frame from right to left while tapping on a metal fence with a wooden stick, thereby explaining the noise that has been heard since the beginning of the shot. At other times, certain objects suddenly enter the frame, such as a bottle, a stone or even a human foot. One way or another, there is always a play between foreground and background, image and sound, what is shown and what is implied: for example, the soundtrack includes extradiegetic sounds like radio recordings, peals of thunder over a shot of a blue sky or an approaching train that never enters the frame (Image 3.1). These sound effects contrast with and comment on the images, suggesting mysteries to the audience through the interplay between the most basic elements of cinematic storytelling: framing, perspective, colour, lighting and sound.

Benning was aware of the anomalous nature of this film, so he decided to 'make it a little more accessible by making it more like a game' (in MacDonald 1992: 235–6). The micro-narratives are thus simple actions that convey complex meanings through scale distortions, unusual repetitions, strange image-sound combinations or stark contrasts between fixed frames and fluctuating sounds, a set of tricks that still draw the audience's attention today, as the filmmaker himself has admitted:

> When I look at ... *One Way Boogie Woogie*, those tricks, and the little narratives I develop, are the least interesting parts of (the) film. What's become more interesting to me ... is how (it) matter-of-factly documented a particular social space; *behind* all my play with off-screen space, there is actually a documentation of that time and place, which has grown more interesting as those places have changed, even disappeared. But when I show *One Way Boogie Woogie* at retrospectives, and say, 'I'm a little embarrassed by the little jokes', I'm surprised at how much interest there is in that youthful play. (Benning in MacDonald 2006: 243)

The passage of time has favoured the film's interpretation as an objective and subjective record of the urban crisis. The formal games do not distract the audience from this issue, but they actually reinforce it by abstracting the cityscape beyond its particular geographical location. In this regard, according to Barbara Pichler, 'the images of Milwaukee ... constitute a kind of meta-narrative about the development of the West's urban industrial zone' (2007: 34), a reading that opens the possibility of decoding the film as a commentary on this historical process. Let us take the final segment as example: shot 52 shows a car that cannot start, 54 a road where several phantom vehicles pass by, 55 a hidden drunk that suddenly reveals his presence, 59 a blue sky that contrasts with the noise of a nonexistent storm, and finally shot 60 a simulated car accident. Each of these shots refers to the urban crisis separately, but all together seem to express a warning message: the car that does not start could symbolise the inability of the industry to revive the economy, the phantom vehicles suggest the gradual disappearance of life in Milwaukee's industrial valley, the drunk makes visible the social exclusion of a growing segment of the population, the contrast between the blue sky and the nonexistent storm could refer to the official discourse that denies the crisis, and finally the car accident closes the film with a metaphor for the plight of the Rust Belt. These meanings, however, are not in the images, but it is the images that make them possible. Benning encourages reflection by avoiding closed or literal meanings, leading some critics to misinterpret the film, as happened with shots 36 and 37 (Images 3.3 & 3.5):

> The image of the woman tied up has been criticized as sexist. The scene
> before that is the baby carriage rolling down the street, a reference to
> Eisenstein and the Odessa Steps sequence – a silly film joke – and in the
> background somebody with an accent is speaking about capitalism and
> the working class. The next shot is the woman who's tied up and gagged,
> which I meant as a reference to the working class. (Benning in MacDonald
> 1992: 236)

Considering this context, the baby carriage would then refer to the downward
trend of the economy – especially because this micro-narrative takes place in
front of a building owned by the American Paper Company – and the woman
tied up would obviously represent the working-class, which struggles for release.
Nevertheless, when these two images were re-enacted in *27 Years Later*, their
meaning changed as a result of their adaptation to a new historical moment. The
resulting film was not exactly a second part of *One Way Boogie Woogie*, but
rather its remake, a postmodern rewriting that updates its content and expands
its discourse. Indeed, both works are currently shown together as a single one in a
juxtaposition that establishes new connections between 'memory, history, longevity, and discontinuance', as Ault has pointed out (2007: 111).[2]

Benning has explained that he decided to re-film each individual shot in *One
Way Boogie Woogie* as a vehicle 'to revisit (his)
past and to meet old friends again' (in Slanar 2007:
176). Accordingly, in the new footage, the camera
is roughly placed in the same spots, usually in front
of the same people, although the exact replica is always impossible: many buildings had been demolished, some people had died, and even the physical
appearance of the two twins who drink and smoke
to the beat of a siren and a phone was no longer
as identical as in 1977. These differences cause,
according to Adrian Martin, 'a massive material
and conceptual displacement' of the entire project,
which has developed 'completely different concerns' regarding its original meaning (2010: 387).
Thus, since 2004, the main subject of *One Way
Boogie Woogie / 27 Years Later* has shifted from
urban decay to 'memory and aging', as stated by
Benning himself (in Pichler & Slanar 2007: 253).

The formal games in the original film have

Images 3.1 & 3.2: *One Way Boogie
Woogie / 27 Years Later*, shot 22

been replaced in its remake by the awareness of the passage of time, which is activated by the explicit comparison of equivalent images: for instance, shot 22, in which the filmmaker and a woman extended a thread across the railroad tracks, is repeated in the same place in the footage and in the same spot in the city, but the thread has been replaced by a measuring tape and the building in the background has disappeared (Images 3.1 & 3.2). Nevertheless, the main difference between the original shot and its rewriting is the absence of suspense: the first time the audience sees this shot, most people believe that the approaching train heard on the soundtrack is going to enter the frame and cut the thread, but the second time everybody knows that the train will never appear, so its sound just recalls the previous suspense. Nostalgia and melancholia are therefore the dominant feelings, because the new footage basically shows that this cityscape has barely improved between 1977 and 2004. The atmosphere of decay is the same or even worse as in the 1970s, especially taking into account the disturbing signs of decline listed by Ault: 'formerly active places turned dormant, absence, distinctive old buildings replaced by nondescript modern ones, and more barbed wire fences' (2007: 110).

Melancholy is emphasised by overlapping the soundtrack of *One Way Boogie Woogie* and the images of *27 Years Later*. The former had already been post-synched (see Benning in MacDonald 1992: 236), but the latter is directly out of synch due to the difficulty of adapting images to sounds instead of sounds to images. Consequently, many original elements remain in the soundtrack despite having disappeared in the images, like the crashed car in the last shot of the film. For this reason, the horn noise that closed *One Way Boogie Woogie* is no longer a warning message in *27 Years Later*, but a reminder of the material and human absences in the new footage. The possibility of reusing the whole soundtrack of a pre-existing film was already explored by Benning in *UTOPIA* (1998), a film about the agricultural landscapes of Southern California in which he literally stole the English soundtrack of *Ernesto Che Guevara, le journal de Bolivie* (*Ernesto Che Guevara, the Bolivian Diary*, Richard Dindo, 1994). In that film, Benning 'wanted to bring revolution to Southern California' (in MacDonald 2006: 241), but this intertextuality has another purpose in *One Way Boogie Woogie / 27 Years Later*:

> By using the same soundtrack twice I was able to provide the audience with a tool to map the second film back onto the first. This of course was necessary since many things had changed in the past twenty-seven years and not always did I reconstruct the narratives in the same exact way. (Benning in Ault 2007: 110)

The changes from one version to another can be accidental or deliberate, which allows the audience to reinterpret each shot. Let us examine a few examples: first, the chimney fire in shot 28 of *One Way Boogie Woogie* becomes extinct in *27 Years Later*, perhaps referring to the exhaustion of the industrial economic model; second, the factory in shot 50 is replaced by a McDonald's restaurant, probably representing the decline of the industrial sector in favour of the service one; and finally, the forklift truck in shot 24 no longer carries a scrapped car but a shopping cart, an inspired joke on the passage from a production-based economy to a consumption-based one.

All these variations document urban change while commenting on the recent political-economic evolution, as in the aforementioned shots 36 and 37. The first one shows a baby carriage pushed by a man in a suit that crosses the frame from right to left, going up instead of down the street, whose appearance seem to have slightly improved since the 1970s – the pavement looks better, the grass is well kept and there is even a little tree, although the American Paper Company building has disappeared (Image 3.4). Since the voice on the soundtrack says the same about capital and labour, shot 36 might be suggesting that some things have changed for the better, despite the vanishing of industrial activity. This interpretation is reinforced by the rewriting of shot 37, which makes explicit its reference to the working class: the bound and gagged woman stands in front of the camera, holding a sickle and a hammer with drooping arms (Image 3.6). The new message is as parodic as contradictory: the working class has certainly been released, although it seems to have given up the active struggle, at least judging by the drooping arms.

Images 3.3 & 3.4: *One Way Boogie Woogie / 27 Years Later*, shot 36

Images 3.5 & 3.6: *One Way Boogie Woogie / 27 Years Later*, shot 37

The meaning of each shot is always open to interpretation, but there is no doubt about the aesthetic functions of this diptych: the first one would be, borrowing Michael Renov's terms, 'to record, reveal or preserve' a particular cityscape, and the second one 'to analyse or interrogate' its historical and emotional evolution (1993: 21; 2004: 74). In other words, Benning's primary concerns were to document a given place – his hometown – and to reflect on its perception over time, therefore depicting Milwaukee as both a place of memory and a synecdoche of the whole Rust Belt.

The California Trilogy: Mapping a Tortured Landscape

Throughout the 1970s and 1980s, Benning continued to film Midwest landscapes, but his geographical interest turned to the Southwest when he moved to Val Verde, California, to teach at the California Institute for the Arts in 1988. The first film in this new period was *North on Evers* (1991), a road movie that chronicles two motorcycle trips from Val Verde to New York and back to Val Verde, first taking the southern route and then the northern one. In these journeys, Benning crossed Utah, where he later filmed *Deseret* (1995) – 'his first western', as David E. James has dubbed it (2005: 422) – and also part of *Four Corners* – a work that explored the quadruple border between Utah, Colorado, New Mexico and Arizona. A year later, this westward shift was completed with *UTOPIA*, in which the filmmaker finally focused on the landscape of Southern California.

The geographical links between these titles are, according to Benning, the result of the influence that every film of his has on the following one (see MacDonald 2006: 242; Ault 2007: 105–6). In this sense, the California Trilogy emerged from a similar dynamic: first, *El Valley Centro* grew directly out of *UTOPIA* as a way of delving into the issue of land use; then, *Los* was conceived as its urban companion; and finally, *Sogobi* showed its opposite, wilderness, which is also understood as the origin of agricultural landscape. This transition from rural to urban and back to the natural environment has been interpreted by James as 'a circular dialectic', according to which 'the industrial urbanity' – if we start with *Los* – 'generates its antithesis, the natural, which in turn generates the agricultural Central Valley as the synthesis between them – though it is itself being transformed more and more into the extended urbanity of Los Angeles, of *Los*' (2005: 423).

The unity of the trilogy is achieved at three levels: first the geographical one, because the set of these films 'aspires to represent the state as a whole' (James 2005: 426); secondly the thematic, given that the entire trilogy deals with different forms of land occupation and exploitation; and thirdly the formal level, inasmuch as each part consists of thirty-five two-and-a-half-minute fixed shots followed by a detailed list of film locations, in which each shot is identified by its action, location and ownership. Thus, according to James, the trilogy suggests 'the class divisions in the social systems that structure California geography' by showing how 'labor is divided and controlled by the wealthy and by corporations' (2005: 427, 428). In

El Valley Centro, for example, the main landowners appear to be transnational companies engaged in the oil industry (Shell Oil Company, Chevron Corporation, Getty Oil, Texaco) or in freight transport (Southern Pacific Transportation Company, Union Pacific Railroad). The landscape is clearly 'permeated by capital and labor', as Claudia Slanar has noted (2007: 171), because every place has an owner and every natural resource has become a commodity, beginning with fresh water. Benning's interest in water politics was already present in *UTOPIA,* but he fully developed this subject throughout the entire trilogy:

> In the Central Valley, corporate farms take advantage of two irrigation systems that were built with public money, one with federal money, one with state money. The corporations paid for none of the construction, but they take full advantage of it: 85 per cent of the water in California is used for farming; only 15 per cent is used for manufacturing and public consumption. And, of course, Los Angeles was expanded by stealing water from the Owens Valley. When I made *El Valley Centro,* I was very aware of the water politics, and I thought, 'Well, when I make this urban companion, I'll have to make a reference to how those politics continue from one place to another.' So *Los* begins with water flowing into LA in the original aqueduct from the Owens Valley. And then, in *Sogobi,* I tried to show where the water comes from. (Benning in MacDonald 2006: 250)

Images of water infrastructures establish a visual and geographical continuity between the end of each part and the beginning of the next one: *El Valley Centro* opens with a shot of a spillway in Lake Berryesa and closes with an image of a pumping station in the California Aqueduct; *Los* begins with the Los Angeles Aqueduct and ends in the Malibu beaches, facing the ocean; and finally *Sogobi* starts with a rocky cliff in the California Sea Otter Refuge to then return to the spillway in Lake Berryesa. This loop closure allows the trilogy to be endlessly reproduced like a video installation which viewers can enter at any point, a formal decision determined by the structural rigidity of these works that actually serves to increase their meaning.

Benning is aware that the current perception of the California landscape is mediated by its multiple representations, whether as a non-humanised land reservation or a space of conflicting interests: the first perspective considers that wilderness must be preserved and protected from human erosion, while the second is rather concerned with its economic potential as a source of raw materials, developable areas, tourist attractions or even film locations. According to Benning's opinion, the California landscape has been shaped by human activity for centuries, to the point that it has become 'a tortured landscape' (in Ault 2007: 92). Indeed, wherever he went while filming the trilogy, he always found the effects of the same process: man endeavours to tame nature, and nature responds by encroaching upon human space. From this perspective, *El Valley Centro* shows the transformation of wilderness into rural landscape; *Los*, the presence of nature in urban areas; and *Sogobi*, the inability to find pure, unspoiled nature.

The way space has been produced in California, and especially in Los Angeles, has been discussed by a long tradition of boosters and critics, among which Mike Davis stands out. In *Dead Cities and Other Tales*, he summarised the main problems of the Sun Belt development model by talking about Las Vegas as a clone of Los Angeles:

> Las Vegas has (1) abdicated a responsible water ethic; (2) fragmented local government and subordinated it to private corporate planning; (3) produced a negligible amount of usable public space; (4) abjured the use of 'hazard zoning' to mitigate natural disaster and conserve landscape; (5) dispersed land-use over an enormous, unnecessary area; (6) embraced the resulting dictatorship of the automobile; and (7) tolerated extreme social and, especially, racial inequality. (2002: 92)

In this excerpt, Davis related the expansion of this territorial model to the worsening living conditions of the underprivileged, an idea previously developed by Edward Soja in *Postmetropolis: Critical Studies of Cities and Regions*: 'the new urbanization processes have built into their impact the magnification of the economic and extra-economic (racial, gender, ethnic) inequalities along with destructive consequences for both the built and natural environment' (2000: 410). In the particular case of Los Angeles, the city's adaptation to the new economic paradigm in the 1970s and 1980s came at the cost of sacrificing the social and territorial cohesion of its different communities: thus, while the closure of factories in the industrial corridor between South Central and Long Beach destroyed thousands of jobs in the African-American community, other activities based on fast, cheap and intensive work attracted hundreds of thousands of Latin American immigrants to the region. Under these circumstances, the imbalance between the economic status and the population ratio of the four main communities in the city led Davis to parody its workforce's racial distribution as follows: 'a white professional-managerial elite, a black public sector workforce, an Asian petty-bourgeoisie, and an immigrant Latino proletariat' (2002: 252–3).

These four communities do not have the same perception of the cityscape because their geographical distribution is neither uniform nor proportional to their number. Nevertheless, a particular community – high-income whites from the Westside – has taken advantage of its privileged socio-economic status to control the spatial representations of the city and thereby impose its cognitive map to the rest of the population: according to them, Los Angeles is a glamorous city of beaches and palm trees where white people can feel at home, instead of a multicultural postmetropolis with its own strengths and weaknesses. In order to counteract this media mirage, Benning depicted a completely different city in *Los* (the most interesting film of the trilogy for this book) by focusing on those landscapes that best define the territorial model of Southern California: sprawlscapes, middle landscapes, non-places and banalscapes.

The first of these concepts, sprawlscape, refers to the landscape produced by 'urban growth spilling out of the edges of towns' (Ingersoll 2006: 3). Since the 1950s, especially in North America, many cities have doubled or even tripled their traditional extension through a process of mass suburbanisation, giving rise to a non-hierarchical succession of juxtaposed single-family houses, shopping centres and empty spaces organised according to their access to transportation networks. Soja has warned that this process 'may be more advanced in Southern California than anywhere else in the United States', to the point that it has actually become 'a mass regional urbanization' (2000: 141). The resulting cities have been praised by scholars like Reyner Banham because 'all its parts are equal and equally accessible from all other parts at once' (1971: 18), but this supposed spatial democracy may also cause problems of perception, as Kevin Lynch found out in the late 1950s:

> When asked to describe or symbolize the city as a whole, the subjects used certain standard words: 'spread-out', 'spacious', 'formless', 'without centers'. Los Angeles seemed to be hard to envision or conceptualize as a whole. An endless spread, which may carry pleasant connotations of space around the dwellings, or overtones of weariness and disorientation, was the common image. (1960: 40)

The sprawl has generated an increase in the middle landscapes within the city, a series of intermediate spaces between the built and natural environment that Lars Lerup has described as 'unfinished, incomplete, waiting somewhere between development and squalor' (2000: 158).[3] In such territory, which is neither urban nor rural, the main hubs are non-places such as airports, motorways, hotels or shopping centres; that is, those 'spaces which are not themselves anthropological places and which ... do not integrate the earlier places', as defined by French anthropologist Marc Augé (1995: 78). The urban fabric surrounding them usually lacks a distinct identity, because it has been shaped from standardised models that can be reproduced anywhere. The ultimate expression of these interchangeable spaces has been termed banalscapes by Francesc Muñoz, a concept that identifies those 'urban morphologies that are relatively autistic regarding the territory' (2010: 190; my translation). This type of cityscape results from the recent thematisation and brandification of central and peripheral areas of the city, a process that seeks to transform each city into a competitive brand in the world market:

> [Banalscapes] are a specific kind of cityscape that, despite being offered to city dwellers, have been produced to serve the interests, needs and requirements of the global economy. It is a hybrid cityscape that, on the one hand, has local character, because it retains some elements of the physical and social space, but on the other hand its appearance allows its standardised consumption by global audiences. This is the device whereby the final outcome of urban renewal looks similar everywhere. (2010: 195; my translation)

In *Los*, Benning portrays Los Angeles as a set of scattered locations that generally fit into one of these four categories, as seen in Table 3.1: the presence of a few sprawlscapes recalls the voracious expansion of the city at the expense of nature, the abundance of middle landscapes links the film with the rest of the trilogy, the numerous non-places confirm their ubiquity in the current urban fabric, and the inclusion of half a dozen banalscapes points out the emergence of new spaces of socio-economic power in West Hollywood, Bunker Hill, Orange County, the Financial District, Koreatown and even Chavez Ravine. A few images may be included in two different categories, and only ten from thirty-five shots (less than a third of the footage) do not correspond to any type of landscape since they are mostly devoted to productive activities.

Table 3.1: *Los*, distribution shots by type of landscape

Type of Landscape	Number of Shots	Shots
Sprawlscapes	5	3, 5, 17, 19, 20
Middle Landscapes	9	1, 3, 12, 14, 23, 26, 31, 32, 35
Non-Places	9	4, 7, 10, 15, 19, 21, 24, 30, 34
Banalscapes	6	2, 8, 9, 16, 21, 24
Productive Activities	8	6, 11, 13, 18, 25, 27, 28, 33

NOTE: Shots 22 and 29 do not appear in this table because they respectively show a police squad and a cemetery. The full list of shots is available in Appendix I, where they are identified by a number indicating their position in the footage.

Table 3.2: *Los*, distribution shots by geographical location

Geographical Location	Number of Shots	Shots
1. Los Angeles	31	
- Los Angeles Plains	16	
· Downtown	5	7, 8, 16, 22, 34
· Westside	5	West Hollywood (2), Westwood (29), Santa Monica (5), LAX (10), Baldwin Hills (23)
· South	3	South Central (31), Vernon (28), Maywood (12)
· Santa Monica Hills	2	Griffith Park (17), Chavez Ravine Hill (24)
· Mid-City	1	Koreatown (21)
- San Fernando Valley	8	1, 4, 11, 14, 20, 25, 27, 30
- Santa Clarita Valley	4	3, 4, 19, 33
- Long Beach	3	6, 15, 18
- Malibu	1	35
2. Orange County	3	9, 13, 26
3. Riverside County	1	32

NOTE: Shot 4 was filmed in the Newhall Pass, the natural boundary between the San Fernando and Santa Clarita Valleys, so it has been counted twice.

The combination of these four landscapes mirrors the high level of entropy that characterised Sun Belt cities: the less organised the territory is, the less defined its identity will be, as suggested by Albert Pope in *Ladders* (1996). In particular, the mass regional urbanisation in Southern California has led the Greater Los Angeles Area to expand into five different counties: Los Angeles, Orange, San Bernardino, Riverside and Ventura. *Los* was almost entirely filmed in the first one, whose large land area – 4,083 square miles, or 10,570 square kilometres – allowed Benning to document a wide variety of places and landscapes, as seen in Table 3.2 and Map 3.1. It is important to note here that Benning's vertex in the region is always Val Verde, his place of residence, which is located northwest of Los Angeles in the upper left corner of the map: that is the place from which he perceives the territory, whether the Greater Los Angeles Area, the Central Valley or the entire state of California. From there, he has to drive up and down the Interstate 5 to get anywhere, a perpetual movement that indirectly documents the car dependence in Sun Belt cities. Hence Benning's landscape films can also be considered travelogues or even road movies.

The overrepresentation of higher-income areas in mainstream film – namely, Westside and Orange County – is counteracted in *Los* by highlighting the demographic and territorial importance of the suburbs in the San Fernando and Santa Clarita Valleys, whose images correspond to almost a third of the footage (eleven shots). In comparison, there are more images from these areas than from Westside and Orange County together (eight shots) or from the pairing of Westside and Downtown (ten shots) in an explicit attempt to balance their real and symbolic presence in the everyday experience of the city for someone, like Benning, who lives in the northern suburbs. For this reason, Downtown is only represented by its two ends: on the one hand, businessmen and skyscrapers (shots 7 & 16; see Image 3.7), on the other, homeless and prison (shots 8 & 34; see Image 3.8). The suture point between these two worlds, the Broadway-Spring corridor, does not appear in the film, perhaps to emphasise the spatial polarisation of the area, which has been described by Soja:

Map 3.1: Film Locations in *Los*.
Map available in the appendix and
http://g.co/maps/ct97j

> With regard to jobs and housing in particular, this enclaved downtown is the site of two striking agglomerations representing the extremes of presence and absence. In the western half, consisting of the Civic Center complex of city, county, state and federal offices, and the corporate towers of the Central Business District and its southern extension around the Convention Center, is the densest single cluster of jobs in the polycentric post-metropolis. In the middle of the tiered enclaves that comprise the eastern half is Skid Row, on any given night the largest concentration of homeless people in the region if not the entire USA. With cruel irony, the homeless, with neither good jobs nor housing, probably outnumber the housed and employed residential population in the downtown core, despite concerted public efforts to introduce middle-class residents to live in the area and to control if not erase Skid Row. (2000: 252-253)

Benning consciously avoided most landmarks of the city because his main purpose was to restore the screen presence of the working class: faced with those discourses that stated its disappearance as a consequence of the industrial crisis, *Los* reveals a cityscape dominated by all kinds of workplaces where workers are metonymically represented. As seen in Table 3.3, two thirds of the footage is devoted to productive land uses, among which tertiary sector activities stand out, from international trade to waste management. Some primary sector activities, such as farming and mining, still remain within the city, while industry appears to have undergone a slight decline: four shots of a total of thirty-five are not too many, but they at least show operating facilities in stark contrast with the ruinscape depicted in *One Way Boogie Woogie / 27 Years Later.*[4] The six shots of transport and water infrastructures have also been counted as productive land uses, because they are essential for the circulation of raw materials and commodities, as water itself. Recreational land uses, in turn, correspond to those places where nature pervades the city, such as parks, beaches, cemeteries or playing fields, as well as meeting places like the Crystal Cathedral in Garden Grove, Orange County. Finally, only two shots represent residential land uses, but they perfectly summarise the dynamics of the sprawl from the first to the last stage (Images 3.9 & 3.10).

Images 3.7 & 3.8: *Los*, Arco Plaza (top) and Skid Row (bottom)

The image of the housing lots in Stevenson Ranch documents a landscape under construction that has just been taken from nature: it is the kind of middle

Table 3.3: *Los*, distribution shots by land use and economic activity

Land Use	Number of Shots	Shots by Economic Activity
1. Productivity Use	24	
- Primary Sector	3	Farming (31), Mining (23, 33)
- Secondary Sector	4	Industry (11, 18, 28), Construction (27)
- Tertiary Sector	11	Trade (6, 15, 21), Real-Estate Market (3, 8), Repressive Institutions (7, 22), Waste Management (13, 25), Finance (16), Advertising (2)
- Infrastructures	6	Transportation Network (4, 10, 15, 30), Water Infrastructures (1, 12)
2. Recreational Use	9	Open Spaces (5, 17, 26, 29, 32, 35), Sports (14, 24), Meeting Places (9)
3. Residential Use	2	3, 20

NOTE: Shot 34 does not appear in this table because it shows homelessness in Skid Row.

Images 3.9 & 3.10: *Los,* housing lots in Stevenson Ranch (top) and a private residence in Encino (bottom)

landscape that precedes the explosion of the sprawlscape. Benning filmed this shot near his home in Val Verde, just on the edge of the urban frontier, where a new suburb was about to be built. These outlying communities bring the American myth of the frontier to the postmetropolitan context, consuming large amounts of land and consequently shaping spaces characterised by their deep unsustainability in functional, environmental, social and cultural terms, as Muñoz has warned (2010: 172). By showing the interregnum between natural and built environment, Benning did nothing but remind us that Los Angeles was, according to Davis, 'the creature of real-estate capitalism: the culminating speculation … of the generations of boosters and promoters who had subdivided and sold the West from the Cumberland Gap to the Pacific' (1990: 25).

The places depicted in *Los* are actually pieces of a historical narrative that accounts for the sustained growth of Los Angeles since the early twentieth century. Beginning with real-estate capitalism (shots 3, 8 & 20), its development was only possible thanks to the construction of a large network of water infrastructures (shots 1 & 12) and several regional transportation networks (shots 4 & 30). The local economy was fuelled by the creation of an artificial harbour in 1907 (shot 6), the establishment of the film industry in the 1910s (shot 2), the discovery of new oil fields in the 1920s (shots 18 & 23), the emergence of the aeronautical industry after World War II (shot 10) and the recent integration of the city into global capital networks (shots 8, 16 & 21). This account of continued economic progress also hides a counter-history of political scandals, social protests and violent uprisings, in which the resort to repressive institutions has been the usual way to maintain social order (shots 7 & 22).

All these places and activities are represented in *Los* with a deep class-consciousness, thereby suggesting that social space has historically been produced in Los Angeles according to class, race and gender criteria (see James 2005: 427). The film is quite clear on this point: the spaces of power – Westside, Orange County, the Downtown Financial District and the San Fernando Valley – are white territories (shots 5, 9, 16 & 20), but most people who appear in the footage are actually Latinos, as already happened in *El Valley Centro* (shots 7, 14, 17, 19, 20 & 31). Moreover, the choice of certain locations indirectly recalls a class- and race-specific history, as in the case of Bunker Hill (shot 8) and Chavez Ravine (shot 24), two former working-class neighbourhoods – the second one mainly populated by Mexican-Americans – that were razed to the ground in the 1950s to make way for, respectively, a new financial district and the Dodgers Stadium. Benning never makes explicit these historical accounts, because he is usually more interested in the present than the past of the cityscape. Nevertheless, this does not mean that he is not aware of the memorial value of his images. On the contrary, he films the present in order to document all that might disappear in the future, like the South Central Community Garden (shot 31), which is currently an empty plot of land.[5]

Within each one of these shots, Benning establishes a series of inner tensions to emphasise their condition as moving landscapes. His usual micro-narratives appear to have been choreographed, but this time he has explained that 'it (was) only a matter of waiting for the right moment' (in Slanar 2007: 169). The resulting effects may be the hypnosis induced by cyclic sequences or continuous flows, the surprise at unusual events, or the uncertainty of not knowing whether an action will be completed within the length of the shot. For two and a half minutes, the audience can explore the landscape with their eyes instead of their feet, as if they were on location with Benning himself. Accordingly, what is supposed to be an objective record of the cityscape actually becomes a subjective journey that links observational and autobiographical landscaping: the thirty-five shots of *Los* are actually thirty-five performances in which the filmmaker visits different parts of the Greater Los Angeles Area in order to record 'how (he) felt at those places at those moments' (in MacDonald 2006: 245). From this perspective, each film location in the entire trilogy is also a lived space that Benning wants to share with the audience:

> I gravitate more and more toward ... experiencing things by myself and perhaps make films about it because I also think that there is something marvellous about ... sharing it with somebody. But if I would be making these films with somebody else along I couldn't do it. I have to have that experience by myself to record it somehow – to actually see it. (Benning in Ault 2007: 90)

By being as observational as performative, the California Trilogy shows a landscape that is simultaneously objective and subjective, material and emotional, epic and lyric: it can be understood as a set of 'sedimentary layers of historical events' (Slanar 2007: 178), 'a map of political denunciation' (Muñoz Fernández 2011; my translation) or a geographical projection of the filmmaker's self. That is to say that even the most detached filming device such as 'observational landscaping' can convey a personal view of the depicted space, inasmuch as the way someone looks at landscape implicitly reveals a way of being in the world and relating to it. Therefore, James Benning's California Trilogy can be regarded as a film mapping of the territory's ongoing transformations as well as a private diary of the filmmaker's journeys and experiences through it. Since the images allow both readings, it is up to the audience to decide which film they want to see.

NOTES

*   A shorter version of this chapter, without the analysis of *One Way Boogie Woogie / 27 Years Later* (James Benning, 1977/2004), has been previously published in Spanish in *Fotocinema. Scientif Journal of Cinema & Photography* (see Villarmea Álvarez 2014b).

1   Benning even made a film on Robert Smithson's Spiral Jetty, an earthwork sculpture constructed on the north-eastern shore of the Great Salt Lake in Utah. Entitled *Casting a Glance* (2007), it shows how Smithson's work changes over time.

2   There is also a digital rewriting of *One Way Boogie Woogie*, which is simply entitled *One Way Boogie Woogie 2012* (James Benning, 2012). Unfortunately, it was not possible to get a copy of this new version at the time of writing this chapter in July 2014.

3   The concept of middle landscape was originally coined by American historian Leo Marx in *The Machine in the Garden: Technology and the Pastoral Ideal in America* (1964).

4   Los Angeles never experienced deindustrialisation to the degree of the Rust Belt cities, given that the city also underwent a simultaneous reindustrialisation process that, according to Soja, 'reconstituted Fordism along significantly different lines' (2000: 172).

5   This place was turned into an urban farm by a group of South Central residents – mostly Latinos – from 1994 to 2006, the year when it was destroyed at the request of its nominal owner. The film *The Garden* (Scott Hamilton Kennedy, 2008) documented the farmers' struggle to preserve the agricultural land use.

CHAPTER FOUR

Psychogeographical Landscaping

Psychogeography has always been a broad and ambiguous concept, indistinctly used in order to refer to 'a literary movement, a political strategy, a series of new age ideas or a set of avant-garde practices', as Merlin Coverley has pointed out (2010: 9–10). Its official definition, established by Guy Debord in the 1950s, identifies the sense of this term and its derivates as follows:

> Psychogeography sets for itself the study of the precise laws and specific effects of the geographical environment, whether consciously organised or not, on the emotions and behaviour of individuals. The charmingly vague adjective *psychogeographical* can be applied to the findings arrived at by this type of investigation, to their influence on human feelings, and more generally to any situation or conduct that seems to reflect the same spirit of discovery. (1981a: 5)

Following these guidelines, different kinds of films may be regarded as psychogeographical documentaries, including those directed by Debord himself, such as *La société du spectacle* (*The Society of the Spectacle*, 1973) or *In girum imus nocte et consumimur igni* (1978). In order to avoid any confusion, the label 'psychogeographical landscaping' is here applied to those documentaries that express the emotional effects of the territory on the subject – who may be the viewer, the filmmaker or a character – through a combination of an observational *mise-en-scène* with an expository, reflexive or performative commentary. The aim of these films would ultimately be the subjective reading of the landscape beyond its objective record, usually depicting it as a lived space or a historical site. Therefore, the main difference between observational and psychogeographical landscaping is the explicit presence of historical references in the latter as a way to emphasise the constructed nature of landscape.

The narrative of these films is usually structured around the search for the *genius loci*, a concept defined by Coverley as 'the spirit of place, through which landscape, whether urban or rural, can be imbued with a sense of the histories of previous inhabitants and the events that have been played out against them' (2010: 33). According to this author, the usual strategies to find the *genius loci* have been the search for new ways of experiencing familiar surroundings, the encourage-ment of unexpected insights and juxtapositions created by aimless drifting and, overall, the imaginative reworking of the city (2010: 31). Many of them have been adapted to film by means of old techniques, such as the reinterpretation of images through a spoken commentary, the contrast between old and new footage, or the use of 'phantom rides', a type of shot in which the camera is placed on the front of a moving vehicle – depending on the type of vehicle, the resulting shot may be a carscape, a trainscape or a boatscape, to name just the most common pos-sibilities. Furthermore, psychogeographical documentaries have also developed specific devices to capture the *genius loci*, among which the visual palimpsest stands out: in this type of dissolve, two images taken from the same camera posi-tion at different times remain superimposed for a few seconds, thereby creating a third image that reveals the main changes in a given place over time. Finally, even fictional reenactments may have a psychogeographical purpose, as happens in a short sequence of *São Paulo, Sinfonia da Metropole* (*São Paulo, a Metropolitan Symphony*, Adalberto Kemeny & Rudolf Rex Lustig, 1929): an image of São Paulo's Independence Park in is followed by a *tableaux vivant* that recalls the Brazilian declaration of independence, the 'Cry of Ipiranga', which supposedly took place right there in 1822. This shot roughly reproduces the composition of Pedro Américo's painting *Independence or Death!* (1888), an example of how the dialogue between different forms of artistic expression helps to recover the past of the territory.

The political dimension of psychogeography was originally developed in Paris first by Surrealists and then by Situationists, who understood it as a tool to trans-form urban life. In this tradition, according to Coverley, 'psychogeography seeks to reveal the true nature that lies beneath the urban surface to overcome the pro-cesses of "banalisation" by which the everyday experience of our surroundings becomes one of drab monotony' (2010: 13). This approach, however, contrasts with that of the London tradition, which rather considers that the *genius loci* is immutable. This concept of psychogeography has more to do with local history than with any transformative project, but this does not mean that the political dimension has disappeared from contemporary psychogeographical practices. In this regard, the three films discussed in this chapter – *L.A.X.* (Fabrice Ziolkowski,

1980), *Thames Film* (William Raban, 1986) and *London* (Patrick Keiller, 1994) – use the observational record of the cityscape and its subsequent historical interpretation to provide the audience with a critical perception of urban change. As we shall see below, these films expose the conflicting interests that have shaped the cityscape of Los Angeles and London, challenging all those official accounts that skip, hide or forget the negative effects of controversial political decisions on the urban fabric.

L.A.X.: Hidden Stories and Foreign Gaze

The opening shot of *L.A.X.* is a ten-minute take filmed from an airplane that shows the Los Angeles cityscape from above (Image 4.1). Viewers who already know the city can easily distinguish many of its landmarks, such as Wilshire Boulevard, McArthur Park, the Hollywood Hills, the Santa Monica Freeway or the Silver Lake Reservoir. This sprawlscape, and especially the aerial view of Downtown Los Angeles, usually appears as a location or transition shot in mainstream cinema,

Image 4.1: *L.A.X.*, aerial view of Downtown Los Angeles in the early 1980s

as in *Un homme est mort* (*The Outside Man*, Jacques Deray, 1972), *Repo Man* (Alex Cox, 1984), *Collateral* (Michael Mann, 2004) or *Drive* (Nicolas Winding Refn, 2010). Aware of this tradition, French filmmaker Fabrice Ziolkowski adopted this point of view to depict the city as a unit, borrowing this idea from Reyner Banham:

> An even greater urban vision than the view of Los Angeles from Griffith Park Observatory is the view of LA on a clear day from a high-flying aircraft. Within its vast extent can be seen its diverse ecologies of sea-coast, plain, and hill; within the diversity can be seen the mechanisms, natural and human, that have made those ecologies support a way of life. (1971: 217)

The sprawl has currently become the most recognisable Los Angeles icon, given that architecture has historically been unable to symbolise a city whose main landmarks are geographical, like hills, freeways, reservoirs and even skyscrapers, if we see them as erections *of* the territory instead of *in* the territory, as Spanish anthropologist Manuel Delgado has suggested (2007: 127). The problem with the sprawlscape, however, is its lack of meaning, at least judging from a European perspective, as Jean Baudrillard has warned:

No elevator or subway in Los Angeles. No verticality or underground, no intimacy or collectivity, no streets or façades, no centre or monuments: a fantastic space, a spectral and discontinuous succession of all the various functions, of all signs with no hierarchical ordering – an extravaganza of indifference, extravaganza of undifferentiated surfaces – the power of pure open space, the kind you find in the deserts. The power of the desert form: it is the erasure of traces in the desert, of the signified of signs in the cities, of any psychology in bodies. (1988: 120–1)

By depicting the city from above at the beginning of *L.A.X.*, Ziolkowski was basically reproducing the shock of arrival in Los Angeles for a European observer like him, for whom the sprawlscape is, at first sight, meaningless. The *voyeur*'s perspective serves here to establish a foreign gaze before descending into the city to explore its urban fabric at street level, in an attempt to expose its hidden history without ever leaving the position of a detached observer.

Once on land, and due to the impossibility of getting around the city on foot, Ziolkowski decided to include three carscapes in the footage: one travelling the freeways, another following Wilshire Boulevard westward in the Miracle Mile area and a third moving west on Fifth Street through Downtown. These kind of shots had previously been used by other European filmmakers to express a feeling of estrangement towards the American city in films such as *Zabriskie Point* (Michelangelo Antonioni, 1970), *Alice in den Städten* (*Alice in the Cities*, Wim Wenders, 1974), *News from Home* (Chantal Akerman, 1977) or *Mon oncle d'Amerique* (*My American Uncle*, Alain Resnais, 1980). The first one, *Zabriskie Point*, even established a highly influential model to depict Los Angeles as 'a *collage* of images, noises and events, a confused overload of activity and an overwhelming amount of advertising images … a blend of chaos and consumerism', as described by British architect Graham Cairns (2007: 133; my translation). Ziolkowski's carscapes, however, follow Chantal Akerman's aesthetic model, in which the camera is placed in the driver's or passenger's seat and records their corresponding perception of the city in a long single take. The outcome of this choice is a continuously changing view that conveys the sprawl experience otherwise: by showing a moving cityscape that always looks the same.

Let us briefly analyse the longer of these carscapes, in which the camera crosses Downtown Los Angeles from east to west: the shot begins in the Warehouse District, then passes through Skid Row, the old Historic Core, Pershing Square and the new Financial District – where the site of the U.S. Bank Tower is still empty – and finally enters the sprawl across the Harbor Freeway. Contrary to James Benning in *Los*, Ziolkowski does show the geographical link between all these places, which are actually much closer than Angelinos think, but he does not record their real soundscape. The music that accompanies these images sets a gloomy atmosphere that emphasises the decline of Downtown in the early 1980s, when Banham's famous curse was closer to reality: 'most of what is contained within the rough central parallelogram of the Santa Monica, Harbor, Santa Ana, and San Bernardino freeways could disappear overnight and the bulk of the citizenry would never even notice' (1971: 190). By going from nowhere to nowhere, this carscape portraits Downtown as an area besieged by the sprawl. Its *genius loci* was, then, marked by the transience of the urban experience, which made Los Angeles an unstable and intangible city without permanence or consistency, borrowing Carlos García Vázquez's terms to describe the urban planning in the Sun Belt (2011: 10–40, 94–122).

The comparison between *L.A.X.* and *Los* was first established by David E. James, who stated that the former anticipated many of the images and formal strategies of the latter. Their main difference, however, is the same that distinguishes observational from psychogeographical landscaping: 'where *Los* simply leaves the cityscape to speak for itself, Ziolkowski's verbal texts specify the histories of exploitation and corruption that have produced it' (2005: 522). The film's discourse thereby arises from the contrast between images of certain symbolic places and eight literary texts that directly or indirectly address their hidden history, a formal strategy that, according to James, recalls the films of Jean-Marie Straub and Danièle Huillet for two reasons: 'its detached yet intensive scrutiny of the environment' and 'its implications that history is somehow sedimented in landscape and can be recovered from it by means of verbal texts' (2005: 419, 420).[1]

A first example of this dynamic is the combination of a shot of the three mammoth sculptures in La Brea Tar Pits and a text that reflects on the shortage of history that characterises American society. Considering the context, the sculptures could symbolise the historical layering of the place, where dozens of prehistoric fossils have been found, as well as the production of history as a simulation, because the sculptures can hardly re-enact the past in a city where there are very few buildings over a century old: they look too new and too crappy. In this particular shot, the connection between the image and the text remains on a metaphorical level, but most times it is much more explicit, especially when the commentary refers to events that took place in the film locations: for example, the images of the Venice Beach canals are accompanied by the account of how the neighbourhood was gradually moving away from its promoter's dream to become a seaside slum; then, the story of the rise of the studio system is told over a shot of the Vista Theatre at the intersection of Hollywood and Sunset Boulevards, the place where the huge Babylonian set of *Intolerance* (David W. Griffith, 1916) was built; and finally, most mentions to interethnic conflicts and insecurity problems go with images of low-income areas inhabited by Latino or African-American residents like East Los Angeles – represented by a Latino mural – or Watts – represented by the Watts Towers, the only landmark in a neighbourhood infamously known for having become a 'gangland' in the 1970s and 1980s. The last case reveals Ziolkowski's interest in the darkest episodes of local history, especially those referring to institutional violence against non-white citizens, from the lynching of Chinese immigrants in the 1871 riots to the internment of Japanese Americans in concentration camps during World War II, the former recalled over a shot of Union Station – the original location of the first Chinatown in Los Angeles – and the latter over a night shot of Little Tokyo. This kind of narrative reveals that the practice of *damnatio memoriae* is quite usual in Los Angeles, its prime example being the controversial construction of the Los Angeles Aqueduct at the expense of Owens Valley's water resources.

L.A.X. is generally organised in a linear fashion regarding time and space, because it reproduces the structure of 'a day in the city' and traces a specific path through the urban grid, going from the Los Angeles International Airport at dawn to Hollywood Boulevard at night. The last section of the footage is composed of a series of images of movie theatres over which Ziolkowski edits Jean-Luc Godard's reflections on the relationship between film and dreams in *2 ou 3 choses que je sais d'elle (2 or 3 Things I Know About Her*, 1967). This sequence depicts an unglamorous cityscape that was about to be turned into a theme park in which 'the gaze of the moviegoer, the shopper, and the tourist become interchangeable' (Stenger 2001: 70). Far from being what the tourist expects, Hollywood, as Carey McWilliams said in the 1940s, 'exists only as a state of mind, not as a geographical entity' (1946: 330), an impression that Ziolkowski emphasises by contrasting the fantasy worlds offered inside movie theatres with the hostile environment surrounding them. In this context, the closing shot – a night view of Hollywood Boulevard dominated by the neon light of a porno theatre – gives a new meaning to the title of the film, which becomes a pun between 'the LAX of the Los Angeles International Airport' and 'the LAX of the X-rated Los Angeles', as suggested by James (2005: 420).

There are many other themes in this documentary, such as the promotion of Southern California as a residential destination during the interwar period or the numerous corruption scandals related to the Chandler family, including the construction of the aqueduct, several media campaigns for or against specific political candidates or its reprehensible tendency towards land speculation.[2] All these stories are told in an incisive but dispassionate manner, putting into practice the teachings of Bertolt Brecht in order to encourage the audience's reflection. The distancing effect increases the feeling of estrangement and, above all, points to the filmmaker's alien status. As initially he has neither emotional bonds nor personal memories associated with Los Angeles, his search for the *genius loci* has to be guided by others, using the camera to mediate between divergent subjectivities: his own one as a foreigner, but also those of the quoted authors, local viewers and foreign audiences. Depending on the observer, the depicted places may have different meanings, but Ziolkowski manages to join all these possible perceptions together thanks to the layering of subjectivities. Thus, his foreign gaze finally finds a way into the city, which ultimately allows him to tell a large number of (hi)stories at once.

Thames Film: The River of Time

> The St Lawrence is water, the Mississippi is muddy water,
> but the Thames is liquid history. John Burns, MP, 1929.

The River Thames has acquired a mythological status in English culture thanks to its role as a perennial witness to the historical, political and economic evolution of London. In feature films such as *Pool of London* (Basil Dearden, 1951), *Alfie* (Lewis Gilbert, 1966), *Bronco Bullfrog* (Barney Platts-Mills, 1970), *Frenzy* (Alfred Hitchcock, 1972), *The Long Good Friday* (John Mackenzie, 1980) and *Eastern Promises* (David Cronenberg, 2007), its mere presence serves to precipitate the development of the plot, taking advantage of its liminal nature to locate important sequences on its banks, as Jez Conolly has explained:

> A river can possess a liminal quality; it is an ambiguous, unclassifiable, transitory space, a marginal state between states, distinctly different from terra firma, which by its very nature can allow individuals to exist temporarily in a situation where social conventions are loosened, thereby allowing for more permissive and open behaviour. There is also something in the character of a river that can provide natural narrative thread, running through a film and precipitating events, often disgorging important plot points onto its banks where the threshold between liquid and solid states are emphasized. (2011: 130)

By the mid-1980s, this power of suggestion led experimental filmmaker William Raban to make a film about London from the point of view of the Thames. In the short documentary *The Frame–William Raban* (Filmmaker Unknown, 2003), he mentions that 'the obvious way I have seen of doing that was to drift all the river

Image 4.2: *Thames Film*, London from the point of view of the river

in a small boat as close to the water surface as possible and record what happened on the banks' (Image 4.2). The outcome, *Thames Film*, understands the riverscape as a geographical and cultural territory fraught with places of memory, whose historical density is depicted through visual materials from different times: first, the present is captured by the footage filmed in 1984; second, the recent past is recovered through old films and pictures; and finally, the distant past is recalled by means of pre-filmic documents, such as paintings, maps, illustrations, engravings or travel literature. The set of all these materials establishes a historical reading of the watercourse in which the decaying riverscape functions as a metaphor for the economic recession of the early 1980s. The Thames, according to Charlotte Brundson, has historically been 'the privileged locus for stories of industrial and imperial decline' (2007: 15), a tradition that Raban updates by showing a panorama of empty wharves, rotting piers, sunken ships and abandoned forts. Wherever the filmmaker went, mist and fog threatened to make invisible the silhouettes of blackened warehouses and other post-industrial ruins, helping to create the impression of drifting over time.

From the beginning, the idea of temporal simultaneity is introduced by a quote from T. S. Eliot's poem 'Burnt Norton' (1935), read by the poet himself: '*Time present and time past / are both perhaps present in time future, / and time future contained in time past*'. Such fusion of historical times is achieved in *Thames Film* by means of the preference for long and static shots and the juxtaposition of past and present images. The soundtrack, meanwhile, emphasises the river's timeless perspective through the combination of the ubiquitous sound of water and the echoes of distant activities. But what definitely symbolises the temporal overlapping is the river's longevity, an idea directly expressed in the following excerpt of the commentary: '*The river journey unwinds a distant memory. Each moment has a particular meaning and relation to the past. Another time, different values, but the river transcends these changes.*'

The narrative structure of the film seeks to reflect the river's geological time by following the tidal cycles in a loop. The opening sequence, for example, goes upstream from the estuary to the city, where Raban changes direction to go to the mouth again. The second journey pays much more attention to the waterfront and tells the historical vicissitudes of riverside areas such as Millwall, Greenwich,

Blackwall, Long Reach, Gravesend or Canvey Island. Once the camera reaches the starting point of the first trip, Raban reinforces the tidal narrative by repeating the opening sequence shot by shot up to the Victoria Embankment, where the film ends with the only image filmed from outside the watercourse: a shot of people walking on Waterloo Bridge.

Throughout the second journey, the most frequently quoted source for links between past and present is Thomas Pennant's *A Journey from London to the Isle of Wight* (1801). John Hurt, the film's narrator, recites several excerpts of this travel book in the commentary, while Raban includes images of the original manuscript in the editing. Indeed, the first and second journey are separated by a series of shots of the spine, the cover and the first pages of the book, after which Hurt reads the beginning in order to highlight the spatial synchronisation of Pennant's and Raban's journeys:

> On Monday May 7th 1787, I took a boat at the Temple stairs to make the voyage to the lower part of the Thames. Monday May 7th 1984. High water, 6:09. Crossing the time and place of your departure. Your voyage following the ebb tide downstream to the sea. Your search on the ebb flow. Looking for the signs of increase, production, exploration and empire.

Raban chronicles the vanishing of these signs as a result of post-industrial crisis, but Pennant's stories increase the haunting atmosphere of the film by describing the waterfront as a succession of power symbols and repressive spaces: the reference to the execution docks in Long Reach, where '*hanging bodies were left there to be covered by three full tides before sentence was completed*', functions as a bad omen for the future, which was then threatened by dystopian visions inspired by George Orwell's *Nineteen Eighty-Four* (1949). In this context, the dry and constant noise of a pile driver can be interpreted as a sound metaphor for the executions and burials on the riverside, because it somehow recalls the sound of driving nails into a coffin.

There are so many references to Pennant's book in *Thames Film* that it could be considered its film adaptation. Nevertheless, Raban also contrasts contemporary footage with other visual materials, such as a few pictures from 1937, four films found in the Port of London Authority Collection, the painting *The Triumph of Death* (Pieter Bruegel the Elder, 1562), and the engraving 'The Idle 'Prentice turn'd away, and sent to Sea', which is the fifth plate of the series *Industry and Idleness* (William Hogarth, 1747). The films, which are *Port of London* (Filmmaker Unknown, 1921), *City of Ships* (Filmmaker Unknown, 1940), *Via London* (Filmmaker Unknown, 1948) and *Waters of Time* (Bill Launder & Basil Wright, 1951), date back to the good old times of the Empire, when the Docklands was a place of bustling activity and an example of paternalist capitalism. They show the repair of ships and the work of longshoremen with an optimistic and even euphoric tone that Raban opposes to the dying stillness of the 1980s: thus, whenever possible, he compares old and new images of the same places in order to increase the impression of sudden decay.

The decline of the Docklands, according to Francesc Muñoz, began in the mid-1960s when large multinational corporations took control of their productive capacity and moved their main activities to Tilbury, at the river's mouth (2010: 98). Later on, in the 1980s, the area was at its worst, which justifies Raban's recurrent comparison between the rundown waterfront and the frightening battlefield painted by Bruegel: *The Triumph of Death* appears up to five times in the film, usually in relation to Pennant's comments about hangings and graveyards on the foreshore, as well as when Raban finds sunken ships and abandoned forts in the estuary. Its violent scenes bring to the 1980s the classical topics of *memento mori* ('remember you will die') and *tempus fugit* ('times flies') in an attempt to announce the definitive burial of industrial Britain under Thatcher's rule.

Hogarth's engraving, in turn, only appears once to confirm Pennant's stories about Millwall's double nature as workspace and execution dock, two functions respectively represented by four windmills and a hanged body. This area would become the new business district of London in the 1990s, a project vigorously supported by the Conservative government of the day, but when Raban made *Thames Film* there was no sign of redevelopment in the Isle of Dogs. The absence of One Canada Square – the tallest building in the United Kingdom from 1990 to 2010 – increases the historical value of *Thames Film*, given that Raban recorded a fleeting avatar of the riverscape in the interregnum between the end of port activity and the construction of the new business district, Canary Wharf.

One Canada Square does appear in Raban's later films, especially in the shorts that form the Under the Tower Trilogy. The first one, *Sundial* (1992), consists of seventy-one shots in one single minute in which the building is always centred in the frame, although the camera changes position from one shot to another in order to explore the visual impact of the tower in the landscape. The second film, *A13* (1994), is a post-symphony that contrasts the construction of a new road scheme in the area – the Limehouse Road Link – with scenes of its everyday life, among which several political demonstrations stand out. Finally, the third film, *Island Race* (1996), documents the political aftermath of the 1993 Millwall by-election, in which the far-right British National Party won its first local council seat. The ubiquitous presence of One Canada Square in all these films reveals the progression of banalscapes in the Isle of Dogs throughout the 1990s, following the pattern described by Muñoz:

Port areas have finally returned to the city as smooth and flat surfaces in which the standardised uses that make up the restricted menu of urban developments are located: a metropolitan aquarium, a sea museum, a multiplex movie theatre with an IMAX screen and a shopping area with its corresponding public spaces, which are inspired by the economy of global franchises and decorated according to the old image of the city, whatever city, from London to Genoa, and from Rijeka to Rotterdam. These plans, far from generating inclusive dynamics and synergies between the renovated port and the existing city, have been characterised by prioritising the functional specialisation of land uses and the visual impact in the short term. They are linear and predictable from an architectural perspective and too limited from the point of view of urban planning, because they are unable to generate new relations between different areas of the city. Their simplicity and univocity therefore result in the increase of port areas shaped as commonplaces. (2010: 207; my translation)

The arrival of Tony Blair's 'New Labour' government after almost two decades of Conservative rule did not change the urban policy in the Docklands: the short film *MM* (William Raban, 2002) chronicles the construction of the Millennium Dome east of the Isle of Dogs, another work of architecture-spectacle that led to the creative destruction of its surrounding area. This kind of project tends to produce a generic city that replaces the historical identity of the places where it stands with a consumer-friendly simulacrum that attenuates the local characteristics that may hinder its consumption. The very term 'generic city' was coined by Rem Koolhaas and Bruce Mau in the mid-1990s, a time when there were many similar redevelopment projects to Canary Wharf all over the world:

> The Generic City is the city liberated from the captivity of center, from the straitjacket of identity. The Generic City breaks with this destructive cycle of dependency: it is nothing but a reflection of present need and present ability. It is the city without history. It is big enough for everybody. It is easy. It does not need maintenance. If it gets too small it just expands. If it gets old it just self-destructs and renews. It is equally exciting – or unexciting – everywhere. It is 'superficial' – like a Hollywood studio lot, it can produce a new identity every Monday morning. (1995: 1249–50)

Faced with this trend, Raban's whole work seeks to recover the historical identity of the Docklands through different formal devices. *Thames Film*, in particular, chooses psychogeographical landscaping to capture the *genius loci* of the area,

73

adopting not only the river's perspective but also its sense of time. Consequently, the film depicts the riverscape from inside out and from the present to the past, setting a clear precedent for the following case study.

London: The Absence of the City

The first part of the Robinson Trilogy begins with the same image that closed *Thames Film*: a ship arriving at the city by the river. This time, the camera's perspective has changed, inasmuch as it frames the river from the city instead of the city from the river. Aboard the ship, the nameless narrator of *London* and the next film in the trilogy, *Robinson in Space* (2007), returns to the country after an absence of seven years, during which he had been working as the ship's photographer. He has decided to quit his job to join an old friend and lover called Robinson in a mysterious psychogeographical research. Despite their former intimacy, the Narrator introduces this character in a detached way, describing his socio-economic status and living conditions even before his personality:

> *Robinson lives in the way that people were said to live in the cities of the Soviet Union. His income is small, but he saves most of it. [...] He isn't poor because he lacks money, but because everything he wants is unobtainable. He lives on what he earns in one or two days a week teaching in the school of fine art and architecture of the University of Barking.*

These lines are heard over a shot of a housing project in Vauxhall, which would supposedly be Robinson's home. Nevertheless, there is no human figure that could be identified as 'Robinson' or 'the Narrator' in these images or in the entire trilogy, because they only exist as narrative entities in the commentary: the Narrator's voice guides the audience during Robinson's journeys through the territory while the images show what he and his travelling companion find in the landscape without ever showing their physical presence there. The Narrator is therefore a chronicler who accompanies the hero in his wanderings, while Robinson embodies a totemic figure in the psychogeographical tradition: he is 'the man of the crowd', a traveller, a visionary, a romantic, a modernist, a misfit, a bohemian, an outcast and even one of the damned, but above all a walker who explores the territory in search of signs that allow him to study 'the problem of London' in the first part of the trilogy, 'the problem of England' in the second, and the possibility of life's survival on the planet in the third, *Robinson in Ruins* (2010).

From a narrative point of view, Robinson is also Patrick Keiller's fictional disguise. The character was initially identified with an autobiographical figure, because Keiller himself is a researcher who teaches architecture and fine arts (see Yates 1994: 55), but Stella Bruzzi has warned that the ambiguity of the narrative device prevents considering Robinson or the Narrator as Keiller's alter ego:

> The relationship of this narration to either Robinson or Keiller is ambiguous (is Robinson, the collator of images, really the Narrator – or is the Narrator, a ship's photographer, Robinson? Are either Keiller's alter ego?). The Narrator, however loquacious, is not given a 'character' as such, but is a site where ideas, observations and fact collation congregate. There are some similarities between him and Keiller ... but to interpret him as a self-portrait would be wrong. (2006: 110–11)

Chris Darke seems to have found a solution to this controversy by saying that 'Robinson is Patrick Keiller's method of deferred narration' (2010: 74). According to him, this name, character or concept serves to express Keiller's gaze at the world, a gaze that captures both the *zeitgeist* and the *genius loci* of a specific time and place:

> Each of the Robinson films has been sensitive to what Marxists would call its moment of historical conjuncture. *London* captured the fag end of Tory rule in its portrait of a shattered, shuttered city. *Robinson in Space,* a grand tour of Britain's new neoliberal non-places, was released in the year of the New Labour landslide. *Robinson in Ruins* is equally self-conscious about the current conjuncture. The camera lingers at length, 'in the manner of Turner', on landscape views of Oxfordshire and Berkshire as the narrator repeatedly details the near collapse of the international banking system in 2008. (Ibid.)

Keiller's landscaping is characterised by a constant interaction between the fictional nature of the narrative and the documentary substrate of the images, which were usually recorded without location sound (except in *Robinson in Ruins*) and almost without camera movements (there are only a few brief pan shots in *Robinson in Space*). This formal strategy has been described by Paul Dave as a combination between 'elements of the performative documentary' and 'a more expository method' (2006: 128, 129), while Patrick Russell has compared it with 'the most primitive of travelogues, postcard views on the screen' (2007: 116). The structure of film diaries has also influenced the trilogy, because each of its parts includes a rigorous temporal dating of most of its shots. Finally, Keiller's work has many elements in common with the essay film, beginning with the way of addressing an immense amount of objective data from an always subjective perspective. It must be taken into account that the images of these films can be interpreted in an objective or subjective manner within their respective fictional stories, because they always show real landscapes from the character's point of view: 'the camera', according to Robert Yates, 'works as the eyes of the *flâneurs*, of Robinson and of the narrator, and drifts with them' (1994: 55).

London, the most urban film of the trilogy, has been defined by Bruzzi as 'a reflexive journey documentary ... part of [a] growing tradition that takes the attributes and ethos of observational cinema (its interest in contemporary life, detail, personalities, mannerisms) as the basis for reflexive films that simultaneously debate these observational foundations' (2006: 109–110). In this documentary, Robinson's journeys are developed in three overlapping dimensions: the first is space, since most of the footage is devoted to three psychogeographical expeditions through London's geography; the second is the time of the story, which expands for a whole year, from 11 January to 9 December 1992; and the third is historical time, which is present almost everywhere through monuments, references, traces or memories. These journeys, however, are motionless and imaginary, because its stages are developed between the shots: the editing neither includes images that can suggest the character's movement nor archival footage or other visual materials representing the historical events mentioned in the commentary. Each shot only shows a specific point in the path, whether an intermediate stop, an unexpected detour or its final destination, that is, places associated with findings or distractions, which can be surprising or disappointing. As 'no image is prioritised over any other' (Bruzzi 2006: 112), their narrative meaning entirely depends on the commentary.

The city, meanwhile, is depicted as a juxtaposition of buildings, streets, parks, commons and streams in which the constant references to history bring to life the fixed frames to recover the successive lost identities of the cityscape. Hence Keiller's reflections can be understood on two levels: on the one hand, regarding representation, which is constructed by means of the interplay between fictional narrative and documentary images; on the other, regarding the historical and political meaning of these representations, which is more suggested than revealed by the narrator's remarks.

Within the fictional plot, Robinson's journeys aim to address 'the problem of London', an expression referring to the historical hostility of the city to European modernity. This attitude, according to Keiller, was represented at the time by the anti-urban policy of Margaret Thatcher's and John Major's governments, whose most controversial measures are explicitly criticised in the film:

London ... is a city under siege from a suburban government which uses homelessness, pollution, crime and the most expensive and rundown public transport system of any metropolitan city in Europe as weapons against Londoners' lingering desire for the freedoms of city life.

The idea of 'a city under siege' is emphasised by the 1992 IRA bombing campaign in London. These terrorist attacks symbolise the material destruction of the city, as well as the growing unrest against the conservative government that poisoned the social climate of the time. In this regard, Mark Fisher has recalled that *London* was made in the wake of a political non-event, the general election of 9 April 1992, when the end of Tory rule was widely expected – even by the Conservative Party itself – but John Major was finally re-elected (2010: 23). The Conservatives maintained a parliamentary majority of 21 seats in the House of Commons that allowed them to govern for five more years, until 1997.[3]

This electoral victory meant the continuation of an urban policy based on the downsizing of local government and the systematic production of banalscapes to attract investors to the city. Regarding the first issue, *London* includes several comments on the abolition of the Greater London Council (GLC) by the Local Government Act 1985, which in practice limited the city's capacity for self-government by dividing the GLC powers among thirty-three boroughs. The lack of a single administrative body for the whole city between 1986 and 2000 – the year Tony Blair's government established the Greater London Authority (GLA) – led to the sale of a large number of plots in the international land market, an operation that Muñoz has regarded as the prelude to their subsequent redevelopment as banalscapes (2010: 96).

Another consequence of this policy was the gradual disinvestment in those services that the government wanted to privatise, such as railways and public housing. In this context, the modernist paradigm of urban planning was definitely abandoned, as Robinson regrets on his way through Elephant and Castle, an area of concrete tower blocks built in the post-war years that needed urgent restoration in the early 1990s. Overall, according to Ewa Mazierska and Laura Rascaroli, Thatcherite politics 'strengthened the position of London as the richest city in Britain and as the political, economic and cultural centre of the country', but it also increased the gap between its rich and poor areas, as well as social fragmentation (2003: 164). Under these circumstances, the city explored by Keiller was characterised by 'the elimination of the local places in between the landmarks ... in favour of an architecture of spectacle', as Charlotte Brundson has said, 'a material montage of shiny surfaces and "no-place" spaces like lobbies and atria' (2007: 218).

Faced with the hostility of these new spaces, Keiller uses psychogeographical landscaping to overcome what Ian Robinson – a real scholar with no relation to the character – has described as 'a crisis in the articulation of local collective memory and global political economy' (2010: 120). Throughout the film, the film-maker gives many examples of how the historical meaning of the cityscape was being blurred and banalised as a result of the implementation of neoliberal economics, beginning with the house where Michel de Montaigne had lived in London: at that particular spot, his very name no longer refers to the French writer, but to a school of English named after him. This finding announces the interpretative possibilities of the characters' psychogeographical drifts, first in small scale, in Vauxhall, and then in three long expeditions that put into practice Guy Debord's definition of '*dérive*':

> A technique of rapid passage through varied ambiences. *Dérives* involve playful-constructive behavior and awareness of psychogeographical effects; and are thus different from the classic notions of journey or stroll. (1981b: 50)

The second sentence of this definition reveals Debord's effort to distinguish the Situationist *dérive* from the Dada visit or the Surrealist deambulation. For him and his travelling companions, urban space was 'an objective passionate terrain rather than merely subjective-unconscious' (Careri 2002: 90), meaning that their *dérive* did not demonstrate 'the pure submission to unconscious desire that characterised the surrealist wanderings or the journeys of the strolling *flâneur*' (Coverley 2010: 96). On the contrary, they drifted to conduct a psychogeographical research whose main purposes were, according to Sadie Plant, 'to notice the way in which certain areas, streets, or buildings resonate with states of mind, inclinations, and desires, and to seek out reasons for movement other than those for which an environment was designed' (1992: 59). This research has to do with Debord's assumption that 'cities have psychogeographical contours, with constant currents, fixed points and vortexes that strongly discourage entry into or exit from certain zones' (1981b: 50). This last idea ultimately led him to state 'the existence of psychogeographical pivotal points', which could be those places where the *genius loci* would be more present in the cityscape, even though they have been completely transformed over time (1981b: 53).

But how to represent the Situationist *dérive* in moving images? Debord tried to draw up maps of influences in his own films – especially in the case of *In girum imus nocte et consumimur igni* – through old maps and aerial views, which have been considered 'the cinematic counterpart of the *dérive*' by Teresa Castro, because they establish 'a dialectics between the act of seeing and surveying the earth from above – intensified by the camera movements across the image – and that of experiencing it by walking' (2010: 153). This dialectics, Castro continues, is part of 'a scaling strategy' that recalls cartographic methods: 'surveying the earth from above, with the eyes, and scanning it and measuring it by field walking, with the body' (2010: 153).[4] However, there are also simpler ways of adapting the Situationist *dérive* to film based on two properties that differentiate this medium from everyday experience, as Amanda Wasielewski has suggested: 'its ability to be edited and rearranged and its mediation of space via the camera' (2009: 2).

Keiller only uses framing and editing to depict Robinson's and the Narrator's journeys throughout the entire trilogy. In the first part, these characters assume a subversive position by exploring London by foot, inasmuch as this activity opposes 'the spirit of the modern city with its promotion of swift circulation', as explained by Coverley: 'the street-level gaze that walking requires allows one to challenge the official representation of the city by cutting across established routes and exploring those marginal and forgotten areas often overlooked by the city's inhabitants' (2010: 12). This insistence on avoiding means of transport is especially striking in a city as hostile to pedestrians as London, which, unlike Paris, Vienna or Rome, has seldom been depicted as a city of strollers, as Mazierska and Rascaroli have pointed out:

> We rarely see people in films walking the streets of London and when they do, it usually ends badly for them – they are raped, mugged or killed, and their bodies are disposed of in the Thames. [...] This suburban and *anti-flâneurian* character is reminiscent of many other cities in the English-speaking world, particularly the USA, and manifests itself in the lack of a distinctive, well-defined centre and of clear pedestrian routes, even if it can be argued that London has several 'centres' around which Londoners stroll and to which they relate. (2003: 169–70)

London questions why the European sensibility towards street life represented by certain modernist writers was unable to take root and flourish in England, but also continues the London psychogeographical tradition by borrowing the narrative structure of Daniel Defoe's *A Journal of the Plague Year* (1722).[5] The simultaneous reference to Debord and Defoe locates *London* halfway between the English and French concept of psychogeography, which were respectively interested in finding out the *genius loci* and in reworking the urban environment in a creative way. In order to reinforce this dual affiliation, Keiller mentions artists and writers that belong to one or another tradition, such as William Hogarth,

Lawrence Sterne and J. M. W. Turner on the British side, and Charles Baudelaire, Paul Verlaine, Arthur Rimbaud and Guillaume Apollinaire on the French one. Anyway, despite all these influences, Keiller also has his own idea of what psychogeography is about: the ultimate aim of Robinson's expeditions is to *'travel through time'*, as the Narrator says more than once. Indeed, at the beginning of *London*, he explains that *'Robinson believed that if he looks at it hard enough he could cause the surface of the city to reveal to him the molecular basis of historical events. And in this way, he hoped to see into the future.'* This idea of using space to travel through time had already appeared in *Thames Film*, but this time the act of walking to every destination entails a more material relationship with film locations. Thus, the spatial practices developed by the characters are a first step to re-appropriate the city in an attempt to overcome the fragmentation imposed by Thatcherite mismanagement.

These practices can be classified into three different groups: the first consists of short pilgrimages to places of memory, the second is the journalistic coverage of political events throughout 1992, and the third refers to three 'official' *dérives*. Regarding the short pilgrimages, the first place of memory visited by the characters is the statue of King Charles I at the intersection of Whitehall and Trafalgar Square, where groups of Anglo-Catholics and other ultra-monarchists lay wreaths every year to commemorate his execution by the revolutionary government of 1649. This ceremony inspires the first of Robinson's many critical comments on history and politics contained in the footage – this time on the failure of the English revolution – thereby establishing the discursive dynamic of the film: wherever the characters go, they will always find something in the cityscape that Robinson can interpret as a symptom or a consequence of 'the problem of London'.

More examples of this dynamic would be the view from the suite of the Savoy Hotel in which Claude Monet lived and worked for several months – the same view that he painted, the same specific frame – whose contemplation leads to a denunciation of the abolition of the Greater London Council (Image 4.3); or a visit

Image 4.3: *London*, view from Claude Monet's room at the Savoy Hotel

to the Brixton Market in search of Apollinaire's trail that includes a brief reflection on the harsh living conditions of Afro-Caribbean immigrants in the post-war years. In both cases, the elements that have given rise to these comments are part of the cityscape: on the one hand, the former seat of the Greater London Council, County Hall, can be seen from Monet's room at the Savoy (it is to the left of the frame); and on the other hand, the presence of many Afro-Caribbean customers in the Brixton

Market establishes the link with the recent history of this community.

The same dynamic is repeated in the journalistic coverage of a large variety of events that reflect the *zeitgeist* of 1992, such as the general election, many terrorist attacks, some political demonstrations and a few royal ceremonies. Some of them speak by themselves, like the bombing of the Baltic Exchange, represented by a long shot of St. Helen's destroyed skyscraper without comments, but the Narrator also echoes the signs of discontent that he witnesses, such as the presence in the City of a deranged man identified as 'the man of the crowd' after the bombing or the unexpected insults against the Royal Family during the reopening of Leicester Square and an homage to Bomber Harris[6] – in the first event, someone shouted to Queen Elizabeth II 'pay your taxes, you scum!', while during the second the Queen Mother was called 'mass murderer'. These situations lead the Narrator to express his own antipathy against monarchy and its anachronistic rituals: when he attends the Trooping the Colour ceremony, he says that he is amazed at the contrast between the precision and splendour of that kind of display and the squalor of the suburbs that he has recently visited. The journalistic approach, therefore, allows Keiller to combine several voices within the same narrative device, given that the Narrator gathers public opinion as heard on the streets and read in the press.

Current issues also appear one way or another in the three official *dérives*: for example, the departure of the first expedition has to be postponed due to an IRA bombing in Wandsworth Common; then, the itinerary of the second *dérive* goes through places that were being transformed at the time, such as Spitalfields or Stoke Newington; and finally, the third journey documents the taking of the suburbs by large companies like Tesco or IKEA. Throughout these psychogeographical expeditions, Robinson and the Narrator find out the contemporary avatars of the city, most of them unusual and unexpected, despite the fact that they are apparently much more interested in looking for the traces of modernist writers in the cityscape.

Map 4.1: Itineraries of Robinson's *dérives* in London [Grey (1st expedition), White (2nd expedition) and Black (3rd expedition)]

These expeditions usually take place in the southern and western suburbs of the city. The first one, marked with a grey line in Map 4.1, begins with a pilgrimage to Horace Walpole's house in Strawberry Hill, Twickenham, southwest of London – the place where he wrote *The Castle of Otranto* (1764) – after which the characters return to Vauxhall through Richmond, Mortlake, Hammersmith and Battersea. The second expedition, represented by a white line in the map, also uses literary references as points of departure and arrival: this time, the characters go to Clapham North, again in the southwest, where Apollinaire was once in search of a former lover, and then head north through Stockwell, Oval, Elephant and Castle, London Bridge, the City, Spitalfields and Shoreditch, to reach Stoke Newington, where they intend to visit Edgar Allan Poe's school but only find the house where Daniel Defoe wrote *Robinson Crusoe* (1719). The literary references decrease in the third *dérive* – the black line in the map – in which the characters track the River Brent downstream from Wembley to Brentford. Their original purpose was to look for contemporary cultural practices in the western suburbs of the city, but once there, they realise that the growing presence of non-places does not seem to inspire any kind of artistic or literary activity.

None of these expeditions is linear in time and space, because the characters continuously stop to eat in modern supermarkets or sleep in traditional inns. Sometimes, they even return home to rest or attend public events before taking up their itinerary again. These interrupted *dérives* are, essentially, the backbone of Robinson's research, his fieldwork, through which Keiller gradually addresses a series of recurrent topics: nostalgia for a future that will never happen, the perception of London as a historical palimpsest, and the slow vanishing of its identity due to its social and administrative fragmentation. Considering the political climate of the time, it is not surprising that Robinson arrives at a negative conclusion at the end of the film:

> For Londoners, London is obscured. Too thinly spread, too private for anyone to know. Its social life invisible, its government abolished. Its institutions at the discretion of either monarchy or state. Or the City, where at the historic centre there is nothing but a civic void which fills and empties daily with armies of clerks and dealers, mostly citizens of other towns. The true identity of London ... is in its absence. As a city, it no longer exists. In this alone, it is truly modern: London was the first metropolis to disappear.

This final remark suggests that absence is the key concept to explain the problem of London. Merlin Coverley has associated it with the lack of effective government, visible economic output, public space, community and even society (2010: 133), while Ian Robinson has interpreted it as the decline of the city as 'a place of encounter, sociability, creativity, unpredictability and history' (2010: 123). Even Rem Koolhaas and Bruce Mau agreed with this interpretation when they wrote that 'London – its only identity a lack of clear identity – is perpetually becoming even less London, more open, less static' (1995: 1248). In Keiller's documentary, this absence is more evident in the non-places inherited from Thatcherism, such as financial skyscrapers, shopping centres, new road schemas or construction sites, a set of transitory spaces in which 'the sociality of the collective', according to Ian Robinson, 'is reduced to suspicion and surveillance' (2010: 118). Such perception is reinforced by Keiller's way of framing symbolic landmarks, like One Canada Square, which is depicted as a disturbing sentinel that controls and masters the city from a position of superiority (Image 4.4). This building and its surrounding area are a prime example of what Marie-Christine Boyer has called 'city *tableaux*': a simulated cityscape that combines the fantastic with the real to compensate the everyday failures of the city (1992: 200). 'These *tableaux*,' according to Boyer, 'are the true non-places, hollowed out urban remnants, without connection to the rest of the city or the past, waiting to be filled with contemporary fantasies, colonized by wishful projections, and turned into spectacles of consumption' (1992: 191). One Canada Square

Image 4.4: *London*, One Canada Square

is arguably Robinson's nemesis, and not only because it has been built for *voyeurs* instead of for walkers, but above all because it symbolises the contempt for and oblivion of the *genius loci*.

Faced with the shallowness of city *tableaux*, psychogeography allows both characters and audience to rebuild an imaginary city from the material remains of all those futures that never came true. In fact, Robinson's interest in English writers of the eighteenth century and the French poets who followed Baudelaire was actually, according to the narrator, '*an attempt to rebuild the city as if the nineteenth century had never happened*'. This agenda accounts for his nostalgia for the modernist approach to city planning associated with the former London City Council (LCC), the first metropolitan authority to be directly elected.[7] Robinson praises its legacy twice in the film, first as he passes through Elephant and Castle and then when he stops at Arnold Circus, in Shoreditch, to contemplate the Boundary Estate for hours. Over a beautiful image of two children playing in the street, the Narrator explains that this place is a fragment of a golden age or a utopia to Robinson, because it is one of the earliest social housing schemes built by the LCC. Keiller holds the shot for a few seconds, turning it into a tribute to the city that could have been if the modernist approach to city planning had prevailed on the suburban approach. This nostalgia insists on the failure of London as a modernist city, a discourse that Paul Dave has related to Perry Anderson's theses on the development of English capitalism:

The examination of public space in *London* ... is influenced by the idea that the energies of the bourgeoisie have historically been contained by an aristocratic hegemony. These energies conventionally include the values of modern urbanism that the narrator remarks are absent in London, places are 'either void or the stage sets for spectacles of nineteenth century reaction endlessly re-enacted for television'. Examples provided of this archaic 'heritage' spectacle in the film, such as the Lord Mayor's and Trooping the Colour, are linked to the *ancien régime* – here Corporation of London and the Monarchy respectively. For Perry Anderson ... the historical explanation for the perceived failings of the national culture lies in the fact that the English Revolution was the 'least pure bourgeois revolution of any European country' (1992: 17). In other words, because the aristocracy was not ultimately displaced the revolution failed to modernise the social structure and the political system. (2000: 342)

In the 1980s, Thatcherism replaced the last attempts at modernity with a post-modern approach to city planning that hid urban decay behind the production of city *tableaux*. Since then, most of the heritage spectacles mentioned by Dave have taken place in the historical, political and financial centre of London, between Westminster and the City, an area that only appears in the journalist sequences of the film. Meanwhile, the psychogeographical *dérives* explore the suburban working-class neighbourhoods in which most of the population lives, such as Vauxhall, Brixton, Clapham, Shoreditch, Notting Hill or Wembley. Many of these places are located south of the Thames, a traditionally under-represented area in mainstream cinema that Keiller depicts as the new battleground between citizenship and capital.

Both the journalistic and psychogeographical expeditions share the same concern with the negative effects of the government's measures on the social and urban fabric, regardless of their scale: Robinson is thus worried about the worsening living conditions in the whole city, but most especially in his own neighbourhood, Vauxhall. The best example of how Keiller uses Robinson's individual situation to address the collective dimension is the long list of exaggerated social and personal problems that the Narrator enumerates over images of the celebration of the fourth consecutive Conservative victory in Downing Street:

> *Robinson began to consider what the result would mean for him. His flat would continue to deteriorate, and its rent increase. He would be intimidated by vandalism and petty crime. The bus service would get worse. There would be more traffic and noise pollution and an increased risk of*

getting knocked down crossing the road. There would be more drunks pissing in the street when he looked out of the window and more children taking drugs on the stairs when he came home at night. His job would be at risk and subjected to interference. His income would decrease. He would drink more and less well. He would be ill more often. He would die sooner.

For the old, or anyone with children, it would be much worse. For London as a whole, there would now be no new elected metropolitan authority. The public transport system would degenerate into chaos as it was deregulated and privatised. There would be more road schemes. Hospitals would close. As the social security system was dismantled there would be increased homelessness and crime with the police more often carrying guns. The population would continue to decline as those who could moved away and employers followed.

This passage repeats the same topics in its two parts: problems with the transportation system, social security, public safety and the job market that may jeopardise the very survival of the city and its residents. Considering that the filmmaker has explained that he wanted to turn Robinson's deprivation into a sort of shared experience (in Dave 2006: 135), it could be said that this character embodies the experience of all the people left behind by Thatcherism. This is the reason why the film does not end with Robinson's final remarks but with the characters' return to Vauxhall, where the last sequence documents the visible consequences of Conservative anti-urban policies: after a spate of vandalism caused by a group of teenagers, most businesses, beginning with the Portuguese driving school that is right in front of Robinson's house, had to protect their shop windows with roller shutters. Moreover, the Narrator says that Robinson's street had just been designated a red route, a device intended to speed the flow of commuters from the suburbs to the centre. These details confirm some of Robinson's predictions – these referred to the increase of traffic and the decrease of public safety – and close the film in an everyday environment, insisting on the subjective perception of London as a lived place.

Contrary to how it may seem, the subjectivity at stake here is not individual but collective: it is a set of historical and everyday experiences that emerges from the cityscape itself as a response to the power discourse. Hence Robinson does not stand for Keiller, but rather Keiller makes up Robinson as a way of taking the pulse of public opinion at different turning points, from the last years of Tory rule in *London* and *Robinson in Space* to the outbreak of the financial crisis in *Robinson in Ruins*. Consequently, in *London*, the filmmaker attempts to counteract the city's lack of identity with a psychogeographical report that links past and present, looking for the spirit of time (the *zeitgeist*) in the spirit of place (the *genius loci*). For him, as for Ziolkowski and Raban, the psychogeographical gaze at the city transcends the here and now, because they all understand recent urban transformations as part of larger processes, whether the historical evolution of a place – a journey through time – or global tendencies in contemporary urban planning – a journey through space.

NOTES

1   The eight texts are, in order of appearance, John and LaRee Caughey's *Los Angeles – Biography of a City* (1977), Stephen Longstreet's *All Star Cast – An Anecdotal History of Los Angeles* (1977), Carey McWilliams' *Southern California: An Island on the Land* (1946), David Gebhard and Robert Winter's *The Guide to Architecture in Los Angeles and Southern California* (1977), David Halberstam's *The Powers that Be* (1975), Raymond Chandler's *The Little Sister* (1949), Tristan Tzara's *Seven Dada Manifestos* (1924) and Jean-Luc Godard's *2 or 3 Things I Know About Her* (1967).

2   The Chandler family kept control of the *Los Angeles Times* for almost a century, from 1882, when Harrison Gray Otis became the paper's editor, to 1980, when his great-grandson Otis Chandler retired from the position of publisher.

3   The composition of the House of the Commons after the general election of 1992 was as follows: Conservative 336 seats, Labour 271 seats and the Liberal Democrats 20 seats.

4   Both perspectives would later be theorised by Michel de Certeau (1984: 92–3), who identified them with the voyeur's and walker's gaze, as we have seen in chapter one.

5   Coverley considers that Defoe's book was the first example of psychogeographical practices in the London visionary tradition, because it foreshadowed 'the figure of an urban wanderer, who moves aimlessly across the city before reporting back with his observations' (2010: 16). Other milestones in this tradition would be, according to him, William Blake's poems, Thomas de Quincey's *Confessions of an English Opium Eater* (1821), Robert Louis Stevenson's *The Strange Case of Dr Jekyll and Mr Hyde* (1886), Arthur Machen's *The London Adventure or the Art of Wandering* (1924) and Alfred Watkins' *The Old Straight Track* (1925) (2010: 31–56).

6   Sir Arthur Harris, commonly known as Bomber Harris, was one of the military men responsible for the bombing of Cologne in World War II.

7   The London City Council was created in 1889 and later replaced by the Greater London Council in 1965. Previously, the main instrument of London-wide government was the Metropolitan Board of Works, which was an appointed rather than elected body.

CHAPTER FIVE

Autobiographical Landscaping

One of the main differences between observational and psychogeographical landscaping is the filmmaker's degree of intervention: James Benning's careful choice of framings is much less explicit than Patrick Keiller's fictional narratives, but both reveal a gradual involvement of filmmakers in urban space. Autobiographical landscaping develops further this link between subject and object – or sender and message, in the usual terms of information theory – by combining the distancing effect of structural films with the subjective dimension of first-person accounts. In these documentaries, the autobiographical content becomes a key element to decode the meaning of the urban surface, despite the differences established by the way in which the first-person is used.

Prior to the 1980s, cinema was not perceived as a suitable medium for autobiography. Literary scholar Elizabeth Bruss asserted that 'there is no real cinematic equivalent for autobiography' (1980: 296) because filmmakers could not embody the filmed subject while they were behind the camera or, conversely, they could not film themselves if they were in front of the camera. She criticised early examples of this film practice such as *Fireworks* (Kenneth Anger, 1947), *Joyce at 34* (Joyce Chopra & Claudia Weill, 1974), *Les quatre cents coups* (*The 400 Blows*, François Truffaut, 1959), *8½* (Federico Fellini, 1963) or *Annie Hall* (Woody Allen, 1977) for their lack of 'truth-value', 'act-value' and 'identity-value', three criteria that have been summarised by Jim Lane as follows:

> Truth-value is associated with reference and autobiography's empiricist claim 'to be consistent with other evidence'. Act-value is associated with performance, 'an action that exemplifies the character of the agent responsible for that action and how it is performed'. Identity-value is associated with the conflation of the roles of author, narrator, and protagonist in au-

tobiography and 'the same individual occupying a position both in the context, the associated "scene of writing", and within the text itself'. (2002: 29)

Since Bruss wrote her article, non-fiction film has undergone a subjective turn that has led many film theorists to defend the opposite idea: the existence of *mise-en-scène* and editing resources capable of overcoming these problems. Philippe Lejeune, for example, pointed out the ability of home movies, film diaries, still photographs and voiceover narration to address the past in a cinematic way (2008: 19); Jim Lane added formal interviews and interactive modes of filming to those resources (2002: 94); Michael Renov reminded us that the filming subject could easily be before and behind the camera at the same time 'thanks in no small measure to ... the mirror and the tripod' (2004: 232); and finally Gregorio Martín Gutiérrez enumerated up to five markers of subjectivity: 'the inclusion of the filmmaker's own voice ... the presence of his body, his gaze bound to the camera's perspective, [the presence of] documents or objects with his own name, or the indicative nature of certain images, such as recording his own shadow' (2010: 372). One way or another, all these resources fit in with the three levels on which filmmakers can inscribe themselves, as defined by Catherine Russell: first-person voiceover, the origin of the gaze and their body image, to which she added editing choices as an indirect form of identity (1999: 277).

As these categories go beyond what Lejeune termed 'the autobiographical pact' – in which author, narrator and character are always the same subject (1989: 3–30) – it is necessary to make a distinction between purely autobiographical filmmakers and those first-person filmmakers who construct a socio-political discourse from their identity. On the one hand, autobiographical filmmakers would be those who strictly fulfil the autobiographical pact, such as Jonas Mekas, Ed Pincus, Ross McElwee, Alan Berliner, Joseph Morder, Alain Cavalier, David Perlov or Avi Mograbi. On the other, directors such as Jean Rouch, Chris Marker, Jean-Luc Godard, Agnès Varda, Werner Herzog, Harun Farocki, Thom Andersen, Michael Moore, Nick Broomfield or Terence Davies should be considered first-person filmmakers, because they 'speak from a first-person position in the role of witness, and sometimes participant observer, without being centred on the autobiographical self', as Michael Chanan has explained (2012: 24). There is even a third type of filmmaker, such as Nanni Moretti, Manoel de Oliveira or Guy Maddin, who practise self-fiction, a hybrid genre in which 'the identity of the filmmaker is maintained, but the events referred to may be imaginary' (Martín Gutiérrez 2010: 372). Self-fictions can be as fictional as fakes or mockumentaries, but their distance from the discourses of sobriety turns them into 'a useful tool to explore what is beyond the appearance of reality' (Catalá & Cerdán 2007/8: 17; my translation).

Thus, in spite of distorting what is usually understood as 'reality', these fantasies can be interpreted as a subjective truth that challenges official accounts, because they convey the way filmmakers perceive their place in the world.

The boundaries between these three groups – autobiographical, first-person and self-fiction filmmakers – tend to be ambiguous, because they can change their style from one film to another, but they all are interested in showing the historical world through their own subjectivity. 'The documentary maker,' Antonio Weinrichter has written, 'sets himself up as a character, as well as an active enunciator, resorts to tactics of identification … and filters our perception of the events that are presented' (2010: 276). This subjective turn involves a double movement: first inwards, to the filmmaker's personality and identity, and then outwards, to his or her historical context, due to the identification between the first person singular and the first person plural proposed by French philosopher Jean-Luc Nancy (2000). This idea, according to which there is no individual existence without coexistence with another, has been applied to the non-fiction field by Alisa Lebow, establishing a bridge between the individual and the collective dimension of first-person filmmaking:

> The 'I' is always social, always already in relation, and when it speaks, as these filmmakers do, in the first person, it may appear to be in the first person singular 'I' but ontologically speaking, it is always in effect, the first person plural 'we'. The grammatical reference reminds us that language itself, though spoken by an individual, is never entirely our own invention, nor anyone else's. Despite the fact that we believe it to express our individuality, it nonetheless also expresses our commonality, our plurality, our interrelatedness with a group, a mass, a sociality, if not a society. This is as true about the expression of individuality and subjectivity in first person films as it is in language itself. And that is precisely what I find most arresting and fascinating about first person films. They are quite the opposite, in most cases, of the singular 'I'; and can even be understood to be a 'cinema of we' rather than a 'cinema of me'. (2012: 3)

Autobiographical landscaping echoes this double movement inwards and outwards by depicting the city as a lived space, using the filmmaker's personal history in order to represent a collective experience. In these documentaries, directors embody all those residents who negotiate their relation with the places they inhabit every day through an account – their account – that might be interchangeable with someone else's. In this sense, the two films analysed below, *News from Home* (Chantal Akerman, 1977) and *Lost Book Found* (Jem Cohen, 1996), combine an observational attitude towards everyday street scenes with a first-person commentary that provides a subjective reading of the images, thereby offering a portrait of life in the city from a collective and autobiographical perspective at the same time. In fact, both documentaries share a similar interest in exploring unusual variations of the first-person commentary: in *News from Home*, Akerman reads up to twenty letters written by her mother and addressed to her during her 1972 stay in New York; while in *Lost Book Found*, the narrator, who is not Cohen, tells a fictional story slightly inspired in the filmmaker's first job when he settled in New York in the 1980s. Therefore, the commentary gives rise to an indirect autobiography in *News from Home* (because Akerman uses her own voice but not her own words) and a third-person autobiography in *Lost Book Found* (in which Cohen's story is told by someone else's voice).

News from Home: Urban Crisis from the Walker's Perspective

Chantal Akerman filmed *News from Home* in the summer of 1976 under the confessed influence of the American avant-garde film (see Grant & Hillier 2009: 154-155; Koresky 2009: 1). A year before the New York City blackout of 1977 – the event that would later symbolise the city's urban crisis – she depicted a cityscape of dilapidated buildings, closed stores, dirty alleys, obsolete infrastructures and graffiti on subway cars. The film can then be interpreted as an objective portrait of New York in the mid-1970s, but it is also something else: a hidden family portrait in which the dispassionate reading of the filmmaker's correspondence creates a distancing effect that turns the cityscape into a state of mind. The contrast between the observational record of street scenes and the personal implications of such a commentary produces a subjective reading of urban space that reveals the emotional gap between the filmmaker and her mother, thereby giving an autobiographical meaning to the film.

The urban crisis had a highly negative impact on public space in the 1970s: streets, parks and even public transportation became dangerous places in which people – especially women – tried to spend the least possible time. Despite the open hostility of the city, Akerman decided to keep a 'ground-level observational strategy' that Jennifer M. Barker has related to Michel de Certeau's walker's perspective (1999: 41). This choice has a feminist background, since the *voyeur* (the opposite figure to the walker) has historically been identified with a dominant male figure: its natural habitat – skyscrapers, penthouses, observation decks, etc. – is usually occupied by male characters, while the places identified with women – family residences, laundries or schools – remain at street level (1999: 53, 56). In order to counteract this gender division, Akerman paid particular attention to those spatial practices through which underrepresented subjects, such as women, children and African-Americans, appropriated public space: a good example of this logic would be a thirty-second shot of an African-American woman who stares at the camera while sitting on a chair outside her home, an image that claims both women's visibility and the right to the city of low-income communities. The decision to emphasise this kind of non-event through duration is what Ivone Margulies has called Akerman's 'hyperrealist everyday', a way of filming focused on those empty moments usually elided in commercial films:

> The label 'Nothing happens', often applied to Akerman's work, is key
> in defining that work's specificity – its equation of extension and inten-
> sity, of description and drama. The inscription of subject matter neglected
> in traditional film tends to involve a corrective thrust, a setting straight
> of the image bank: if conventional cinema contains too few positive im-
> ages of women and ethnic or other minority groups, it becomes the realist
> filmmaker's task to represent these groups. The inclusion of such 'images
> between images' begets a spatio-temporal, as well as moral expansion of
> cinema. This interest in extending the representation of reality reflects a
> desire to restore a phenomenological integrity to reality. (1996: 22)

Women filmmakers are often interested in the representation of the everyday as a way to render women's activities visible, especially those that are socially characterised as banal, mundane or ordinary. Akerman herself achieved worldwide recognition thanks to *Jeanne Dielman, 23 Quai du Commerce, 1080 Bruxelles* (1975), a film made just before *News from Home* in which she represented a single mother's domestic routines through fixed frames and long shots. Such minimalist *mise-en-scène* serves in *News from Home* to draw the audience's attention to transit spaces that are below the threshold of visibility, such as empty alleys, crowded intersections, parking lots or subway stations. There, Akerman attempted to embody all those invisible women who move across the city every day, representing their experience in both objective and subjective terms: at first sight, her images seem anonymous, because they show 'what you see every day when you live there' (Akerman in Grant & Hillier 2009: 154), but they also express her own self as a foreign woman filmmaker, given that they contain information about her attitude towards the filmed space. In this regard, 'the construction of the self', as Barker has suggested, 'becomes a spatial issue':

> Through forms of architecture and urban planning, and through forms of
> *being in* architecture and urban spaces, subjects of the city write and are

themselves written in spatial, corporeal terms. [...] The deep resonance between body and city, between corporeality and 'city-ness' ... allows Akerman to cast her autobiography as a 'tour' of this city. By tracing the spaces of the city in which she now lives, for which she has left her family and home town, she seeks herself as a subject. (1999: 46, 48)

Akerman's corporeal relationship with New York takes the form of a travelogue in which her body and her own words are absent both on the screen and in the commentary. Her voice, on the contrary, is heard from the third shot as she reads aloud her mother's letters, whose text is usually trivial, repetitive and redundant. They all essentially tell the same story – conventional family accounts about work, money, holidays, illnesses and moods, besides motherly advice and comments on the weather – to the point that their most remarkable feature is the phatic function: the mother constantly asks about the daughter's new jobs and addresses in New York, claims for news from her and complains about the delay of her letters, simple requests that actually mean, according to Janet Bergstrom, 'I love you, I miss you, so please, answer me' (2004: 181; my translation). Akerman's fast, cold and detached reading conveys the growing distance between her and her mother, and ultimately erases the original signature of the letters, thereby creating a strange superimposition of roles that Margulies has interpreted as a response to the mother's complaints (1996: 151).

Taking into account that the mother's words end up being drowned by the sounds of the city, Akerman's answer has to be necessarily in the cityscape. Her confusion, loneliness and alienation as a foreigner in New York can be found in the images that reveal her alien status there: in one of the sequences shot inside a subway car, two men react with clear discomfort when they realise that they are being filmed by a stranger – the first one gets off at his stop and the second blatantly escapes from the camera by changing to another car. Their returned gazes emphasise the distance between the filmmaker and the city, to which she does not belong and in which she cannot be recognised by anybody. Accordingly, Akerman's gaze at New York can be compared with Ziolkowski's foreign gaze at Los Angeles, in which the explicit gap between the perceiving subject – the filmmaker – and the perceived object – the city – establishes a strong sense of defamiliarisation towards the filmed space.

Inside the crowd, however, the filmmaker acts like a female *flâneur* fascinated by the comings and goings of people, a character that is quite different from its male counterpart, as Maria Walsh has highlighted: 'unlike that masculinist discourse, where the *flâneur*'s vision is both possessed by and possesses the city, here the gazer becomes more and more absorbed by the image of the city' (2004: 193).

This is the reason why Akerman focuses on those places where anyone can go unnoticed, that is, 'the "lived" spaces of everyday life, with which the city's residents would be more intimately familiar' (Barker 1999: 42). For example, there is a sequence made of twelve similar shots of people crossing the street at the geographic centre of Manhattan: the intersection of Fifth Avenue and 46th Street. There, Akerman moves her camera around the four corners of the intersection three times over the course of a day and a night, filming in both the crowded rush hours and the empty night time. Such an interest in the act of crossing a street recalls psychogeographical practices like the static *dérive*, in which the observer had to spend an entire day without leaving a given place (see Debord 1981b: 52). Likewise, Akerman just settled down in that particular intersection in order to let her camera record what happens when people believe that *nothing* happens, as she also does in subway cars and stations.

One of the longest shots of the film simply shows people waiting in a subway station to get on the trains (Image 5.1). Passengers cross the platform at different paces, hurrying up or killing time, getting on and off trains that suddenly arrive, stop for a few seconds and then they go again, leaving behind a completely different scene. The unusual length of this shot – nine minutes – captures the real experience of waiting: how many trains and minutes have to pass before a change of view? Gilles Deleuze (1985) defined this kind of take as 'time-image', because they entail a more direct representation of time than the 'movement-image', the visual regime commonly associated with mainstream film. The main differences between these two conceptions of cinema have been summarised by Walsh as follows:

> In the cinema of the direct time-image, the coordinates of the sensory motor schema of the movement-image are abandoned. Instead of characters being able to extend their perceptions into action, their internal mental states pervade the image, often immobilizing it or causing images to succeed one another by means of false continuity shots, thereby creating what Deleuze calls aberrant movement. [...] In a cinema of the time-image an intensive, infinitely expanding duration or interval suspends action, whereas in the movement-image the interval no longer assures continuity in space and succession in time. (2004: 200)

The temporal logic of time-image is used above all in the shots filmed from means of transport, such as private cars, suburban trains and even a boat in

Image 5.1: *News from Home*, micronarratives in a subway station

the last sequence. The first carscape, for example, is a ten-minute tracking shot in which the camera remains static inside a vehicle moving up 10th Avenue. From that perspective, the West Side is depicted as a volatile cityscape: streets and buildings follow one another throughout twenty-one blocks of shop and garage fronts, parking lots, urban voids, parked cars and passers-by (Images 5.2 & 5.3). There is only enough perspective in the cross streets to make out some blurred skyscrapers, but the camera avoids landmarks to focus on the experience of driving through the city. The carscape can then be interpreted as a 'cut' in the urban fabric similar to Gordon Matta-Clark's building cuts, a series of artworks in abandoned buildings in which he removed sections of floors, ceilings and walls in order to reflect on urban decline. These interventions, according to Marta Traquino, demonstrate that 'understanding the meaning of inhabiting depends on the observation and relation with the surrounding environment, as well as on recalling the possibility of

Images 5.2 & 5.3: *News from Home,* two instants of the first carscape

transforming the space by showing new openings on old surfaces' (2010: 55; my translation). This idea can be applied to *News from Home* since its representational strategy also seeks to transform everyday spaces through new ways of seeing them. Furthermore, considering that Matta-Clark made most of his works in the years prior to the making of this film, the cityscape filmed by Akerman was practically the same on which he worked.

The iconic dimension of New York, meanwhile, only emerges in the final boatscape, another ten-minute tracking shot in which the camera is placed aboard the Staten Island ferry. This sequence begins with a confused jumble of buildings that gradually fall behind as the boat moves away from the city. After a few minutes, the well-known Manhattan skyline can be finally made out in the distance, although it immediately begins to fade in the mist like an impressionist painting. By leaving the city, Akerman seems to adopt the *voyeur*'s

perspective, but this frame also coincides with the immigrant's perspective: it is the first panorama that Europeans who migrated to New York between the late nineteenth century and the 1930s could see on arrival. *News from Home* ends with this view, but the filmmaker rewrites it in the reverse direction: instead of approaching the city, she moves away from it. This choice expresses her status as a misplaced immigrant in a hostile city, as well as her emotional distance with respect to her native country. The Upper New York Bay thus becomes a no-man's-land that dissolves the lived city into an abstract mood related to the transnational experience of living simultaneously here and there, a mindscape in which the new home and the old one are superimposed.

News from Home is therefore a cinematic mapping of Akerman's wanderings through New York City that not only shows where she was but also how she felt there. Such performative dimension comes first and foremost from the different roles that she plays through the images, each one associated with a particular emotion: walker / curiosity, passenger / routine, *flâneur* / fascination, filmmaker / creativity, foreigner / loneliness and, above all, daughter / weariness and affection at the same time. Akerman pretends to be tired of her mother, but she still shares a close intimacy with her: why else would she choose her letters as commentary for the film? As in a sketchbook or a diary film, the filmmaker's subjectivity is behind every image, and consequently the film depicts the New York cityscape as an emotional experience, always unpredictable, instead of as a series of soulless views of iconic motifs.

Lost Book Found: The Subconscious of the City

Jem Cohen is a filmmaker who simultaneously comes from the New York tradition of street photography and the artistic and political spirit of the avant-garde. He identifies himself with 'certain truly independent independents, often formally adventurous and deeply engaged politically, working outside of traditional social issue documentary but also not so easily placed within the so-called avant-garde' (in Cerdán *et al.* 2009: 76). This kind of filmmaker, such as Jonas Mekas, Robert Frank, Peter Hutton, James Benning or Chantal Akerman, usually feels at home in non-fiction territory for its openness to different formats and styles, a key feature to explain the way they work, as Cohen has written in a text about the essay film:

> This is a realm that simply makes sense for those who need to do most of it on their own; collagists and collectors, drawn to build from fragments of actuality (which are cheaper, after all); filmmakers who relish untethered histories, juxtaposed scraps, who make work indisposed to focus groups, pitch sessions, funder control, and even clear definition. The work then has always been an uncomfortable mix of documentary, narrative, and experimental approaches, something you can hardly claim to have pioneered, and which has certainly become more common in recent years. That said, the mixture of genres and approaches is not really the point;

it is not so much about documentary techniques as about documentary *openness*; being open to the world as it unfolds, being open to the film as it makes itself from that world. (2009a: 18)

Talking about his travelogues – *Buried in Light* (1994), *Amber City* (1999) and *Blood Orange Sky* (1999) – Cohen has defined his works as 'sketchbooks in film, sometimes shaped into essays' (in Cerdán *et al.* 2009: 45). Their final form is always conditioned by his method: he usually spends much time walking the city with his camera in hand as a postmodern *flâneur* and capturing raw images of unexpected events and unusual details of street life as 'someone else might jot down ideas or quick sketches in a notebook' (Halter 2009: 228), a never-ending process during which he also edits and writes the voiceover texts. This system has led him to create a huge image archive that threatens to exceed his working capacity due to its wide variety of formats: Super 8, 16mm, ¾" Umatic, beta SP, open

Images 5.4 & 5.5: *Lost Book Found,* street vendor and urban fisherman

reel 1", D2, digibeta, dv, dvcam, audio cassettes, mini-discs and lately many hard drives (see Cerdán *et al.* 2009: 72–3). The use of the archive, as well as the overlapping of two or even more long-term projects, entails a clear tendency to the aesthetic of the fragment, which has a prime example in *Lost Book Found*. This film, according to Ed Halter, summarises much of Cohen's work, because it explicitly theorises his method and philosophy of filmmaking (2009: 234).

Its meagre plot tells the story of a pushcart vendor in New York's West Side who receives a mysterious book from a man who fishes for objects through the underground ventilation system grilles (Images 5.4 & 5.5). The book is full of hand-written lists and enumerations of '*places, objects, incidents, all having something to do with the city*', as the unseen narrator says; and suggests to him a new way of looking at urban space. This story is and is not autobiographical, because it is roughly inspired by Cohen's first job in New York as a pushcart vendor, but many details are fictional, and, what is most important, the first-person narrator's voice is not Cohen's but Todd Colby's. For all these reasons, the film can be considered an example of third-person autobiography, as the filmmaker himself has hinted:

I wanted it to be *somewhat* autobiographical, but I still wasn't interested in it being a*bout* me. Many of the details are true and come directly from my experience, but that just wasn't the point. The film is about attempts to make sense of the city, about ways of looking, and about the way the city operates in its hidden layer. But the details of the narrative and of the narrator as a particular person aren't so important in themselves. So, the voice is somewhat like mine, but it isn't mine. I preferred to stand back a little. (Cohen in Cerdán *et al.* 2009: 64)

Similarly to the Robinson Trilogy, *Lost Book Found* documents the places where the filmmaker has been and the things that have caught his attention there. The film also echoes *News from Home* for several reasons beyond its autobiographical content: both are interested in street scenes and everyday environments, which are almost always showed from the walker's perspective, and curiously they share a similar cinematic geography. In Cohen's film, the narrator says that '*on most days, I rode the cart from a parking garage to the same spot on 9th Avenue, near the mouth of the Lincoln Tunnel*', a place located just one block east of where Akerman shot her longer carscape. Therefore, there is a spatio-temporal continuity between *News from Home* and *Lost Book Found*, because together they cover two decades in the city's history, from the urban crisis of the 1970s to the beginning of Rudolph Giuliani's first term as Mayor of New York City.

Cohen's experience as a pushcart vendor allows him to discover the gift of invisibility and extend his perception of the city: '*I discovered that simply by standing behind the cart and selling, I had put up both a wall and window, from which I could watch what happened on the street [...] And as I became invisible, I began to see things that had once been invisible to me.*' Sonia García López has related this awareness of urban life's smallest details to Cohen's apprenticeship as a filmmaker, given that he has applied the idea of becoming invisible to most of his films since *This is a History of New York* (1987) (2009: 94–5).[1] In that short, the filmmaker tried to merge past and present in the same space by imagining 'a flattened history ... in which different eras exist simultaneously' (Halter 2009: 232), a fantasy that somehow reappears in *Lost Book Found*.

Cohen usually records his images in a few seconds, by chance, which identifies him with the character of the urban fisherman: both collect their materials from the depths and fringes of the city, they 'glean' them from the debris of late-capitalism, as Agnès Varda does in her documentary *Les glaneurs et la glaneuse* (*The Gleaners and I*, 2000). Again, *Lost Book Found* skips the landmarks of the city – the only one that briefly appears is Times Square through a steamed up windshield – and focuses instead on fleeting impressions of what the pushcart vendor might have seen and heard: 'bits of paper and plastic swirling ghostlike in eddies of wind, weathered storefronts surviving from decades past, cheap and forlorn shop-window displays, notes on walls, passing conversations and the sounds of machines at work' (Halter 2009: 225). These images are organised in descriptive series which go beyond the objective record of reality to become metaphors for contemporary society: the shot in which a man disappears through a trapdoor in the sidewalk, for instance, suggests the existence of a hidden city beneath its surface, and the fisherman's book might be the key to enter it.

The narrator remains hypnotised by the content of the book, to the point that some of its lists and enumerations *'come back in flashes'*. Suddenly, everything in the city can be interpreted as part of 'a text waiting to be uncovered, read and deciphered', as Halter has said, from the hand-scrawled broadsheets taped everywhere to the spatial practices of commuters and homeless (2009: 226). Cohen's ability to discover *'signs hidden behind other signs'* allows him to capture 'the subconscious of the city' (Luc Santé quoted in Cerdán *et al.* 2009: 120), an idea that seems to have been inspired by Walter Benjamin's *The Arcades Project* (1927–1940).[2] This work consists of hundreds of quotations from all kind of sources – from high to low culture – through which the German writer attempted to build an account of Paris's cultural history in the nineteenth century. Accordingly, by structuring the film as a collage of non-hierarchical stories and testimonies, Cohen was actually updating Benjamin's notion of the city as a repository of anachronistic objects, as Halter has explained:

> Cohen's way of seeing the city is ... textual, archival, and archaeological. It is reminiscent of Benjamin's concept of literary montage, an act of picking through 'the rags, the refuse' of past and present society, reading the city as a palimpsest, roughly layered with accretions of time, the cast-off objects of many generations lying together like accelerated geological strata that have crumbled into one another with the speed of their never-ending creation. Rather than the epitome of modernity's newness, the city becomes an essential instance of the 'wreckage upon wreckage' and 'piles of debris' of collapsed time. (2009: 232)

The places depicted in *Lost Book Found* were far from their heyday when Cohen filmed them, as he has remarked: 'when Benjamin's talking about the arcades, they're already passé, they're already like [New York's] 14th Street used to be a few years ago' (in Halter 2009: 229). This fascination with retail stores, however, is precisely what reinforces the identification between narrator and filmmaker: while the first falls silent before the spectacle of consumption, the second records it in order to save it from oblivion. This attitude, on the one hand, fuels the documentary nature of Cohen's work, as he has stated: 'I believe that it is the work and responsibility of artists to create such a record, so that we can better understand, and future generations can know, how we lived, what we build, what changes and what disappears' (2009b: 105). On the other hand, Cohen's need to film the smallest detail allows him to develop a critical cinematic cartography through what Les Roberts has termed 'an *archaeology* of the city in film':

> This takes as its guiding metaphor the *layering* of urban cinematic geographies: that is, the city's landscapes conceived in terms of a spatial palimpsest; constantly inscribed and reinscribed by multiple, imbricated forms of urban spatial practice (architectural, socio-political, cultural and aesthetic, psychoanalytical, environmental, planning and developmental, etc.). (2010: 198)

To the current viewer, these stores seem to belong to another time, but this impression is achieved, above all, by technical choices: regarding the film format, Cohen shot most images of *Lost Book Found* on Super-8 – except for one of the last sequences, which was filmed on 16mm – and later edited them in video, adding some visual and colour effects, such as slow motion. Super-8 images convey the imminent obsolescence that threatens the 14th Street stores, because this format was already obsolete in the 1990s: it was launched in 1965 and became popular in the 1970s and 1980s, so its grainy texture unconsciously transports the audience to that time. Sound, in turn, is another key element to give an anachronistic appearance to the cityscape: Cohen usually concocts the soundtrack of his films apart from the images, creating 'ghost versions of real places', because most of the time he films without recording sound (in Cerdán *et al.* 2009: 58). The New York cityscape is then depicted as if it had been perceived by a sleepwalker, someone who had really been there but who could only remember it as a dream. After all, Cohen is not so much interested in capturing the present as in revealing the permanence of the past in the present. From this perspective, all those places, objects and characters that were about to pass into non-existence in the 1990s recall a bygone era and bring the past to the present, as the narrator says towards the end of the film:

> *What is a city made of? Sometimes it seems as if the city is the rubble of stories and memories, layers and layers, and that objects, all of the layers of things, are like the city's skin. Many of these objects, these leavings, are the relics of commerce, of the simple exchange of goods and services.*

Most people spend most of their lives earning a living. One man's loss is another man's gain. Time is money.

The last lines of this excerpt raise the issue of the objects' economic nature, which the film attempts to replace with an archaeological meaning: if capitalism operates through a totalising allegory in which 'all events and objects must ultimately correspond to commodities', as Halter has written, 'then *Lost Book Found* and its titular, mythical notebook provide a counter-allegory, an alternative way of ordering and understanding the artefacts of the city as an ever-expanding archive: a critical way of seeing' (2009: 234). What if the real value of these objects is not in their price but in their symbolic component? Most of them embodied an earlier stage in the development of capitalism in which the spectacle of consumption was still in the streets, before being enclosed in shopping centres. Contrary to the latter, which are 'drained of all history and regional character', retail stores helped to define the identity of a place by encouraging the spatial practices of many types of people – vendors, suppliers, customers, *flâneurs*, etc. – that ultimately created a sense of belonging to that place, something hard to achieve in non-places and banalscapes because they exist 'everywhere, repetitive, commonplace and anaesthetized' (Cohen in Cerdán *et al.* 2009: 38).

The narrator of *Lost Book Found* is an inhabitant of these commercial spaces, an insider, regardless of whether it is a vendor, a *flâneur* or a filmmaker. These three characters are equally subject to the hostility of public space. The narrator complains that '*there are very few public bathrooms in the city and very few places that would even give you a free drink of water*', a situation that has worsened in the twenty-first century, in both the streets and non-places, as Cohen's later films show. *Chain* (2004) describes the behavioural impact of non-places on two female characters – Tamiko, a Japanese woman embarked on an endless business trip, and Amanda, a girl who has run away from her family home – while the act of filming itself takes centre stage in *NYC Weights and Measures* (2005) and *One Bright Day* (2009), as part of a strategy to claim the right to film in public spaces after the announcement of the Patriot Act in October 2001.[3]

In conclusion, *Lost Book Found* offers another view from below that becomes an experience of engaged observation, in which the filmmaker embraces the usual markers of subjectivity in the essay film: the first-person commentary, an aesthetic of the fragment, a tendency towards reflection rather than narration, and a focus on atmospheres instead of events. Similarly to Benning or Akerman, 'the distance between the subject who observes and the object represented gets narrower until it disappears' (García López 2009: 103), although Cohen's camera work is much more expressive than Benning's or Akerman's, as he himself has described it:

There are two main poles to my camera work. On one hand, I use the camera as a kind of extension of the body that can be handled roughly and instinctively. On the other hand my camera work can be very spare and simple – usually using a tripod and often with no camera movement. In the latter case there is the possibility for a kind of remove, a coldness even, where my own presence, the physical sense of self, is in some ways erased. One could say that I tend towards extremes of both subjectivity and objectivity, depending on the film, or even on the moment within one film. (Cohen in Cerdán *et al.* 2009: 37)

Thanks to this hybrid style, Cohen may simultaneously be considered a chronicler and a poet. His images, in addition to being a testimony of a particular time and place, teach the audience how to explore the imaginary worlds that exist within this world, either in New York or anywhere else. This approach makes the coexistence of the old and the new easier, documenting the city both in and through time, that is, as it was in the 1990s and as it could have been before, in an undated past closer to mythology than to history. The most remarkable feature of *Lost Book Found* is therefore its ability to feed the social imaginary of New Yorkers, establishing a set of guidelines to decode the urban surface that would then be applied by Guy Maddin to Winnipeg. Thus, autobiographical landscaping provides both filmmakers and audiences with a link between cityscape and mindscape, using images from the real city to actually depict an inner geography.

NOTES

1   Cohen firmly believes in the possibility of becoming invisible. In an interview, he stated that 'you can become someone invisible, like a phone box, if you stay enough time in the street with a tripod' (in Reviriego & Yáñez 2008: 18; my translation).
2   There are many clues that point to Benjamin's influence in *Lost Book Found*, from its very title – which may refer to both the fisherman's book and Benjamin's, due to the latter's status as an unfinished work – to the final dedication: '*For Walter Benjamin / Who Knew / And Ben Katchor / Who Knows.*' Ben Katchor, in turn, is a cartoonist best known for his comic strip *Julius Knipl, Real Estate Photographer* (1988–), in which he depicts the fading small-business community of New York.
3   The complete name of the Patriot Act is Uniting and Strengthening America by Providing Appropriate Tools Required to Intercept and Obstruct Terrorism Act. It reinforced the systems to watch over and control citizens and even banned filming in certain places such as airports, supermarkets, subway stations and buses for a few years (see García López 2009: 94). In the late 2000s, Cohen was one of the leaders of the protests against

such a ban: he sent out a couple of open letters and co-founded a group, Picture New York, which gathered over 35,000 signatures against the restrictions. After a year of struggle, the protests finally achieved their goal: 'the City changed course and instigated improved rules which actually safeguard the right to film and photograph in the city' (Cohen 2009b: 107).

URBAN SELF-PORTRAITS

Self-portrait, both written and filmed, is an autobiographical subgenre that places the author at the centre of the discourse without necessarily following a narrative logic. One of the first critics interested in its film translation was Raymond Bellour, who explained its specific features as follows:

> The self-portrait clings to the analogical, the metaphorical, the poetic, far more than to the narrative. Its coherence lies in a system of remembrances, afterthoughts, superimpositions, correspondences. It thus takes on the appearance of discontinuity, of anachronistic juxtaposition, of montage. Where autobiography closes in on the life it recounts, the self-portrait opens itself up to a limitless totality. (1989: 8–9)

A few examples of self-portrait films would be *Speaking Directly: Some American Notes* (Jon Jost, 1973), *Film Portrait* (Jerome Hill, 1973), *Self Portrait* (Jonas Mekas, 1990), *JLG/JLG – autoportrait de décembre* (*JLG/JLG: Self-Portrait in December*, Jean-Luc Godard, 1994) or *Cinéma, de notre temps: Chantal Akerman par Chantal Akerman* (Chantal Akerman, 1997). Similarly to other forms of autobiography, the self-portrait developed its film version as a consequence of the global tendency towards subjectivity that arises from the rift between oneself and the world, as suggested by Marta Andreu (2009: 151). This subjective turn was simultaneously developed in Europe and America thanks to the mutual influence of their respective findings: on the one hand, Chris Marker's and Jean-Luc Godard's essay films opened the possibility of a first-person cinema, while on the other Jonas Mekas's and Ed Pincus's film diaries offered an alternative to the orthodoxy of direct cinema. Regarding the American case, Jim Lane has related the origins of this autobiographical impulse to the following four historical factors:

> First, the autobiographical avant-garde film of the 1960s paved the way for self-inscription in documentary. Second, autobiographical documentarists rejected the realist conventions of the popular American direct cinema of the same period. Third, the reflexive turn in international cinema strongly influenced experimentation with autobiography in documentary. Fourth, the rise of autobiographical documentary coincided with a larger turn to the politics of selfhood in the United States. (2002: 8)

In a broader sense, the subjective turn has to do with the linguistic and cultural turns that the social sciences and the humanities underwent after the collapse of the rational-structuralist paradigm. In fact, the emergence of the reflexive and performative modes in the 1980s may be interpreted as their film counterparts: the reflexive mode would be the outcome of the linguistic turn, while the performative one rather seems a specific sign of the cultural turn. This link between the evolution of academic discourses and documentary film can be extended to many other fields, from politics and economics – in which Keynesian solutions were replaced by neoliberal policies – to urban planning and social tendencies – among which stood out the separation between public and private spheres or the rise of individualism and narcissism. This is the reason why the paradigm shift of the 1970s affected up to five interrelated levels: first, the political and economic decisions to face the post-industrial crisis; second, their social consequences; third, the physical space in which they took place; fourth, the academic discourses that tried to explain them; and fifth, the cultural practices that echoed the new *zeitgeist*.

Personal issues have always been political, as claimed by the feminist movement. In *Doc: Documentarism in the 21st Century*, Antonio Weinrichter mentions that self-reflexive practices are, above all, 'part of the ideological project of the film, which does not stop being political simply because it allows the intervention of the narrator' (2010: 276). In the same book, the resurgence of documentary forms in the 2000s is directly considered by Josep María Catalá as 'an act of resistance to the flattering of reality instigated by the neoliberal neoculture', in which aesthetic concerns work as 'a way of recovering power over reality, usurped by the media and the propaganda apparatuses of a military-industrial imagery' (2010: 281). Inside this hostile mediascape, the autobiographical approach has given voice – and visibility – to the people willing to challenge dominant discourses, especially those filmmakers who come from underrepresented or misrepresented groups such as women, gays and lesbians, ethnic minorities or Third World nations (see Nichols 2001: 133, 153; Renov 2004: xvii; Chanan 2007: 7).

The emergence of autobiographical documentaries has been linked with the displacement of the politics of social movements by the politics of identity in the United States (see Nichols 2001: 153; Lane 2002: 21; Renov 2004: 176–7). The inability of the American New Left to defeat the Establishment in the short-term led its activists to focus on the specific demands of their communities, replacing collective struggle with identity issues. The feminist movement pioneered this attitude change by realising that gendered hierarchies persisted in the counterculture, and was also the first group to understand the potential of autobiographical documentaries for community building. Following their example, and regardless of their gender or race, many contemporary filmmakers have used their personal experience in order to express the problems, standpoints and worldviews of their respective communities, thereby counteracting the ideologies that attempted to hide their particular history and culture behind the myths of national unity and universal identities. The new formulation of performative documentaries – 'we speak about ourselves to them', or even 'we speak about ourselves to us' – has provided them with a useful tool to convey their political messages to society, as summarised by Nichols:

> [Performative documentaries] contribute to the social construction of a common identity among members of a given community. They give social visibility to experiences once treated as exclusively or primarily personal; they attest to a commonality of experience and to the forms of struggle necessary to overcome stereotyping, discrimination, and bigotry. The political voice of these documentaries embodies the perspectives and visions of communities that share a history of exclusion and a goal of social transformation. (2001: 160)

According to Nichols, the performative mode offers a meeting point for several opposite pairs, such as the general and the particular, the individual and the collective or the political and the personal (2001: 133). In his 'official' definition, Nichols explains that this mode 'emphasizes the subjective or expressive aspect of the filmmaker's own engagement with the subject and an audience's responsiveness to this engagement', and in addition rejects 'notions of objectivity in favor of evocation and affect' (2001: 34). This move away from 'a realist representation of the historical world' has encouraged filmmakers to explore 'more unconventional narrative structures and more subjective forms of representation', to the point that sometimes these documentaries may lean towards fake, combining 'the actual and the imagined' in order to include the filmmaker's fantasies as another element of the historical world (2001: 131). In short, all these features make this mode the most suitable for autobiography, since it usually gives an added value to 'the sub-jective qualities of experience and memory that depart from factual recounting' (ibid.).

The development of the self-portrait film as a documentary subgenre is a con-sequence of this rise of performativity in the non-fiction field. Nowadays, the ethnographic film has become 'autoethnography' or 'domestic ethnography' (see Russell 1999: 275–314; Renov 2004: 216–29), the conventions of direct cinema have evolved into 'an aesthetics of failure' (see Arthur 1993: 126–34), and even in-stitutional documentaries have lately been commissioned to filmmakers willing to tell their life story, as in the case of Manoel de Oliveira's *Porto da Minha Infância* (*Porto of My Childhood*, 2001) or Terence Davies's *Of Time and the City* (2008).[1] Urban self-portraits would then be those performative documentaries in which the filmmaker's self is constructed in relation to his or her hometown, as well as any urban documentary that depicts a city through the filmmaker's personal experi-ences, especially when he or she has left places of memory there. According to this definition, documentaries such as *News from Home* and *Lost Book Found* could also be urban self-portraits, but this does not mean that all urban self-portraits necessarily adopt the *mise-en-scène* of autobiographical landscaping.

The first examples of this subgenre were made after the post-industrial crisis, when many cities were transformed by factory closures and the subsequent urban decay. In the 1980s, the interest in endangered cityscapes was initially associated with a nostalgic reaction before the end of a long growing period, a feeling that was first analysed by British cultural historian Robert Hewison in his book *The Heritage Industry: Britain in a Climate of Decline*:

> The impulse to preserve the past is part of the impulse to preserve the self. Without knowing where we have been, it is difficult to know where we are going. The past is the foundation of individual and collective identity, objects from the past are the source of significance as cultural symbols. Continuity between past and present creates a sense of sequence out of aleatory chaos and, since change is inevitable, a stable system of ordered meanings enables us to cope with both innovation and decay. The nostal-gic impulse is an important agency in adjustment to crisis, it is a social emollient and reinforces national identity when confidence is weakened or threatened. (1987: 47)

Within the field of urban planning, this nostalgia involved a fetishisation of the past that led to the construction of city tableaux and banalscapes in central loca-tions and gentrified areas, but not to an extensive programme of restoration in those neighbourhoods inhabited by low-income citizens. Rem Koolhaas and Bruce Mau have described this situation with their peculiar sense of humour: 'In spite of its absence, history is the major preoccupation, even industry, of the Generic City. On the liberated grounds, around the restored hovels, still more hotels are constructed to receive additional tourists in direct proportion to the erasure of the past' (1995: 1256). Like this type of urban planning, the urban self-portraits of the 1980s and 1990s recalled missing cityscapes as part of an idyllic past, but they simultaneously denounced the gradual disappearance of endangered places. However, as industrial cityscapes were disappearing, this nostalgia gave way to a more lyrical approach that included a pinch of irony as antidote against idealisation. Thus, instead of depicting the filmmakers' places of memory through a series of recollections frozen in the past, the urban self-portraits of the 2000s rather showed their evolution over time.

The six case studies in this section – *Lightning Over Braddock* (Tony Buba, 1988), *Roger & Me* (Michael Moore, 1989), *Les hommes du port* (Alain Tanner, 1995), *Porto of My Childhood* (Manoel de Oliveira, 2001), *My Winnipeg* (Guy Maddin, 2007) and *Of Time and the City* (Terence Davies, 2008) – summarise the evolution of urban self-portraits from the 1980s to the 2000s. In these films, their directors, most of them born and raised in industrial cities in the 1940s and the 1950s, develop a similar elegiac discourse about the loss of their childhood's cityscape.[2] They all combine their creative work behind the camera with an awareness of the successive gazes with which their hometowns have been depicted throughout film history. Indeed, Braddock, Flint, Porto, Winnipeg and Liverpool have always been present one way or another in their works, to the point that they have become metacritics of the film representation of their hometowns – only Genoa, the city portrayed in *Les hommes du port*, does not regularly appear in Alain Tanner's films, due to the latter's condition as travelling filmmaker.

All these urban self-portraits directly address the emotional relationship between these filmmakers and their places of memory, thereby providing a critical account of the decline and subsequent renewal of their hometowns or host cities. Since these films can be compared in terms of similarities (their autobiographical approach) or differences (their political commitment) they will be analysed in pairs according to their belonging to three different documentary traditions: first, *Lightning Over Braddock* and *Roger & Me* stand for the subjective turn of the American socio-political documentary in the 1980s; then, *Les hommes du port* and *Of Time and the City* are urban self-portraits highly influenced by the European essay film; and finally, *Porto of My Childhood* and *My Winnipeg* are representative examples of a recent trend within the fake documentary: self-fiction.

NOTES

1   Both *Porto of My Childhood* and *Of Time and the City* were the official films of different editions of the same event: the subject city as European Capital of Culture.
2   Tony Buba was born in Braddock, Pennsylvania, in 1944; Terence Davies in Liverpool, UK, in 1945; Michael Moore in Flint, Michigan, in 1954; and finally Guy Maddin in Winnipeg, Canada, in 1956. Only Manoel de Oliveira (Porto, Portugal, 1908) and Alain Tanner (Geneva, Switzerland, 1929) were born before World War II, although the latter also returns to the post-war economic boom in his urban self-portrait.

CHAPTER SIX

Self-Portrait as Socio-Political Documentary

After the 1973 crisis, the transition from an industrial economy to a service one caused a deep change in the socio-economic structures of Western countries: many factories closed and were relocated to other regions, dispensing with hundreds of thousands of skilled industrial workers who had to look for a new place for themselves in the service economy. Class-consciousness and intra-class solidarity were undermined by Ronald Reagan's and Margaret Thatcher's governments, whose neoliberal policies aimed to dismantle the welfare state in the United States and the United Kingdom respectively. Their aggressive opposition to free public services was interpreted by Gilles Lipovetsky as part of 'the postmodern tendency to favour freedom instead of uniform egalitarianism, but also to hold individuals and companies responsible for themselves' (1986: 134; my translation), a breach of the post-war social contract between corporations, unions and states termed 'The Great U-Turn' by Bennett Harrison (1988). These policies, according to Edward Soja, turned 'what was initially described as a process of *deindustrialization*' into 'a polarizing of America that was intensifying poverty, decimating the blue-collar workforce, ruining once-thriving communities, and significantly pinching middle-class households as corporations sought new pathways to profitability' (2000: 168). This gradual disintegration of the social fabric, along with the falling apart of effective agencies of collective action, have been considered by Zygmunt Bauman as 'the unanticipated "side effect" of the new lightness and fluidity of the increasingly mobile, slippery, shifty, evasive and fugitive power' (2000: 14). Inspired by French economist Daniel Cohen (1998), Bauman argued that the breaking down of the invisible chain that tied the workers to their working places was 'the decisive, watershed-like change in life experience associated with the decline and accelerated demise of the Fordist model' (2000: 58).

The workers' change of position in the productive system involved the decay of their towns and neighbourhoods. In the luckiest cases, these places still preserved their architectural heritage after having been gentrified, but most were razed to the ground in order to make way for new developments, especially in the United States, where 'the vindication of social and urban heritage did not go hand in hand' (García Vázquez 2004: 70; my translation). Anyway, the original identity of these areas disappeared with their historical residents in those industrial and port cities that lost part of their population and former functions as regional centres in favour of global cities (see Sassen 2007: 111–12). In this context, two urban self-portraits such as *Lightning Over Braddock* and *Roger & Me* described the decline of the American Rust Belt cities in the 1980s through first-person narratives in which the directors themselves appeared onscreen: initially, Tony Buba and Michael Moore played the role of investigative reporters in what was supposed to be journalistic documentaries about the plight of their hometowns, but they soon became characters as important as the depicted cities by using their own body and subjectivity in order to convey the main concerns of their community. Such a way of addressing urban transformations in the American Rust Belt says more about the social perception of the process than about the process itself. Consequently, instead of providing the audience with an objective chronology of the events, these films basically show the emotional impact of the post-industrial crisis among the residents of these cities.

Roger & Me: The Industrial Town in Global Times*

Michael Moore's critical and commercial success has turned him, according to Paul Arthur, into 'the public face of contemporary non-fiction cinema' (2010: 106). Having won an Academy Award and a Palme d'Or in the 2000s – the first for *Bowling for Columbine* (2002), the second for *Fahrenheit 9/11* (2004) – his best *mise-en-scène* and editing ideas actually come from his first documentary feature, *Roger & Me*, in which he already explored the quest structure, the practice of ambush interviews and the *détournement* of found footage. In this film, his well-known character – dubbed 'a schlump in a ball cap' by Sergio Rizzo (2010: 32) – appeared for the first time as 'a combination of common citizen, investigative reporter, simple-minded buffoon and guerrilla performer' (Oroz & Ambruñeiras 2010: 330). His close relationship with Flint, his hometown, is an important part of the character, since it allows him to introduce himself as part of the working-class rather than as a part of the elite (see Studlar 2010: 54). Indeed, Moore has regularly returned to Flint in later documentaries in order to reaffirm his film persona as an ordinary citizen concerned about his community.

Despite his constant allusions to his working-class origins, Moore has never been an autobiographical filmmaker but a first-person one: in his films, the expression of subjectivity is just a way to develop what Douglas Kellner has called 'a unique genre of filmmaking, the personal witnessing, questing and agit-prop interventionist film that explores issues, takes strong critical point of view, and targets villains and evils in US society' (2010: 100). This genre, according to Elena Oroz and Iván G. Ambruñeiras, has established 'a bridge between the social documentary based on the principles of minimum interference adopted by American direct cinema ... and the autobiographical and journal approach that had begun in the United States in the early 1970s' (2010: 331), a combination so unusual for its time that critics have had much difficulty in locating *Roger & Me* in Nichols' schema of documentary modes. Miles Orvell has declared it 'a hybrid of interactive and reflexive modes', Matthew Bernstein has analysed its expository elements, and finally María Luisa Ortega has drawn attention to its performative strategies (see Orvell 2010: 128; Bernstein 1998: 397–415; Ortega 2007: 36–7). Contrary to what might seem, there is no contradiction in these three approaches, given that all of them point to what may be Moore's main contribution to documentary film: his particular use of first-person narratives and ironic editing for updating the tradition of the socio-political documentary.

The best example of this device is the opening sequence of *Roger & Me*: the autobiographical approach is established by introducing the filmmaker himself as a character, summarising his origins, personality, wishes and current situation through a vertiginous editing of all kinds of materials, from industrial films to home movies. This beginning is already an accelerated self-portrait that serves to create a contrast between Moore and his antagonist, Roger Smith, the chairman of General Motors (GM) from 1981 to 1990. In this opposition, Moore embodies the everyman, that is, someone completely irrelevant, while Roger Smith is described as one of those people who run the world from the hidden controlling centre of which Guy Debord talked about at the time (1990: 9). The sequence also introduces the space where the confrontation will take place, Flint, which is depicted through a naïve account of its heroic past as a wonderful place to live, a discourse that seemed to be still in force in the 1980s.

In order to be perceived as part of the affected community by the audience, Moore proudly exhibits his working-class credentials: his father worked on the assembly line at the AC Spark Plug factory and his uncle took part in the historic GM Flint Sit-down Strike of 1936, the biggest milestone of the workers' struggle in Flint. No matter that he himself has never directly worked for GM: his status as outraged citizen from Flint automatically gives him moral authority to level criticism at the company. The construction of his film character thus relies on the loss of his emotional referents, which are sometimes identified with places of memory, to the point that the description of Flint's social situation and his own self-portrait go hand in hand.

Regarding the narrative structure, *Roger & Me* follows Moore's political discourse and not a chronological order, sacrificing 'historical accuracy in order to achieve the unity of satiric fiction' (Orvell 2010: 135). The manipulation of facts and figures, as well as the way the filmmaker handles the power relationships in his interviews, have stirred up much controversy, starting with a famous conversation in which critic Harlan Jacobson accused Moore of tampering with the chronological sequence of events. In that interview, Moore defended *Roger & Me* by saying that 'it's not fiction, but what if we say it's a documentary told with a narrative style?' (in Jacobson 1989: 23), but even so he could not alleviate the harshest attack on the film: the following year, Pauline Kael described his discourse as 'gonzo demagoguery', denouncing that the film used 'its leftism as a superior attitude' and thereby encouraged the audience to 'laugh at ordinary working people and still feel they're taking a politically correct position' (1990: 91). Gary Crowdus, in turn, took advantage of the title's opposition to criticise the film, writing that '*Roger & Me* might have acquired a little more political bite if it had focused a little more on "Roger" and somewhat less on "Me"' (1990: 30). This statement, however, simultaneously recognised and missed the point of the film, as noted by Arthur, who was one of its first advocates (see 1993: 128–31). A few years later, once the initial criticism turned into a growing appreciation,

Orvell also hailed the film for its ability to deliver 'the oblique truth of satire' instead of 'the straight truth of documentary' (2010: 136).

Overall, *Roger & Me* has been criticised for three main reasons: its lack of structure, its manipulation of chronology and its failure to create a coherent socio-political analysis (see Studlar 2010: 53). Nevertheless, beyond the debate on authenticity and accuracy, this documentary did manage to

Image 6.1: *Roger & Me*, Moore's final confrontation with Roger Smith. Centre: Smith's face. Right: Moore's back.

convey the local perception of Flint's urban decay, equating Moore's failure to interview Roger Smith with the feeling of powerlessness experienced by many laid-off workers at the time (see Ortega

2007: 36; Orvell 2010: 138).[1] Although the credibility of *Roger & Me* has been seriously damaged since the documentary *Manufacturing Dissent* (Rick Caine & Debbie Melnyk, 2007) revealed that Moore actually did get an interview with Smith but finally chose not to include it in the final editing (see Bernstein 2010: 7), the metaphorical meaning of the chase after Smith does not change, because it is based on the political impotence of individual subjects to face corporate power (Image 6.1). In this sense, the solitude and isolation of the autobiographical self becomes a symptom of the social fragmentation characteristic of post-industrial capitalism, as Jim Lane has explained:

> [Moore's] own representation as the autobiographical narrator in search of answers of Roger becomes a disabled self, armed with the critical apparatus to understand what is going on in his hometown but incapable of effecting change as much as the working people whom [he] indicts. The film becomes a self-portrait of political impotence and futility within the larger frame of social and economic conditions with which the subject maintains a perplexing autobiographical connection and moral detachment. (2002: 138)

When *Roger & Me* was theatrically released, Reaganomics had completely transformed the US labour market, shattering the idea of a life-long job in a secure company. Later on, Bauman warned that 'in the world of structural unemployment no one can feel truly secure', because there are no 'skills and experiences which, once acquired, would guarantee that the job will be offered, and once offered, will prove lasting' (2000: 161). The new labour paradigm imposed uncertainty through flexibility, replacing 'secure jobs in secure companies' by 'the advent of work on short-term contracts, rolling contracts or no contracts, positions with no in-built security but with the "until further notice" clause' (2000: 147). Under these circumstances, the individual has to cope with 'a life without protection, without class culture, without a collective framework [and] without a political project to transform the world', as Gilles Lipovetsky and Jean Serroy have highlighted (2009: 192; my translation).

Such a situation, according to Bauman, was caused by a sea change in 'the managerial science' of capitalism: initially, the system focused on 'keeping the "manpower" in and forcing or bribing it to stay put and to work on schedule', but after the post-industrial crisis it was rather concerned with 'letting "humanpower" out and better still forcing it to go' (2000: 122). Moore denounced these practices in *Roger & Me* without aiming at the macroeconomic system yet, as his *Capitalism, A Love Story* (2009) would do two decades later. On the contrary, by focusing on Flint's situation as an example of what was happening in the Rust Belt, he captured the deep disorientation of his own community: the film thereby emphasises the workers' lack of historical consciousness and perspective in the face of the bitter defeat that they were suffering, showing their alienation with junk television products and pop culture sponsored by GM, such as the Newlywed

Game – a TV programme hosted by an anchorman born precisely in Flint, Bob Eubanks – or Pat Boone's and Anita Bryant's concerts.

These kinds of celebrities – including Miss Michigan 1987 – were the people who went to Flint to lift the spirits of the unemployed. Their interventions show how the public debate on the crisis was simplified to the point of banality: most of them simply repeat that the best way to overcome the recession is to take initiative and stay positive, a naïve discourse that ignored the serious impoverishment of the working class. By letting them speak, Moore ridicules the 'bread and circus' policy that GM offered to Flint as only compensation after eight decades of active service, also warning that the promises made during the post-war economic boom can no longer be fulfilled within the neoliberal paradigm. In fact, throughout his entire film career, Moore has denounced that the alliance between large corporations and Republican administrations has betrayed the ideals of the American Dream, such as a decent job for life, a home of one's own or a public helth care system, the issues respectively addressed in *Roger & Me*, *Capitalism, A Love Story* and *Sicko* (2007). For this reason, his identification with the working class has been interpreted by Gaylyn Studlar as 'a nostalgic desire for a return to the past' (2010: 62).

Moore, however, also loves the same cultural debris that he criticises, at least as source materials: among a wide variety of footage related to Flint, *Roger & Me* includes home movies, newsreels, TV news clips, automotive TV commercials, clips from industrial training films and excerpts from studio-era Hollywood. All this visual waste is mobilised, according to Arthur, 'for purposes of editorial comment as well as illustration of factual statements', thereby producing not only 'humorous asides' but also decentring 'effects of a unified enunciative presence' (2010: 112). The outcome seems a film adaptation of the Situationist *détournement*, a practice that consists in 'the integration of present or past artistic production into a superior construction of a milieu' (Knabb 1981: 45). Moore's main influence was probably *The Atomic Cafe* (Jayne Loader, Kevin Rafferty & Pierce Rafferty, 1982), a compilation film that used humour and irony to distort the original meaning of the footage.[2] Both documentaries would be what Sharon Sandusky has called a 'toxic film artifact': a work that exposes the dangerous engineering and manipulation that the original material already had in its original context (1992: 6). These kinds of compilation films usually recycle footage from the 1950s, a period in which America 'was constructed in the media as a culturally specific domain of family values, democracy, and free enterprise with the small town and suburban nuclear family as its focal point' (Russell 1999: 242). Moore, in particular, goes back to that Golden Age in search of images that recall its unfulfilled promises: he applies the same demystified logic to both old and contemporary materials in order to subvert his opponent's message while promoting his own, as Situationists did by means of *détournement* (see Coverley 2010: 96).

Humour consequently pervades the film, producing ironic dichotomies that further Moore's political argument: in one of the most significant sequences of *Roger & Me*, he uses the musical score as counterpoint to images, playing the Beach Boys' song 'Wouldn't It Be Nice' over several tracking shots that depict the worst effects of urban decay – business closures, loss of population, dilapidated buildings, empty houses and a worrying increase in the rat population. The choice of this particular song is not arbitrary, but it was suggested by a friend of Moore's who suffered an anxiety attack as result of his fear to be fired for the umpteenth time. Thus, while images provide visible evidence of the effects of the crisis on the cityscape, the upbeat lyrics of 'Wouldn't It Be Nice' contrast with the friend's depression and also parody all those positive messages unable to improve Flint's situation. This type of *détournement* – placing a song out of its original context as ironic commentary – entails the expression of two different discourses, one based on well-intentioned statements and another on their factual verification, allowing the audience to build a new meaning through their comparison. Like documentary landscaping, this device provides a critical tool to challenge the official discourse on urban change, given its implicit suggestion that this process might have developed otherwise.

The lack of prospects in Flint led its residents to demobilisation, as revealed by the statements of politicians and trade unionists included in the film: during the parade that commemorates the Great Flint Sit Down Strike, the president of the UAW – United Auto Workers – admits that '*we have to accept the reality that [the plants] are not going to remain open*'. Despite the rejuvenation attempts undertaken by local authorities, which are also parodied in the film, the industrial city where Moore grew up was disappearing in the 1980s, at least as he remembered it: according to US census figures, the population of Flint dropped from 159,611 residents in 1980 to 140,761 in 1990, a decrease of 11.8%. To make matters worse, this downward trend had already started in previous decades and has spanned until today, causing the loss of almost half of its population: from 196,940 residents in 1960 to the current 102,434 registered by the US census in 2010. Like other Rust Belt cities, Flint should have been 'nice', but the post-industrial crisis spoiled it, to the point that *Money* magazine chose it as the worst of three hundred urban areas to live in the United States for 'its high crime rates, weak economies and relatively few arts and leisure activities', an affront to the local self-esteem also included in the film.

This depressive *zeitgeist* is depicted by recording Flint's endangered cityscape and constructing a nostalgic discourse on its loss – the loss of a place of memory, but also the loss of what it symbolised. For example, by filming the last truck made in the Flint factory, Moore and his crew also captured the workers' contradictory attitude towards their redundancy: most employees clapped their hands, perhaps to present their last respects to the factory and their old jobs, or simply to encourage themselves, but there is a man who verbalises the collective concern: *'What's everybody so happy about? We just lost our jobs!'* Unfortunately, their alternatives of a new job, as suggested in the film, were not exactly very promising: the first was migrating to the Sun Belt, which threatened community survival; the second, self-employment, which rarely had the desired success; and the third, retraining, which almost always entailed a deterioration in working conditions.

The tendency to frequently move from one region to another has to do, according to Kevin Lynch and Michael Southworth, with the American way of life and 'the expression of our free spirit' (1990: 95). These authors warned that 'regional shifts may be accounted favorable only when costs are paid by the migrant enterprises that benefit, when the old and the poor are not unwillingly left behind, and when social and psychological ties are not unnecessarily broken or traditions lost' (1990: 169). The massive migration from the Rust Belt to the Sun Belt in the 1980s, however, did not always follow this advice, especially in those cases in which it was actively encouraged by the Reagan administration as the only solution to economic stagnation: 'The 1980 President's Commission for a National Agenda proposed that national policy should encourage this mobility, rather than seeking to check it. [...] Present subsidies to declining places, in their opinion only trap the poor, since they tempt them to stay and survive, when they might move and prosper' (1990: 95). Faced with this logic, *Roger & Me* shows the other side of this policy: as so many people voluntarily left Flint in the mid-1980s, the truck rental companies did not have enough vehicles to provide their services to the most needy, beginning with evicted families. Moore's interest in this particular side effect of the internal migration policy is coherent with his personal decision to return to Flint after the failure of his own move to San Francisco, because he wants to tell the story of the people who have no choice but to stay in Flint despite the evident lack of prospects.

Regarding attempts at self-employment, the film highlights the absurdity of many situations in order to discredit the neoliberal praise of entrepreneurial attitude. Among other individual cases, Moore follows the stories of Rhonda Britton, a woman who sells rabbits as pets or meat, and Janet K. Rauch, a former feminist turned distributor for Amway – a direct-selling company specialised in health, beauty and home care products. Considering Moore's love for unsubtle metaphors, Rhonda's rabbits seem to symbolise the awful fate of the working class – becoming pets/slaves or dying to feed your owner/employer – while Janet's obsession with winter or summer colours is shown as proof of feminism's defeat by the conservative backlash of the 1980s.

The retraining stories are not much better either. Moore tells us how ex-auto workers were hired as prison guards in jails that held former colleagues turned criminals by unemployment, while others found jobs in the fast food sector, just to immediately lose them due to their inability to keep up with the hectic pace of the kitchen. According to a Taco Bell manager, '*many [workers] say that this is a lot of hard work because assembly work is easy. [...] [Instead], fast food demands a fast pace because we want to present a food item within so many seconds, if we can do it. [...] Some of them just couldn't develop that speed.*' This comment bespeaks the social stagnation of industrial workers, unable to adapt to the requirements of the service industry of the 1980s. In light of this situation, the only man with '*a secure job*' that Moore could find in Flint did not precisely work for community building, but just the opposite: the main activity of sheriff's deputy Fred Ross was to evict those who could no longer pay the rent.

The desperation of the unemployed contrasts with the upper classes' lack of social conscience. Moore asks affluent people about their opinion on the crisis, and their answers reveal that they sincerely believe that the economic recession can be overcome with assertiveness. By editing their most unfortunate statements, Moore puts on display the class privilege, racism and sexism of those who are apparently not affected by the crisis, as has been noted by Douglas Kellner (2010: 84), thereby revealing their 'steadfastly held sense of superiority over and indifference to the suffering of their fellow citizens' (Studlar 2010: 61). The ruling class, however, has also been conditioned by neoliberal policies since the 1980s, to the point that any contemporary government, no matter its ideology, has to adapt its decisions to the demands of corporate power, even when they are not appropriate for their particular situation, as Bauman has explained:

> A government dedicated to the well-being of its constituency has little choice but to implore and cajole, rather than force, capital to fly in, and once inside, to build sky-scraping offices instead of staying in rented-per-night hotel rooms. And this can be done or can be attempted to be done by (to use the common political jargon of the free-trade era) 'creating better conditions for free enterprise', which means adjusting the political game to the 'free enterprise' rules – that is, using all the regulating power at the government's disposal in the service of deregulation, of dismantling and scrapping the extant 'enterprise constraining' laws and statutes, so that the government's vow that its regulating powers will not be used to restrain capital's liberties become credible and convincing. (2000: 150)

In the case of Flint, the best example of how corporate power kidnapped the local government was the promotional campaign to attract tourists and investors in the mid-1980s, a project that included the building of a luxury hotel, a shopping centre and a theme park dedicated to the automotive industry, AutoWorld, as well as the spread of institutional advertising on how to welcome visitors. The main idea, according to Miles Orvell, was 'the creation of an economy of the "simulacrum"', in which the production of consumer goods was replaced by 'a story about the production of consumer goods' (2010: 139). This episode is addressed in the film through another *détournement* in which Moore juxtaposes footage of this promotional campaign with its poor results: as tourists never came, the hotel was sold, the shopping centre remained half empty and AutoWorld closed in January 1985, only six months after its opening in July 1984. Meanwhile, the only business that seemed to succeed in Flint was a company that made lint-rollers, Helmac Co., which is mentioned by GM lobbyist Tom Kay as an example of the business opportunities that were still in Flint. Thereupon, Moore inserts a couple of shots of lint rollers and compares this product with the auto industry, reminding viewers of the huge scale differences between both activities. By ridiculing his opponents' messages again, Moore turns Kay's suggestion into a fallacy before the audience, who takes sides with the filmmaker not only because he may sometimes be right, but mainly because his arguments are more fun.

To sum up, Moore's personal involvement with the community remains the key factor in conveying the bitter experience of industrial decline. The choice of self-portrait as supporting subgenre for socio-political documentary reinforces his arguments, inasmuch as it creates an emotional link between subject and object. This does not mean, however, that 'Moore is Flint' and 'Flint is Moore', paraphrasing Rudolph Hess's ominous speech about Hitler and Germany in *Triumph des Willens* (*Triumph of the Will*, Leni Riefenstahl, 1935). On the contrary, Moore introduces himself as an ordinary citizen who wants to explain the problems of his community to a wider audience, talking from below and not from above, that is, from the residents' perspective instead of from a position of power. Accordingly, *Roger & Me* documents the time when the people from Flint realised that 'GM was not Flint' and therefore 'Flint was not GM either', despite having been its birthplace in 1908. Moore certainly represents '*a private interest*', as the workers' spokeswoman says when she refuses to make any statement to the camera, but at least it is his own one: that of a first-person filmmaker who attempts to expose an awful truth (GM no longer cares about Flint) while simultaneously exposing his own self (who does care, greatly).

Lightning Over Braddock: A Rustbowl Fantasy: The Big Fish in a Little Pond

Tony Buba might have inspired Jim Lane's definition of 'autobiographical documentarist': he is 'a filmmaker working in anonymity, at a very local level, under low-budget constraints' (2002: 4). Contrary to Michael Moore, Buba is rarely known outside the United States, and he can only be considered a celebrity in the Pittsburgh area, where his hometown, Braddock, is located. His urban self-portrait, *Lightning Over Braddock: A Rustbowl Fantasy*, anticipated some of the features popularised by Moore, such as the aesthetics of failure, personal politics or ironic selfhood, although its main novelty was probably the inclusion of fictional fantasies within the non-fiction context (see Lane 2002: 139). In this film, Buba assumes a wide variety of roles, 'from recorder to social actor to scripted fictional character to commentator', as Paul Arthur has pointed out, but all of them can be summarised in the following two: on the one hand, Buba is Braddock's official chronicler, its 'bard', as John Anderson (2012) has called him; while on the other he is the main subject of this documentary, at least as much as Braddock itself (Arthur 1993: 131).

Both roles are established from the very beginning of the film. Its opening shot is an image of a postcard sent by Buba to his brother Pasquale, which reads as follows: '*Dear Pat, Carrie Furnace is now closed. The Homestead Mill might be next. I'm glad Dad retired when he did. Starting a new film on mill closings, might need your help. Take care. Your brother.*'³ Like the beginning of *Roger & Me*, these lines introduce the filmmaker as the main character of the film (Image 6.2), reveal the setting (his hometown) and the subject (its decline) and consequently locate *Lightning Over Braddock* between the traditions of socio-political documentary and domestic ethnography. Nevertheless, the blend of collective and individual issues is deeper here than in *Roger & Me*, to the point that it is never clear if the self-portrait is simply a device for depicting the post-industrial crisis, as it was in Moore's documentary, or if the crisis is rather a backdrop against which to develop the self-portrait.

The combination of a macro and micro approach continues in the following sequence, in which Buba alternates landscape shots of the Pittsburgh area with Braddock street scenes while providing information about the crisis. Here is the transcription of the introductory commentary:

Image 6.2: Tony Buba, posing with Carrie Furnace in a publicity still of *Lightning Over Braddock*

The Pittsburgh renaissance of the 1980s was deceptive. High technology was the corporate buzzword. High technology means Carnegie Mellon University, computers, software contracts. To corporate leaders, high technology meant the chance to build new factories in El Salvador, South Korea, the Dominican Republic. Anywhere where there was a friendly, repressive government and the promise of no unions and low wages. Office buildings rose, factories were razed. Towns went bankrupt. Water became undrinkable. Infant mortality rates among blacks were higher than in Third World countries. Once-proud communities were reduced to playing the state lottery in the hopes of keeping their towns alive. Over a hundred thousand people moved out of the area. Homes were lost. Suicides increased. All of the mill towns were hit hard. One of the towns hardest hit was my hometown, Braddock. Braddock is a small mill town six miles from Pittsburgh. In Braddock, the unemployment rate was thirty-seven percent. The per capita income was less than five thousand dollars. Loans were taken out to meet the town's payroll. These were hard times. There was a lot of poverty, a lot of anger, and a lot of daydreaming.

These lines could also refer to Flint, but Braddock's situation was even worse: on 15 June 1988, it was declared a 'distressed municipality', that is, a town in bankruptcy, a status from which it has not recovered yet (see Stewart 2012). A quick overview on the historical evolution of its demographic statistics reveals an advanced level of urban decay: in the three decades before the commercial release of *Lightning Over Braddock*, the town lost 62% of its population, going from 12,337 residents in 1960 to 4,682 in 1990. Currently, according to the 2010 Census, Braddock only has 2,159 inhabitants. The following table may help to see the big picture of American Rust Belt cities' depopulation after the 1960s, taking as examples the three cases referred to in this book: Milwaukee, Flint and Braddock, each one representative of a particular film – *One Way Boogie Woogie / 27 Years Later, Roger & Me* and *Lightning Over Braddock* – and of a particular type of city – the centre of a metropolitan area, a medium-sized city and a small mill town.

Year	Milwaukee, WI		Flint, MI		Braddock, PA	
	Population	Variation	Population	Variation	Population	Variation
1960	741,324		196,940		12,337	
1970	717,099	−3.3%	193,317	−1.8%	8,682	−29.6%
1980	636,212	−11.3%	159,611	−17.4%	5,634	−35.1%

1990	628,088	−1.3%	140,761	−11.8%	4,682	−16.9%
2000	596,974	−5%	124,943	−11.2%	2,912	−37.8%
2010	594,833	−0.4%	102,434	−18%	2,159	−25.9%
Total Decrease		−20.2%		−48%		−82.5%

Source: US Census Bureau.

This chart shows that the worst population decline occurred in the 1970s, when James Benning shot *One Way Boogie Woogie*. In the 1980s, the percentages eased, but the same negative trend remained, creating a feeling of irreversible deadlock when Moore and Buba made their films. With the exception of Milwaukee, the situation does not seem to have improved in the 1990s and 2000s, especially in the case of Braddock, which lost even more population in percentage terms in the 1990s than in the 1970s. In order to present the particular case of Braddock within a national context, Buba sometimes echoes macroeconomic figures in his film, as when he comments that '*90% of the baby-boom generation has a lower standard of living than their parents*' or when he films the following statistics in a local bulletin board:

> For every 1000 manufacturing jobs lost, we lose: 1000 service jobs, 17 doctors, 17 eating places, 13 food stores ... 11 gas stations, 6 clothing stores, 5 dentists ... 3 auto dealerships, 2 hardware stores, 2 drug stores ... 2 auto accessory stores, 1 jewellery store, 1 sports store [and an] unknown number of teachers and government workers. These statistics are from the US Department of Commerce and the Federal Office of Budget and Management.

All this information awakes the nostalgic desire to return to better times, whether in terms of quality of life or social commitment. As the 1970s were not precisely a time to remember fondly, Braddock residents had to go back to previous decades to find something to be proud of: towards the end of *Lightning Over Braddock*, an old man recalls the successes of the workers' struggle in the 1930s and encourages young people to '*take to the streets*' again. This discourse is assumed by Buba himself, who ironically pretends to be a modern political filmmaker instead of a postmodern one: '*With statistics like this*', he says over images of the Saint Patrick's Day parade, '*you'll think there'll be mass demonstrations: people taking to the streets. But there didn't seem to be much interest in saving manufacturing jobs. I thought this is a perfect time for a political filmmaker. I can make the film that will raise consciousness! People will take to the streets.*'

There is a good deal of political rallies and demonstrations in the film, but even so Buba is far from fulfilling his stated intentions: before raising the consciousness of the audience, *Lightning Over Braddock* awakes his own one, compelling him to face his feeling of guilt for taking advantage of the situation. *'The ironic thing,'* he admits in the commentary, *'is [that] as Braddock and the Monongahela Valley declined, my fortune increased.'* This confession, according to Lane, questions those filmmakers 'who use the plight of others to promote their own careers' (2002: 142), that is, anyone who crosses the boundary between social documentary and porno-misery.[4] Thus, when it is assumed that the film should go deeper into Braddock's case, it instead exposes the contradictions of the filmmaker by including the footage of one of Buba's appearances on television: a television portrait within a film self-portrait.

Considering that Buba was – then and now – a complete unknown, this footage allowed him to summarise his film career, from his first short documentary, *J. Roy: New and Used Furniture* (1974), to his modest success, *Sweet Sal* (1979), both included in the collection *The Braddock Chronicles* (1972–1985).[5] His commentary, however, does not sound as proud as it might: *'My exposure on TV was directly proportional to the number of layoffs,'* he says. *'The one question I was always asked was "do you ever think about moving?" Of course, the one answer I never give is that "no, I like being a big fish in a little city".'* This is Buba's drama: he would like to be famous around the world, but he is actually satisfied with being famous in Braddock. Therefore, what seemed a shameless act of self-promotion turns into a sample of the possibilities that first-person filmmaking opens for a secondary revision of our memories (see Renov 2004: 114). Indeed, Buba's critical remarks on his media persona are a prime example of post-modernity's narcissistic humour, as Gilles Lipovetsky has described by talking about Woody Allen's films:

> The self becomes the prime target of humour, an object of derision and self-predation. The comedy character no longer uses the burlesque, as Buster Keaton, Charles Chaplin or the Marx Brothers did. Its humour does not come from the failure to adapt to the logic nor from its subversion, but from self-reflection: a narcissistic, libidinal and corporeal hyper-awareness [of its own self]. The burlesque character was unaware of the image that it offered to the others, it made people laugh despite itself, without observing itself or seeing its performance. The absurd situations that it caused triggered the comedy according to an irremediable mechanism. On the contrary, Woody Allen makes people laugh by means of narcissistic humour, endlessly analysing himself, dissecting his own ridicule,

introducing his devalued self mirror to himself and the audience. (1986: 144–5; my translation)

In this quotation, where Lipovetsky wrote 'Woody Allen' it is possible to read many other names, such as 'Tony Buba', 'Ross McElwee', 'Nanni Moretti' or 'Guy Maddin', to name just a few first-person filmmakers. Through his narcissistic humour, Buba sabotaged his position of power as a way of remaining close to his neighbours, admitting one sin after another in a recurrent joke about his Catholic background: '*I started to feel guilty,*' he says right after his televisual incarnation states the opposite, because '*my success seemed dependent on the failure of others.*' Those 'others' are basically his own friends and actors: Jimmy Roy, Stephen Pellegrino, Natalka Voslakov, Ernie Spisak and especially Sal Caru, the local street hustler who starred in *Sweet Sal*.[6] *Lightning Over Braddock* should have been another film about Sal, but apparently his unstable personality spoiled this possibility. In another example of the aesthetics of failure, the documentary focuses instead on the troubled relationship between Tony and Sal, who respectively embodied the friend who succeeds and the friend who fails to succeed, as well as the filmmaker and his star. In these sequences, it is never clear what was real and what was staged because their characters replace their real identities, leading the film towards the field of self-fiction.

Sal's failure to become an actor is just one of the many personal stories that symbolise Braddock's decline. According to Buba, the local entrepreneur Jimmy Roy also failed in business twelve times despite his blind faith in the American Dream: '*You are born to succeed,*' he states in a sequence of *J. Roy: New and Used Furniture,* '*and if you don't succeed it's your own fault because you didn't take control on what you think. What you think is gonna decide what you do, and what you do is gonna decide what you get.*' Such a speech somehow echoes business theories about self-confidence, but Roy's failure in achieving his purpose turns him into a Don Quixote, the opposite myth from the self-made man. Buba, meanwhile, also fails in his project to make '*the film that will raise consciousness*' and becomes another Don Quixote: as the grant money was running out, his doubts about how to make the film apparently prevented him from finishing it, or at least from making it as he would have like.[7] For instance, he could not even show his old short films as they really were, as happened with Steve Pellegrino's musical performance in *Mill Hunk Herald*, a sequence in which Buba replaced the original soundtrack with an explanation about why he had to remove it:

In this part of the film, Steve Pellegrino plays 'Jumping Jack Flash' on the accordion ... but you won't get to hear him play. I called about acquir-

ing the rights to the song, but they wanted $15,000 for it. I told them, 'I don't want Mick Jagger to come to Braddock to sing it. I have a friend who plays it on the accordion.' They still wanted $15,000. $15,000 is three times the per capita income of a Braddock resident. I didn't think it would be a politically correct move to pay that kind of money for a song. In fact, it's crazy. This isn't a Hollywood feature we're making here. I know some of you are going to think this sounds real Catholic, but when I die and get to heaven, what if instead of St. Peter being at the gate, it's Sacco and Vanzetti, and they say to me, 'You paid $15,000 for a song instead of spending that money for political organizing?' I wouldn't get in. So talk to the person sitting next to you and try to remember how the song goes, and then sing along with Steve.

Paul Arthur considers that this aesthetics of failure is the film counterpart of all those stories about frustration and defeat embodied by Buba's friends. The filmmaker, his project, his friends and his hometown are thereby bound in 'a concordance of nonfulfillment' that ultimately guarantees 'authenticity and documentary truth' (1993: 132). By means of a *mise en abyme* similar to that used by Federico Fellini in *8½* (1963), the account of the impossibility of making a film finally becomes that film, although the final reunion of the characters in *Lightning Over Braddock* is not a happy party but a campy sequence in which Jimmy Roy sings a theme song entitled 'Braddock City of Magic', the one that had already opened the film. Despite the intentional excess of Buba's *mise-en-scène* and Roy's performance – described as 'Las Vegas nightclub-style' by Pat Aufderheide (1989) – the sequence is a sincere wail for a dying place of memory that uses ironic detachment to express primary emotions. The song's chorus leaves no doubt about Buba's feelings: '*Braddock ... city of magic. Braddock ... city of light. Braddock ... where have you gone?*'

This kind of staged sequence depicts the aforementioned tendency of Braddock residents to daydream. Throughout the film, Buba unleashes his fantasy and parodies Hollywood popular genres such as the musical, the gangster film or the action film. Thanks to his troupe of amateur actors, he shoots his own versions of the film icons of the time, reflecting on and also criticising 'the seduction of mainstream cinema' (Lane 2002: 139). Thus, along with the opening and closing sequence, *Lightning Over Braddock* includes up to four fictional set pieces that freely combine genres and characters: a local staging of Gandhi's assassination that rather resembles John F. Kennedy's; an 'ethnic detective story' filled with Italian stereotypes and inspired by *The Godfather* (Francis Ford Coppola, 1972); an action sequence in which Sal, characterised as Rambo, takes revenge on Buba's snubs and shoots him to death, and a techno-pop musical composed by Steve Pellegrino and entitled 'Death of the Iron Age Café', in which the dancers are industrial workers whose choreography bears a reasonable likeness to the movements of the living dead, whether because it is a metaphor for industrial decline or perhaps because the dancers' only previous acting experience was in a horror movie directed by George A. Romero, another Pittsburgh-based filmmaker.

All these daydreams are also part of the historical world, given that they documented the filmmaker's mindscape, which is itself a reflection of his time and place. Officially, Buba mixed fiction and documentary because 'I wanted the viewers to be in doubt about what was real and what wasn't, instead of just sitting there and being a good consumer' (in Aufderheide 1989), although that combination can also be interpreted as a cover letter to Hollywood, an 'advertisement' of the filmmaker's skills, as Arthur has pointed out (1993: 132). Hollywood escapism is the exact reverse of what a social documentary should be, but the temptation of selling out to mainstream cinema is so strong that the filmmaker apparently surrendered to it: '*Father, I no longer want to make social documentaries,*' he says to a priest, in a parody of his own confession, '*I want to make a Hollywood musical!*'[8] In this sense, the images of Buba visiting the Chinese Theatre in Los Angeles, where he pretends to leave his fingerprints on the pavement, serve as incriminating evidence of his sin as committed documentary maker. These grandiose delusions contrast with his everyday life in Braddock: like Sal, who summarised his days as '*wake up, walk around, same garbage*', part of Buba's self-portrait consists of sequences in which he is alone at home watching television and wondering how to make his film. Like everyone else, he also wants '*money, power and fame*', the usual promises of the American Dream according to its Hollywood version. The acknowledgement of his self-centredness, however, frees him from guilt because it places him closer to people than to artists, counteracting any haughty pose. Consequently, by showing 'the precarious link between individual and community in an America captivated by media images and fame' (Aufderheide 1989), Buba actually constructs 'an authentic individuality that also speaks for [his] community' (Lane 2002: 143).

Lightning Over Braddock thereby challenges the authority of journalistic documentaries to depict what was going on in the Rust Belt. In fact, during a protest against a plant closing in Duquesne, Buba openly criticises their supposed objectivity by means of a staged interview with a television critic:[9]

> Margie Strosser (TV critic): *Finally, sophisticated media who know how to tell a story are getting involved. [...] Local people ... fail to see the big picture, and also contribute to misappropriations of political struggle.*

Woman reporter: *My father worked for the mills for forty years. You mean to tell me that someone from out of town can tell the story better than I could?*

Margie Strosser: *Yes, that's precisely what I'm saying, because you can't be objective. And your subjectivity may be poetic and well-intentioned but is probably provincial.*

This interview was scripted from a conversation that Buba overhead at a cocktail party, and it raises the question of his own ability to depict the plight of his hometown (see Aufderheide 1989, Lane 2002: 143). Was he – or any other local filmmaker in whatever city – qualified to do so? The film clearly states that yes, he was. A decade before the outbreak of digital technology, Buba was already fulfilling Francis Ford Coppola's prophecy about the future of filmmaking announced at the end of *Hearts of Darkness: A Filmmaker's Apocalypse* (Fax Bahr, George Hickenlooper & Eleanor Coppola, 1991):

To me, the great hope is that now these little 8mm video recorders and stuff have come out, and some ... just people who normally wouldn't make movies are going to be making them. And you know, suddenly, one day some little fat girl in Ohio is going to be the new Mozart, you know, and make a beautiful film with her little father's camera recorder. And for once, the so-called professionalism about movies will be destroyed, forever. And it will really become an art form. That's my opinion.

In stark contrast with the professionalism of mainstream media, Tony Buba claims his right to be the accredited voice of Braddock after having documented its decline for the fifteen years that precede the making of this film. That activity allows him to show the changes in the cityscape through his own footage, comparing images framed from the same camera position in the 1970s and 1980s, the same device that William Raban had already used in *Thames Film*. *Lightning Over Braddock* thereby offers an insightful portrait of the post-industrial crisis that works on two levels: on the one hand, it is a digest of Buba's guilty pleasures that summarises and expands his amateur film career; on the other, it ultimately becomes the social documentary that he strove so hard to make. In short, by combining an ironic self-portrait based on the aesthetics of failure with committed activism and guerrilla practices, both Tony Buba and Michael Moore widen the discursive possibilities of the socio-political documentary film, joining the defence of their respective communities with the expression of their own subjectivity.

NOTES

*   A shorter version of this section has been previously published in the Revue LISA / LISA e-journal (see Villarmea Álvarez 2014c).

1   *American Dream* (Barbara Kopple, Cathy Kaplan, Thomas Haneke and Lawrence Silk, 1990), another well-known documentary of the time, also recorded the same feeling among the striking workers of a meat packing company based in south-eastern Minnesota, Hormel Food. Its directors, however, depicted the workers' defeat through a completely different device from Moore's because they remained faithful to the conventions of the observational mode. Orvell's article is precisely devoted to comparing *Roger & Me* with *American Dream* (see 2010: 127–40).

2   The presence of Kevin Rafferty in the film crew of *The Atomic Cafe* and *Roger & Me* is the most evident link between these documentaries: he co-directed the former and was the cinematographer of the latter.

3   At the time, Pasquale Buba lived in Los Angeles, where he worked as film editor in features such as *Day of the Dead* and *Monkey Shines* (George A. Romero, 1985, 1988).

4   The term 'porno-misery' was popularised by Colombian filmmakers Carlos Mayolo and Luis Ospina through their mockumentary *Agarrando pueblo* (*The Vampires of Poverty*, 1979), in which they parodied the haughty attitude and superficial approach of those filmmakers who take advantage of their position of power to highlight the worst aspects of poverty and squalor without delving into their causes.

5   *The Braddock Chronicles* includes the following short films: *To My Family* (1972), J. Roy: *New and Used Furniture* (1974), *Shutdown* (1975), *Betty's Corner Café* (1976), *Sweet Sal* (1979), *Washing Walls with Mrs G.* (1980), *Home Movies* (1980), *Homage to a Mill Town* (1980), *Mill Hunk Herald* (1981), *Peabody 7 Friends* (1983), *Braddock Food Bank* (1985) and *Birthday Party* (1985). In addition to these works, Buba had filmed another short documentary entitled *Voices from a Steeltown* (1983) before undertaking the project of *Lightning Over Braddock*. A complete list of his works, including the most recent ones, is available at www.braddockfilms.com.

6   Sal Caru is the screen name that identifies Sal in *Lightning Over Braddock*, but his real family name is Carollo. The multiple spellings of this surname, which sometimes appears as Carulli or Carullo, suggest Sal's changing personality.

7   *Lightning Over Braddock* was financed by fellowships from the National Endowment for the Arts, the Pennsylvania Council on the Arts and the John Siman Guggenheim Foundation.

8   The desire to make a musical film also appears in Nanni Moretti's urban self-portrait, 'In Vespa', the first section of *Caro Diario* (*Dear Diary*, 1993). In that film, in order to enter those houses that he likes, Moretti tells their owners that he is looking for locations for his next film, a musical about a Trotskyist pastry chef in the Italy of the 1950s. Later on, Moretti ended his following self-fiction, *Aprile* (*April*, 1998), by pretending to film that musical.

9   Duquesne is another mill town located across the Monongahela river from Braddock.

CHAPTER SEVEN

Self-Portrait as Essay Film

The development of urban self-portraits in Europe has been highly influenced by the essayistic tradition, to the extent that among critics it is often regarded as a specific form of the essay film. This, however, is not exactly a closed genre but an open domain that includes a wide variety of practices: Laura Rascaroli has devoted several chapters of her book *The Personal Camera* to the diary, the travelogue, the notebook and the self-portrait film (2009: 106–89), while Timothy Corrigan has done the same in *The Essay Film: From Montaigne, After Marker*, in which he discusses the travelogue, the editorial approach and metafilmic practices, among other topics (2011: 79–204). All these essayistic modes, as Corrigan has called them, share a similar authorial voice that, according to Rascaroli, 'approaches the subject matter not in order to present an ostensibly factual report ... but to offer an overtly personal, in-depth, thought-provoking reflection' (2009: 33). Consequently, she considers the essay film 'a cinema in the first person, a cinema of thought, of investigation, of intellectual searching and of self-reflection' (2009: 189), a description that echoes old definitions of its literary counterpart, by, for instance, philosophers Eduardo Nicol – 'a theatre of ideas in which the rehearsal and the final performance are combined' (quoted in Renov 2004: 186) – or Max Bense, who had already drawn attention to the experimental nature of this type of writing:

> The person who writes essayistically is the one who composes as he experiments, who turns his object around, questions it, feels it, tests it, reflects on it, who attacks it from different sides and assembles what he sees in his mind's eye and puts into words what the object allows one to see under the conditions created in the course of writing. (Quoted in Ibid.)

The essay film has therefore become, according to Paul Arthur, 'the leading non-fiction form for both intellectual and artistic innovation', as well as 'a meeting ground for documentary, avant-garde, and art film impulses' (2003: 58, 62). The filmmakers who have entered this hybrid domain organise all kinds of visual material guided by their subjectivity, speaking from themselves, as Antonio Weinrichter has written (2010: 266), but not necessarily about themselves. This subjectivity has affected both form and content, to the extent that social and political issues currently coexist with an emphasis on self-documentation and the private sphere: hence the recent blend of collective and individual accounts, historical and personal sources or archival footage and home movies, a series of binomials that have lately caused the pairing of representation and reflection (Weinrichter 2010: 266). By shaping real elements through an explicit authorial voice, the essay film extracts 'the truth and reality of those real elements', Josep Maria Catalá has said, 'a truth and reality that are not outside the *dispositif*, but inside it, because they are the outcome of the hermeneutic process launched by the *dispositif* itself' (2005: 144; my translation).

The origin of this film form dates back to the French documentary tradition, within which titles such as *Nuit et brouillard* (*Night and Fog*, Alain Resnais, 1955), *Les maîtres fous* (*The Mad Masters*, Jean Rouch, 1955), *Lettre de Sibérie* (*Letter from Siberia*, Chris Marker, 1958), *Le Joli Mai* (Chris Marker & Pierre Lhomme, 1963) or *2 ou 3 choses que je sais d'elle* (*2 or 3 Things I Know About Her*, Jean-Luc Godard, 1967) are usually mentioned as 'crucial milestones' in its genealogy (Arthur 2003: 59). Its development was also nurtured by other national film traditions, especially the German, the American and the British ones: Weinrichter has pointed out the role of filmmakers such as Helmut Bitomsky, Harun Farocki, Alexander Kluge or Hans-Jürgen Syberberg within the first; the importance of Ralph Arlyck, Craig Baldwin, Alan Berliner, Su Friedrich, Trinh T. Minh-ha and Mark Rappaport for the second, and the work of Patrick Keiller, Peter Greenaway, Chris Petit and Steve Hewley within the third (2004: 98). Michael Moore is sometimes added to this list, by Arthur and Renov for example, but his documentaries nonetheless lack two key features of the essay film, as Rascaroli has explained: on the one hand, they do not 'problematize his authorship, which is not subjected to self-searching scrutiny', and on the other hand, they do not 'present [either] their subject matter as a subjective reflection on a problem, but as an objective investigation of factual events' (2009: 41). Accordingly, *Roger & Me* would be outside the essayistic domain since its main line of argument is not primarily constructed from the filmmaker's subjectivity but from gathering journalistic information.

Some European urban self-portraits have resorted to the essayistic tradition because its layering of different time frames allows their directors to recall old places of memory from a present in which they no longer exist. These documentaries do not only represent missing cityscapes, but also the way filmmakers attempt to recover them: they are 'fragmentary, full of gaps, associative, abbreviated, dis-orderly, and [have] no respect for chronology', a description that summarises what Michael Chanan considers 'the general rule of memory' (2012: 29). These films usually get lost in 'the chasm between our desire to recapture the past and the impossibility of a pristine return', a contradiction that Michael Renov has found, for example, in Jonas Mekas' diary films (2004: 77, 114). Nevertheless, rather than simply record the present or visualise the past, they mainly focus on the act of remembering itself: even when there is a present from which the past is recalled, this second type of urban self-portrait usually goes beyond the dichotomy of 'then and now' by revealing the emotional ties that bind people and places together over time.

The endless revision of old footage is a usual way of addressing issues related to memory, especially when images and commentary belong to different times and tenses. In those cases, the lack of agreement between what we see and what we hear allows the superimposition of past and present, also emphasising 'histori-cal gaps or tonal clashes inherent in the visual-linguistic interface', as Arthur has said (2003: 60). According to Catherine Russell, the intertextuality of archival footage provides the audience with 'an allegory of history … by which the film-maker engages with the past through recall, retrieval, and recycling' (1999: 238). This means that travelling through time in these essayistic self-portraits is also travelling through images, whether recovered – those that have been preserved – or absent ones – those that only exist as a memory or an emotion. Today, as Àngel Quintana explains, any image may have a great memorial value because the transition from modernity to postmodernity has deleted the distinction between archival footage and waste material:

> A few years ago, filmmakers thought that the useful historical archive was kept at film libraries, on 35mm films, and that its value was clearly infor-mative or sociological. This notion, however, has changed since orthodox documents of the past are no longer the only archive-worthy footage, but also old amateur films, home movies, commercials and all types of ignoble materials. (2010: 70; my translation)

This extended archive has become 'a second reality', as Català has termed it, which 'defamiliarises the real and reveals those haunting elements that the coetaneous gaze did not know how to detect or was unable to' (2010: 283–4, my translation). The replacement of reality by its image has been so intensive in recent years that it has also affected our personal memories: we do not always remember our past experiences directly, but rather through sentimental items or cultural productions ranging from postcards and souvenirs to popular songs or archival footage. In order to describe the mental associations between mediascapes and memoryscapes, Alison Landsberg has developed the concept of 'prosthetic memory' (2004), suggesting that the continuous encounters with popular forms have conditioned our memory to the point that 'it becomes increasingly difficult to differentiate personal experience from the mediating technologies that have (re)constructed both personal and collective experience of past times' (Hallam 2010a: 72). This is to say that media images are currently so intermingled with our direct experiences that cinema itself has become 'a repository of memory', as Rascaroli has stated (2009: 64).

The two case studies in this chapter, *Les hommes du port* (Alain Tanner, 1995) and *Of Time and the City* (Terence Davies, 2008), use the essayistic approach to explore what happens when port cities are threatened with the loss of their local identity. It is necessary to take into account, as Francesc Muñoz has pointed out, that the film iconography of waterfronts has historically symbolised much of what a city is supposed to be: mobility, exchange, intensity, diversity, chance, danger, conflict, etc. (2010: 204). However, if these areas lost their original purpose, to what extent do they preserve their old social meanings? In these two documentaries, Alain Tanner and Terence Davies return to Genoa and Liverpool respectively after an absence of several decades, during which the two cities' architectural and social heritage was completely transformed. As they could no longer find their places of memory in the cityscape, they had to look for their traces in oral testimonies and archival footage, contrasting their own memories with old images. Their first-person narratives convey feelings ranging from topophilia to homesickness, although the explicit nostalgia of previous urban self-portraits gradually gives way to a bitter melancholy of loss. Therefore, *Les hommes du port* and *Of Time and the City* are not exactly documentaries about the longing of missing cityscapes, but rather about the emotional quest for those significant memories that took place there.

Les hommes du port: Self-Portrait in First-Person Plural

Alain Tanner is arguably the best-known Swiss filmmaker thanks largely to feature films such as *La salamandre* (*The Salamander*, 1971) or *Jonas qui aura 25 ans en l'an 2000* (*Jonah Who Will Be 25 in the Year 2000*, 1975). Nevertheless, his lack of attachment to his country and his position outside the industry has led him to become a travelling filmmaker: his first documentary, *Nice Time* (Alain Tanner & Claude Goretta, 1957), was filmed in London within the Free Cinema movement, and since then he has worked in more than half a dozen countries, including France, India, Ireland, Italy, Portugal and Spain, besides Switzerland itself.[1] Contrary to Tony Buba, Tanner preferred exploring the world to staying in his hometown, Geneva, as he has admitted:

> Switzerland is too small, too civilised, and not particularly 'erotic'. Furthermore, cinema is a large consumer of territories: grass grows very slowly when a movie has gone through a small area. In this sense, I do not mind being a foreigner. I feel good and bad at the same time everywhere, so I can move without too many problems. I have partners in different countries where I can easily find funding, but I also face the problems of co-productions and language. (Tanner in Dimitriu 1993: 266; my translation)

In addition to feature films, Tanner also made thirty documentaries in the 1960s, most of which were socio-political reports for SBC, the Swiss Broadcasting Corporation. After the success of *Charles mort ou vif* (*Charles, Dead or Alive*, 1969), he left this format convinced that 'the creative period within television [had] already gone', since its supposed claim at objectivity was 'the opposite end of any form of personal expression' (in Dimitriu 1993: 204; my translation). With the only exception of *Temps mort* (1978), Tanner did not accept any other proposal from television until the French-German channel ARTE invited him to take part in a documentary series about port cities (Julie Z. 2012).[2] Despite the fact that the project was never completed, Tanner filmed his episode in Genoa about the slow decline of the dockers' local union, the CULMV, 'Compagnia Unica fra i Lavoratori di Merce Varie'.

At first sight, *Les hommes du port* may seem another talking heads documentary, but its interviews are punctuated by a first-person commentary, made by the filmmaker himself, that introduces several autobiographical references and essayistic digressions in the film. In fact, the audience soon realises that Genoa is not an unknown city for Tanner: his own voice tells how he visited it for the first time in 1947, when he was eighteen years old, because he was so impressed by Italian Neorealism that he wanted to verify his impressions on location. Later on, in 1952, he was hired by a shipping company based on Genoa as a clerk, a job that he left the next year in order to work as a purser in a cargo ship. From these experiences, he established an emotional bond with the stevedores in *Les hommes du port*, many of whom belong to his own generation. Thus, by means of an essayistic voice, he introduces himself as a mediator between past and present who wants to chronicle the story of the CULMV, a fulfilled utopia threatened by the economic and ideological shifts that followed the 1973 crisis and the fall of the Berlin Wall.

This company was founded after World War II, when Genoese dock workers joined forces to reconstruct the port. Without employers or shareholders, the cooperative allowed them to own their means of production and ultimately released them from dependence on ship owners. Guided by the principles of self-management and direct democracy, they organised themselves through meetings in which they elected two representatives, known as 'consuls', for a non-renewable term of two years. Thanks to this system, they kept control of their job until the 1990s, when the company was forced to change its internal organisation due to the privatisation of docks undertaken by Silvio Berlusconi's first government. In this context, *Les hommes du port* became, at best, a praise of their way of life, and at worst, a hagiography of the company. This approach is quite different from American documentaries of the time that dealt with similar issues, such as the aforementioned *Roger & Me* and *American Dream* (Barbara Kopple, Cathy Kaplan, Thomas Haneke & Lawrence Silk, 1990), in which the defeat of GM and Hormel employees was depicted as a dramatic and irreversible process.

Similarly to Barbara Kopple in *American Dream*, Tanner puts his camera at the workers' service and remains on the sidelines in the interviews, which are usually conducted by Italian philosopher Giairo Daghini. His casting solved the problem of the language barrier between the filmmaker and the filmed subjects, but also reproduced the television hierarchy that Tanner had previously rejected:

[Television executives] distrusted filmmakers because our framing and editing choices could ignore objectivity. In order to avoid this kind of manipulation, power soon passed from filmmakers to journalists, who were best-trained in the codes of practice since they came from the mainstream media. (Tanner in Dimitriu 1993: 204; my translation)

The formal contradiction between the journalistic gathering of testimonies and the essayistic elements of the commentary reveals that *Les hommes du port* is located halfway between the breakdown of the objective paradigm and its replacement by a subjective one. At the beginning of the film, Tanner reserves a few sequences for himself and tells us about his youth in Genoa, but most of the footage is devoted to the interviews with the characters. The narrative split of these two stories, one individual and another collective, echoes the social gap that distanced the filmmaker from dock workers forty years ago: '*There was the society and there was the world,*' Tanner says in the commentary, '*and at the time, I chose the world.*' This separation had a spatial dimension that reappears in *Les hommes du port*: the cargo ships anchored in the harbour and the offices in the Palazzo della Meridiana are the filmmaker's places of memory, whereas the waterfront and the *chiamata* – the area where stevedores go every day in search of a job – are the workers' territory. The CULMV headquarters are precisely located in the *chiamata*, as well as many bars and restaurants in which dock workers used to meet, socialise and, overall, spend most of their lives. For this reason, this place is a key spot in the emotional geography proposed by Tanner: most interviews were shot there or in nearby areas, except for the consul's, which was made aboard a boat while sailing in the harbour, perhaps as an unintended sign of his position of power within the company.

Tanner's places of memory, in turn, are usually represented through evocative images that attempt to capture, or at least to convey, the *genius loci* of Genoa: a few examples are the pan shots taken inside his favourite café, the ubiquitous presence of cargo ships – a fetish image that already appeared in his previous films *Les 100 jours d'Ongania* (1966), *Les trois Belgiques* (1968) and *In the White City* – and, above all, the footage filmed inside the Palazzo della Meridiana, his old workplace. The only inscription of his body in the film is included in this sequence: it is a brief shot in which he is seen from behind while entering the building to visit the exact corner where his desk was located. Thus, like psychogeographical documentaries, *Les hommes du port* explores the urban surface in search of any trace of the past in the old café or the dockers' gestures.

This body language symbolises the association between intelligence and work culture: both at the beginning and the end of the film, Tanner shows several close-ups of these gestures accompanied by classical music, implicitly establishing a comparison between the task of directing the movements of port cranes and the work of an orchestra conductor. This communication system, however, was endangered in the 1990s due to the transformations of dock work itself: as the commentary says, the widespread acceptance of containers as standard format in maritime trade speeded up the process of loading/unloading and fragmented work crews, which replaced old gestures with walkie-talkies. This paradigm shift is visually expressed in *Les hommes du port* through the contrast between the black-and-white footage of dock work recorded by stevedores themselves in the early 1970s and the colour images shot by the filmmaker more than twenty years later, some of them significantly taken from a modern port crane.

This is the first of the two occasions on which Tanner uses archival footage: later on, there is a sequence that dates back to 30 June 1960, when dock workers led a political demonstration against the attempt to held a conference of the Italian neo-fascist party in Genoa. That protest ended in violent clashes with the police and ultimately caused the fall of Fernando Tambroni's government. In those days, dock workers played a key role in local politics, but their influence gradually faded as their number decreased: in the mid-1990s, the CULMV had lost ninety percent of its workforce, going from 9,000 to 900 employees in thirty years. The archival sequences work therefore as testimony of the company's heyday and as illustration of old practices, but without going beyond the dialectic between then and now: given that Tanner undertook his search for traces of the past when many were still visible in the cityscape, he usually keeps his essayistic digressions for contemporary images, limiting himself to describing and identifying the content of the archival footage. In reference to the privatisation of the Genoa port and the transformation of the CULMV into a private firm, he states that '*it's the end of an era and the beginning of another*', a commentary that explicitly locates the film within the interregnum between the end of collective utopias and its replacement by the ideal of good management.

Since *Les hommes du port* does not adopt all the features of the essay film, it must be interpreted as a transition between the urban self-portraits about endangered cityscapes, such as *Roger & Me* and *Lightning Over Braddock*, and others about missing cityscapes, such as *Of Time and the City* and *My Winnipeg*. Indeed, unlike the latter, *Les hommes du port* is still a nostalgic film: to dispel any doubt, Tanner includes a song entitled 'Nostalgia' at the beginning, followed by an interview with his composer in which he reflects about this feeling. This retired worker argues that the city itself as it was has disappeared along with its old social routines. '*There is no more Genoa*,' he says, '*it no longer exists.*' Such idea is further developed in the commentary over a series of carscapes filmed from the '*Sopraelevata Aldo Moro*', an elevated highway that crosses Genoa from east to southwest through its waterfront (Image 7.1):

Image 7.1: *Les hommes du port*, carscape through the elevated highway

The highway is a physical barrier: the first façade of the city over the port can only be seen by those who drive at fifty miles an hour. It is an American solution at the heart of a medieval city. The old town, its houses and arcades faded into the background. They no longer face the coast, forming a whole with the old port, but bump against a viaduct. The barrier is not only physical, but also made of noise and pollution. The historic core of the city steps backwards, disappears into the shadows and becomes a marginalised ghetto; a sad and dark labyrinth for drug addicts and prostitutes. All that thereby enters the shadows is an important part of the historical memory of the city.

The *Sopraelevata* was built in 1965 as part of a circulation plan that attempted to improve vehicular traffic within Genoa's historic city centre. Although a well-intentioned project, this structure nonetheless embodies the usual flaws of Brutalist architecture: it lacks aesthetic dimension, needs constant maintenance and in the long term has had a negative impact on the city since it has broken its historical link with the sea. Consequently, the *Sopraelevata* has turned the Genoa waterfront into what Rem Koolhaas termed junk-space:

> Junkspace is the residue mankind leaves on the planet. The built ... product of modernization is not modern architecture but Junkspace. Junkspace is what remains after modernization has run its course, or, more precisely, what coagulates while modernization is in progress, its fallout. (2002: 175)

After these carscapes, the film enters the historic city in order to show its contemporary appearance: a two-minute tracking shot goes around a section of Via di Prè, a popular street that used to be crowded with sailors and stevedores in the 1950s, but that forty years ago looks half-empty, especially after the stores' closing time. This tracking shot is repeated a few sequences later by night, when the street is practically deserted: in forty-five seconds, the camera only meets a man and a cat in a scene characteristic of a ghost city. In both cases, Via di Prè is dark and dirty, but it does not look especially decayed, at least not yet. This footage is quite similar to some sequences of *In the White City*, a film in which Tanner surrendered to the charms of picturesque aesthetics: in most sequences, he depicted the wild beauty of Alfama – a popular neighbourhood located on a hill over the Lisbon waterfront – without realising that he sometimes confused its *genius loci* with the effects of urban decay. In Genoa, on the contrary, this atmosphere upset him, because he was not a foreigner there. After all, *In the White City* describes the exploration of an unknown cityscape, but *Les hommes du port* deals with the return to a beloved place. Accordingly, the mood of the latter depends on the distance between Tanner's memories of the 1950s and what he actually found in the 1990s: another city, another waterfront and, above all, another emotion.

Les hommes du port was made a few years before the launch of the 'Operating Plan for Genoa's Historic City Centre' (see Galdini 2005). At the time, sailors and stevedores had already been replaced by the first tourists, whose presence announced the imminent gentrification of the area, whereas traditional residents had given way to immigrants who were not always welcomed: in the summer of 1993, a series of attacks against foreign residents ended in a violent clash with police, an incident that warned about the deterioration of living conditions in the neighbourhood. Dock workers were aware of the importance of urban renewal for the future of the city, but Tanner was not as interested in this issue as they were: the only interview that addresses this topic in the film only serves to highlight the stevedores' involvement in local politics.

Contemporary global trends in urban planning usually seek to recover and increase the property value of depressed or neglected areas, such as historic centres and waterfronts, which are ultimately understood as spaces of consumption (see Muñoz 2010: 203–7). In view of redevelopments like Canary Wharf in London, Tanner probably feared that the Genoa waterfront might also become a banal-scape or just remain as a junkspace. In both cases, the past is understood as a commodity, as something that can be marketed as an idea, an image or an experience in order to make a profit from investors and tourists. Since its traces are simply regarded as economic assets for the city, their preservation usually entails some type of forgery: at best, their original appearance is softened by removing any annoying detail or controversial meaning; but at worst, they are not restored or destroyed, but simply preserved 'just in case'. At the turn of the century, when most Western cities, including Genoa, were undergoing similar processes of urban renewal, Koolhaas drew attention to the deep disorientation of local governments regarding what to do with their architectural heritage, an idea that appears in both his well-known text 'The Generic City' (Koolhaas & Mau 1995) and the later article 'Junkspace' (2002):

> The Generic City had a past, once. In its drive for prominence, large sections of it somehow disappeared, first unlamented – the past apparently was surprisingly unsanitary, even dangerous – then, without warning, relief turned into regret. Certain prophets – long white hair, gray socks, sandals – had always been warning that the past was necessary – a resource. Slowly, the destruction machine grinds to a halt; some random hovels on the laundered Euclidean plane are saved, restored to a splendor they never had... (1995: 125–6)

> Junkspace happens spontaneously through natural corporate exuberance – the unfettered play of the market – or is generated through the combined actions of temporary 'czars' with long records of three-dimensional philanthropy, bureaucrats (often former leftists) that optimistically sell off vast tracts of waterfront, former hippodromes, military bases and abandoned airfields to developers or real-estate moguls who can accommodate any deficit in futuristic balances, or through Default Preservation™ (the maintenance of historical complexes that nobody wants but that the *zeitgeist* has declared sacrosanct). (2002: 184)

These urban change agents' perception of the past has nothing to do with Tanner's: his deep admiration for dock workers leads him to praise their legacy, which he considers a source of knowledge for younger generations. '*I thought that it was important to convey their unique experience and their truth at a time in which the lie abounds*', he concludes before closing the film with a shot of a cargo ship sailing away. Stevedores are thus depicted as agents of social cohesion, people who gave an emotional meaning to those areas that were successively affected by the post-industrial crisis, the subsequent abandonment, the loss of functions and population, and a partial renewal that was not always respectful with their historical identity. The set of their testimonies constructs a collective narrative about the disappearance of their way of life, but also chronicles the transformation of the waterfront into junkspace. Tanner's autobiographical account apparently remains in the background, but it is more than an anchor for the story. Indeed, it is the same story, but told from a different perspective, a variation that widens the scope of the film by merging micro and macro approaches: from individual to collective, from generational to historical and from social to spatial. In short, *Les hommes du port* is an urban self-portrait narrated in the first person plural, because whenever an interviewee speaks, Tanner implicitly endorses his words; and whenever someone recalls a memory, including the filmmaker himself, any Genoese could feel it as his or her own.

Of Time and the City: Memories from the Dirty Old Town[3]

'*We love the place we hate / then hate the place we love. / We leave the place we love / then spend a lifetime trying to regain it.*' These lines, recited by Terence Davies at the beginning of *Of Time and the City*, summarise his contradictory relationship with Liverpool, his hometown. While he lived there, from his birth in 1945 until he left in 1972, he could not stand it; but later, after settling in London in the late 1970s, he has not stopped returning to those years throughout his film career. His autobiographical cycle, composed of the shorts *Children* (1976), *Madonna and Child* (1980) and *Death and Transfiguration* (1983), as well as the feature films *Distant Voices, Still Lives* (1988) and *The Long Day Closes* (1992), explore the traumatic memories of his childhood, to the extent of developing a series of recurrent obsessions: the love of a devoted mother, the death of a violent father, a hypocritical and emasculating Catholicism and a troublesome homosexuality experienced as closer to sin than to pleasure.

The three shorts were later reunited in a feature film entitled *The Terence Davies Trilogy* (1983), which tells the life story of Robert Tucker – Davies's alter ego – in a three-act narrative: the first, *Children*, introduces the character as a young man who remembers his traumatic childhood; the second, *Madonna and Child*, focuses on his dependency relationship with his mother and shows his frustrations as a gay man; and the third, *Death and Transfiguration*, directly imagines his lonely death. A few years later, *Distant Voices, Still Lives* re-enacted the filmmaker's family life from his mother's and siblings' memories of the time when his father was still alive; and finally *The Long Day Closes* recalled the short and happy period between his father's death and his discovery of homosexuality in adolescence by means of another alter ego, this time called Bud.[4] All these works describe a mindscape located at a particular time and place – Liverpool in the post-war years – but they are not intended at all to faithfully depict its cityscape (see Everett 2004: 42, 46, 52).

Davies considers that 'cinema is the only art form that can show the passage of time visually' (in Yáñez Murillo 2008: 228), to which he has added that 'cinema recalls memory better than any other art because its effect is instantaneous' (in Reviriego 2008: 81; my translation). Hence the Liverpool portrayed in his films does not match the real city, but an imaginary place that only exists in the filmmaker's memories, an intimate geography that unfolds on the screen without a linear narrative, always following an emotional order instead of a chronological one. The best example of this complex storytelling is the temporal structure of *Distant Voices, Still Lives*, whose logic Davies has explained through the metaphor of a pebble dropped in a pool:

> The idea was that because the film is about memory, and memory moves in and out of time all the while, I had to find a way of saying, you're not going to see 'what happens next'. And once you've set it up, people will know instinctively. They may not say, this is a non-linear narrative, but they'll just know. It seems to me that 7/10ths of the film is in that first scene: it's the day of her wedding, she remembers her dad. That's the pebble dropped in the pool, and then there are those ripples of memory, which is what the film is all about. (Davies in Floyd 1988: 295)

In this film, most sequences are actually located outside the flow of time, that is, they do not come from a specific present but from the act of remembering itself. The evocation of the past, as Antonio Weinrichter says, is usually triggered by insignificant objects that symbolise previous life periods, like Marcel Proust's famous madeleine (2008: 258). This idea already appeared in a sample study of North Chicago residents made by Eugene Rochberg-Halton in 1977, according to which the most valued objects in the home were those artefacts that embodied 'ties to loved ones and kin … and memories of significant life events and people'

(1986: 173). *Distant Voices, Still Lives* therefore works, according to Weinrichter, as an emotional zapping of temporal leaps in which 'echoes, associations, embellishments, forgeries and other instances of self-fiction [produce] a montage of *souvenirs*' (2008: 258). Social ceremonies, such as weddings, christenings or burials, as well as everyday routines, mainly represented by the morning awakening, seem to be endlessly repeated in the film, because they are not conventional flashbacks, in the sense that someone remembers something in particular, but interrelated scenes that coexist in a kind of eternal return, as Quim Casas has pointed out (2008: 186).[5]

Davies's favourite element to bind them together is music, especially the popular songs from the 1940s and 1950s that 'gave ordinary people a voice for their feelings' (in Everett 2004: 206). He chooses these songs for 'their ability to convey a certain mood along with the images, and as a representation of collective feeling', as Ricardo Aldarondo has written, 'but never to create an easy association of ideas between what the song says and what is narrated in the scene' (2008: 201). This is to say that the resulting contrast between the image track and the musical score allows the filmmaker 'to *de-privatise* his own feelings', an expression borrowed from Gonzalo de Lucas that refers to the way he turns his personal memories into collective experience (2008: 85; my translation). Thus, as argued by Wendy Everett, the use of popular songs fulfils a triple function in Davies's autobiographical cycle: 'to recreate a remembered past but also, simultaneously, to interrogate and deconstruct that past' (2004: 167).

This strategy reappeared again, along with Davies's recurrent obsessions, in *The Neon Bible* (1995), a transitional work between his Liverpool films and subsequent literary adaptations like *The House of Mirth* (2000) and *The Deep Blue Sea* (2011).[6] In view of this new direction in Davies's film career, it seemed that he would never make another film about his hometown, but he actually did, under certain circumstances: *Of Time and the City* was produced as an essay film about the city where he grew up within the context of Liverpool's year as the European Capital of Culture in 2008, an event that promoted many works and projects related to the city, its identity and its evolution through time. In this documentary, as Julia Hallam has noticed, Davies finally showed 'the exterior spaces and places of his childhood and adolescence that were evoked but never seen in [his] earlier films' (2010a: 69): for the first time, the domestic topography of his autobiographical cycle was extended to the public space beyond '*home, school, the movies and God*', the places in which the filmmaker spent most time of his childhood, as he states in the film's commentary. The reason for this novelty is the temporal structure itself: contrary to *Distant Voices, Still Lives* or *The Long Day Closes*, *Of Time and the City* does have a specific present from which the post-war cityscape is recalled: 2008. Consequently, Davies establishes a dialogue between past and present that suggests an emotional reading of Liverpool's urban change, as Matthew Gandy outlines in the introductory text to the DVD edition of the film:

> At the heart of this meditation on the city lies a tension, between urban change as a process that is brutal and unremitting, and the persistence of memory as something that is delicate and filamentary. We weave our memories into a palimpsest of dreams where time and place melt into each other. Memories become maps through places to which we can never return in a world that is changing all about us. (2009)

The main topic of this documentary is thus 'the process of aging, whether for the city, the filmmaker or cinema itself' (Davies in Yáñez Murillo 2008: 222). In order to find the traces of old social rituals that disappeared along with popular neighbourhoods, *Of Time and the City* examines archival footage filmed in Liverpool between the 1940s and the early 1970s. This time, instead of re-enacting the past, Davies appropriates real images in which time had been recorded 'as it was being lived' (Bruno 2002: 259): according to Hallam, the film is composed of 85 percent archival footage, mostly taken from professional films such as *A Day in Liverpool* (Anton Dyer, 1929), *Morning in the Streets* (Denis Mitchell, 1959), *Liverpool Sounding* (Ken Pople, 1967), *Who Cares?* (Nick Broomfield, 1971) or *Behind the Rent Strike* (Nick Broomfield, 1974) (2010a: 69–70).[7] Almost all these materials come from public archives, except for a few sequences that also include amateur footage obtained thanks to local collectors, among which Hallam mentions Clive Garner and Angus Tilston (2010b: 284).[8]

Despite professional films currently being part of the 'official' record of the cityscape, Davies uses them as if they belonged to his own collection of home movies, an impression emphasised by his first-person commentary. The combination of these three elements – professional documentaries, amateur films and Davies's memoryscape – creates an urban self-portrait that '[brings] to the foreground contested spaces and [reveals] emotional attachments and attitudes to place' (Hallam 2010a: 79). In a broader sense, paraphrasing Michael Zyrd's definition of found-footage filmmaking, this device ultimately serves to comment on the cultural discourses and narrative patterns behind history, giving a metahistorical meaning to pre-existing images (2003: 42). This new reading is constructed through essayistic elements, such as the poetic tone of the commentary, the rhetorical questions addressed to the audience or the juxtaposition of archival footage and a present-tense commentary. The latter echoes Davies's working method, which has been described by producers Roy Boulter and Sol Papadopoulos as a process of 'reflection and viewing, contemplation and reviewing, selecting the archive footage for its evocation of very specific emotions and memories' (Hallam 2010a: 69). Accordingly, the essayistic component of the film is not only a formal choice, but mainly the outcome of its creative process.

Hallam thematically relates *Of Time and the City* with 'the celebration of northern working-class identity found in the black and white realism of the films of the British New Wave' (2010a: 72). Those works established a pattern of representation that has later conditioned most films set in northern cities of Great Britain. In the entry devoted to Glasgow, Manchester and Liverpool of the encyclopaedia *La ville au cinéma*, Stefano Baschiera and Laura Rascaroli pointed out the main features of this approach:

> The common historical evolution of Glasgow, Manchester and Liverpool explains their similar representations on the screen within stories focused on working life and the miserable living conditions in urban slums and poor suburbs. The house, the favourite place in these films, opens to a middle ground: the courtyard opened to all eyes. The films deal with working-class communities, their belonging to a neighbourhood and their conflicts with rival communities. The three cities are usually shown as a mosaic of fragmented spaces, collections of disjointed neighbourhoods characterised by their unequal living conditions: beautiful gardens or rubbish dumps, rows of little houses or tower blocks, parks or dirt roads, churches or derelict factories, old monuments or skyscrapers. These spaces perfectly reflect the unemployed characters, the outcast or the petty criminals that inhabit them. Within this cityscape, the recurring theme is the escape from the city in search of a more promising place, a desire that contrasts with the threat and insecurity of the urban environment. (2005: 390; my translation)

Davies's autobiographical cycle follows this pattern of representation, but Liverpool is no longer the post-industrial wasteland that it used to be: its current identity has more to do with a business, shopping or tourist city than with its old role of industrial and port city, as also happened to Genoa right after the making of *Les hommes du port*. Curiously, film production has played a key role in the regeneration of Liverpool, as Julia Hallam and her colleagues in the research project 'A City in Film: Liverpool's Urban Landscape and the Moving Image' have extensively analysed:[9]

Liverpool City Council's determination to attract film production to the city as part of its regeneration strategy in the late 1980s was a defining moment in acknowledging the role that the creative industries (and film production in particular) could play in reversing the economic fortunes of the city during a decade in which public images of civil strife, social unrest and industrial disruption were perceived to be major factors in the decline of inward investment in the city. It was not however the prospect of projecting an image of the city, positive or otherwise, that was a primary concern at this time; basing their strategy on post-industrial cities such as Philadelphia in the USA, the city council sought to attract major film production companies to use derelict industrial sites as film locations to create freelance opportunities for local film and media workers and develop supporting industries such as catering and hospitality, a strategy that has proven to be very successful. (Hallam 2010b: 290)[10]

Given that the old pattern of representation is no longer appropriate to depict the contemporary Liverpool, Davies decided to begin his urban self-portrait with a distancing device that marked the temporal gap between the old image of the city and the new one. In the opening sequence, a screen emerges from the floor and opens its curtains in order to show old street scenes, suggesting that this cityscape can only exist as a projection of archival footage. Among these first analogical images, a phantom ride taken from the now demolished overhead railway stands as a film quote to one of the first icons of the cinematic city: the arrival of a train to the city, a usual image among the silent pioneers since *L'arrivée d'un train à La Ciotat* (*Arrival of a Train at La Ciotat*, Auguste and Louis Lumière, 1896) that was later canonised by both avant-garde and mainstream traditions, from *Berlin: Die Sinfonie der Grosstadt* (*Berlin, Symphony of a Great City*, Walter Ruttmann, 1927) to *La bête humaine* (*The Human Beast*, Jean Renoir, 1938). This shot includes a glimpse of the Royal Liver Building, one of the 'Three Graces of the Pier Head' (the other two are the Port of Liverpool Building and the Cunard Building) that symbolise the waterfront, the city centre and even public space. The presence of these and other recognisable landmarks in the film, such as Saint George's Hall, the Liverpool Metropolitan Cathedral or the Albert Dock, emphasises the stark contrast between the representations of the imperial, economic or religious power and the streetscape where people hustle and bustle in their everyday life.

This spatial opposition has been defined by Wendy Everett regarding *The Terence Davies Trilogy* as the clash between 'the wide-open, masculine confidence of the public spaces at [the] centre' and 'the close intimacy of the women's spaces, hidden behind the net curtained windows of the terraced streets on the periphery of the town' (2004: 45). Davies clearly feels more comfortable in the latter, as his editing choices confirm: he usually shows architectural landmarks from the outside, as symbols or visual surfaces, while focusing his attention on customs and rituals already disappeared: from leisure time (soccer, movies, wrestling, etc.) to domestic routines (lighting the fire, cleaning the house, doing the washing) without forgetting the scenes of industrial and port work. This life was probably as mediocre, boring and lacking in prospects as *a long Sunday afternoon: nothing to do, nowhere to go*, as he says in the commentary, but the experiences of that time, like those of any other, left a deep emotional trace in Liverpudlians. This idea is expressed in the following passage, in which Davies invites the entire audience to remember with him, even those who were too young to have lived that period:

Do you remember, you who are no longer young, and you who still are? Do you remember the months of November and December? Wet shoes and leaking galoshes, and for the first time ... chilblains, with Christmas in the air. God was in his heaven, and oh, how I believed! Oh, how fervent I was! And on Christmas Eve, pork roasting in the oven, the parlour cleaned, with fruit along the sideboard. A pound of apples, tangerines in tissue paper, a bowl of nuts and our annual exotic pomegranate. Do you remember? Do you? Will you ever forget?

These words recall a particular time and place, but they can also be interpreted as a general evocation of childhood memories, regardless of the time to which they belong. The temporal distance turns them into '*happy days*', as a recorded voice suggests right after Davies's speech, even though they were actually not happy. Thus, although the filmmaker refers once again to his particular memoryscape, his words urge to remember any past that may have a similar mood.

The insistence on the act of remembering implicitly expresses the topics of *tempus fugit* and especially *memento mori*, which William Raban had already invoked in *Thames Film*. In particular, over an image of people walking down the street in the 1970s, Davies recites a quote taken from James Joyce's *Ulysses* (1922): '*as you are now, we once were*'.[11] These words actually come from the medieval story of 'The Three Living and Three Dead', a narrative that tells the meeting of three living men, usually kings or knights, and three corpses or skeletons who warn them '*as you are now, we once were / as we are now, you may become*' (see Rotzler 1961; Sandeno 1997; González Zymla 2011). By reproducing the first part of this sentence, Davies assumes the role of the three dead, reminding the audience that any city and any person has a past doomed to disappear and, for this reason, worthy of being remembered. Later on, after a sequence about summer afternoons in New Brighton, he insists on the idea of *tempus fugit* by means of another literary quote, this time from Anton Chekhov: '*The golden moments pass and leave no trace.*'[12] Certainly, the material traces of the past cannot be found in the cityscape, since much of Liverpool's urban fabric was razed to the ground between the 1940s and the 1970s, but the emotional traces will survive as memories as long as there are people who may recall them.

The aftermath of World War II created the appropriate circumstances for urban renewal in most cities of the United Kingdom. On the one hand, as John R. Gold and Stephen V. Ward have pointed out, urban policies had receded into the background due to the war effort: house-building stopped, the slum clearance programme was suspended and there was practically no investment in transport and services (1997: 60). On the other hand, the war time experience of mass production and planning served to launch a nationwide programme of reconstruction and reorganisation described by David Harvey in these terms:

> Britain ... adopted quite stringent town and country planning legislation. The effect was to restrict suburbanization and to substitute planned new-town development (on the Ebenezer Howard model) or high-density infilling or renewal (on the Le Corbusier model) in its stead. Under the watchful eye and sometimes strong hand of the state, procedures were devised to eliminate slums, build modular housing, schools, hospitals, factories, etc., through the adoption of the industrialized construction systems and rational planning procedures that modernist architects had long proposed. And all this was framed by a deep concern, expressed again and again in legislation, for the rationalization of spatial patterns and of circulation systems so as to promote equality (at least of opportunity), social welfare, and economic growth. (1989: 69)

In the case of Liverpool, the city council took advantage of war damage to completely reshape the historic centre: the area between the Pier Head and Lime Street Station was practically demolished in full in order to make way for 'an inner-city motorway network and modernist "concrete and glass" offices with integrated shopping precincts and amenities' (Hallam 2010a: 76). Such a project took so much time that vast tracts of the city remained derelict and empty for years, creating an alienating ruinscape from which Davies wanted to escape in the 1970s but to which he attempts to return in *Of Time and the City*. His mixed feelings towards this avatar of his hometown protect him from nostalgia, because he has not precisely good memories of that time, but even so he cannot help but miss it. The best tool to convey this emotional state is music, as usual in his films, thanks above all to its ability to arouse memory. The unconscious association between a melody and the time at which we heard it for the first time has been perfectly explained by Iain Chambers:

> Music serves as a multi-dimensional map, it is simultaneously connected to fashion (repetition of the new) and to memory (moments lost in time). It permits us to maintain a fragile bridge between consciousness and oblivion. It introduces the history of the event into the fluctuating, atemporal regime of memory by permitting us to mark time and recall it, admitting the past to the present, and allowing us to trace in its echo other dreams, further futures. (1997: 234–5)

Davies always relates his works to musical forms, especially the symphony, to the point that this genre has inspired the emotional structure of most of his films, including *Of Time and the City* (see Everett 2004: 168–9). In this sense, its main theme is the passage of time in the city, while its variations revolve around the filmmaker's usual topics: working-class life, homosexuality, Catholicism and cinema. Davies's primary reference to organise these materials was the musical documentary *Listen to Britain* (Humphrey Jennings & Stewart McAllister, 1942), but the tone and meaning of both films is quite different:[13] while Jennings and McAllister's work celebrated British national unity in wartime, *Of Time and the City* is instead 'a love song and a eulogy' for the defunct industrial city of the working class, as its subtitle indicates. Again, the soundtrack includes several popular songs, such as 'Dirty Old Town', 'He Ain't Heavy, He's My Brother', 'The Folks Who Live on the Hill' or 'The Hippy Hippy Shake', as well as a long list of classical pieces, among which there are two that work as counterpoint to the images of urban renewal: Salvador Bacarisse's Concertino for Guitar and Orchestra in A Minor Op. 72 (1957) and Gustav Mahler's Symphony No. 2 in C Minor, 'Resurrection' (1895). This soundscape reinforces the haunting nature of archival footage, maximising what Michel Chion calls 'the added value of music':

> The expressive and informative value with which a sound enriches a given image so as to create the definitive impression, in the immediate or remembered experience one has of it, that this information or expression 'naturally' comes from what is seen, and is already contained in the image itself. (1994: 5)

'The Folks Who Live on the Hill', for example, provided Davies with the foundational image of the documentary: 'When I imagined Peggy Lee singing this song over images of Liverpool's public housing estates in the late 1950s, I knew that this was what we had to do' (in Reviriego 2008: 81; my translation).[14] This sequence summarises the evolution of the cityscape from terraced houses to concrete tower blocks through a device similar to that used by Michael Moore in *Roger & Me*, in which the visual narrative collides with the upbeat lyrics of the song: while Peggy Lee sings about a bright future that never became true for many working-class Liverpudlians, the footage juxtaposes scenes of family life in Arcadian neighbour-hoods, images of their subsequent decay and demolition, and finally a series of shots in which people looked trapped in their new habitat – men and women standing isolated on their balconies, a tiny man walking beside a huge building, an old lady removing a used can from the lift, etc. All these images, as well as the deliberate contrast between old and new spaces, come from *Who Cares?*, but Davies re-edits them to the rhythm of the song. The outcome extends the meaning of the original footage by expressing the filmmaker's personal discomfort regard-ing post-war urban renewal: he explicitly criticises the replacement of 'a citizen-friendly town planning approach that fostered communication among people' by 'another, overcrowded [one] based on concrete tower blocks, graffiti and neglect' (Aldarondo 2008: 204), that is, a misapplication of Le Corbusier's modernist principles.

The only image in this sequence that was not filmed by Broomfield is a photo-graph entitled 'The Long Walk' in which a lonely man walks down Everton Brow amid ruins and rubble [Image 7.2]. This panorama is part of 'Liverpool: The Long Way Home', a series of pictures that photographer Bernard Fallon took between 1966 and 1975, when he was living in Crosby, a suburb located six miles north of the city, and almost every day took the bus to the Liverpool College of Art. At the time, according to Fallon, 'buildings were bulldozed everywhere in an orgy of destruction. It was said, "What the Luftwaffe failed to do, the city corporation finished off". And it was truly a fascinating place to photograph' (2009). 'The Long Walk', in particular, conveys the depressing atmosphere of the interregnum between demolition and reconstruction: it is an image so powerful and poignant that it is usually considered an icon of urban decay. Being aware of this meaning, Davies uses it to split his remix of *Who Cares?* in two halves, the first devoted to old popular neighbourhoods and the second to modernist new spaces, thereby identifying the point of no return of urban renewal.

The traumatic nature of this process is addressed in all its harshness in the musical sequences that resort to classical compositions: in the case of Bacarisse's Concertino, the guitar solo of its second movement is associated with terraced houses, whereas its immediate repetition by the full orchestra accompanies im-ages of neglected tower blocks where people, especially children, strive to live with

Image 7.2: *Of Time and the City*, Bernard Fallon's picture 'The Long Walk'

dignity. The resulting effect suggests that Brutalist architecture created a hostile environment to community life that Davies politely describes as '*the anus mundi*'. The most overwhelming images are nonetheless reserved to the penultimate musical sequence, in which a particularly gloomy passage of Mahler's symphony emphasises the awful experience of living through urban rejuvenation: children, young couples, immigrants and elders look like castaways left to their fate in a post-industrial nightmare, while old buildings are depicted as lifeless bodies rather than useless structures. This ruinscape is vaguely reminiscent of those included in Akerman's *News from Home* because they were all filmed by means of a similar apparatus: the grainy texture and colour temperature of the images correspond to the visual standards of the 1970s, the decade of the post-industrial crisis and also the last years that Davies spent in his hometown. Accordingly, this musical sequence works as a farewell to the dirty old town that he left behind, putting an end to his memoryscape before returning to the present.

Unfortunately, the recent reunion between Davies and Liverpool was anything but happy, as he himself has said:

> Almost everything had been pulled down in the area where I grew up. It's really the dregs what's left of it. Of the sixteen cinemas that were in Liverpool there's only one remaining. It was upsetting because you suddenly realised that fifty years had gone by and that was what was left of

it. At the end of the 1950s we moved house into these new places. It was the new 'Jerusalem', but it really wasn't. It was even worse than our old houses. And, not because I want to be Catholic again – I don't – but our parish church seated about two thousand people and on occasions it was filled. Six people were there now. They'll eventually pull it down, but it's a good example of Gothic Catholic revival built in the 1880s. It's just sad to see everything tatty and ruined at the edges. I'm a stranger there now. I'm an alien. (Davies in Yáñez Murillo 2008: 245)

Being a foreigner in his own land did not prevent Davies from realising that life went on beyond his frozen memories: as the narrative of the film relies on 'the friction between the artist anchored in the past, and the World that continues turning' (Gilbey 2008: 45), it was essential to show to what extent Liverpool had changed. His solution was to appropriate a long-established metaphor in the British documentary tradition: the image of children playing in the open street as a symbol of the city's future (see Lebas 2007: 46–7; Shand 2010: 66). These children look at the city as something new, with the same curiosity that Davies felt at their age, but they will not miss the old industrial city at all: in fact, if they are lucky, their places of memory should be much more pleasant and beautiful than the filmmaker's. Their gazes certify that Liverpool had re-emerged from its ashes in the late 2000s, a real 'resurrection' confirmed by the epic fragment of Mahler's symphony that closes the film.

The final image of the fireworks over the city's waterfront may seem a happy ending, but it is actually as grandiose as ironic. Davies is aware that Liverpool's resurrection was achieved only after having sacrificed its old cityscape in the process, removing most traces of the past from its urban surface. In the late 1980s, David Harvey had already warned that the fabric of traditional working-class communities was being taken over by a lobby formed from the alliance of real state developers and local politicians who surreptitiously exchanged the concepts of restoration and imitation (1989: 303). Following the usual practices of postmodern urbanism, these urban change agents certainly did their best to rehabilitate many degraded areas, but they were only superficially interested in preserving the historical identity of places. Nowadays, for instance, the Albert Dock looks much better than in the 1970s, but its *genius loci* has gone along with the human landscape that inhabited it. This case exemplifies the inherent contradiction of many urban renewals, as exposed by Richard Koeck:

While it is perhaps possible to imitate a cultural past in architectural terms, it is an impossible task to bring back the socio-economic tissue that defined the character of those various historical building types, such as dock warehouses and other site-specific buildings. Paradoxically, such urban planning strategies counteract the natural evolution of a place and its identity, which is not a static agent, but a force that is in constant flux and dialogue with the present. (2010: 215)

Cityscapes, understood as a network of social and cultural relations, cannot be created or recovered by urban planning, not unless they have been simplified as images (Muñoz 2010: 50–1). This process usually develops through two strategies, both based on the manipulation of history, that ultimately lead to the production of banalscapes: the first one, termed 'brandified cosmopolitanism' by Muñoz, consists of selecting and reproducing elements and typologies of vernacular architecture in order to simulate certain urban atmospheres; while the second, identified as 'consumer romanticism' by the same author, borrows local stereotypes, most of them inspired by the idiosyncrasies of the former residents in the area, to recreate a fictional version of disappeared communities (2010: 191; my translation). Much to their regret, Genoa's and Liverpool's dock workers are clear examples of the latter: once they were expelled from historic waterfronts, their iconography was recycled by urban change agents to decorate city tableaux, making profit from their symbolic capital and offering them little more than a nostalgic tribute in return.

Liverpool's waterfront is currently a simulacrum as artificial as South Street Seaport in New York or the Docklands in London, a banalscape in which Davies is so out of place that he had to dive into archival footage to find his way back to the city that shaped his personality. Nevertheless, if there is any hint of nostalgia in *Of Time and the City*, it is not for a better past or for a place in particular, but for a way of living that no longer exists. Like Michael Moore and Alain Tanner, Davies identifies the old cityscape with that lifestyle, but contrary to them, he never idealises it since he is convinced that post-war years were not precisely the best time to live in Liverpool. He was basically unhappy then, but even so he enjoys recalling his past pleasures as much as anyone, no matter how mediocre they were. Thus, while Moore's and Tanner's approach may sometimes be a bit ingenuous, Davies's is more ambiguous thanks to his sincerity. By trying to be honest to himself, he rather lines up with Tony Buba, since they both bear a love-hate relationship to their respective hometowns. Consequently, *Of Time and the City* simultaneously works at several levels, ranging from the personal to the social: depending on who sees the film, it may be interpreted as a process of self-healing, a repository of scenes of everyday life or a chronicle of Liverpool's urban change over half a century. Without ever losing the beat, Davies synchronises his personal memories with archival footage, merging history and story, past and present, facts and feelings in an ambitions combination that manages to bring back the old city-scape to the screen.

NOTES

1   There are many examples of his itinerancy, especially from the 1980s: *Light Years Away* (1981) was filmed in Ireland; *Dans la ville blanche* (*In the White City*, 1983) and *Requiem* (1998) in Portugal; and many sequences of *L'homme qui a perdu son ombre* (*The Man Who Lost His Shadow*, 1991) and *Le journal de Lady M* (*The Diary of Lady M*, 1993) in Spain.

2   *Temps mort* is a SBC program in which Tanner reflects about cinema and television during a round trip between Geneva and Bern.

3   This section has been previously published as a chapter in the volume *Cityscapes: World Cities and Their Cultural Industries* (see Villarmea Álvarez 2014d).

4   Davies's father died of cancer when the future director was only six-and-a-half years old (see Everett 2004: 9).

5   Casas argues that this device pioneered narrative experiments later popularised by films such as *Reservoir Dogs* (Quentin Tarantino, 1992), *Irreversible* (Gaspar Noé, 2002) and *21 Grams* (Alejandro González Iñárritu, 2003) (2008: 186-187).

6   *The Neon Bible* and *The House of Mirth* respectively adapt John Kennedy Toole's first work (1989) and Edith Wharton's homonymous novel (1905), while *The Deep Blue Sea* is the second film version of Terence Rattingan's play (1952) that had previously been brought to the screen by Anatole Litvak in 1955.

7   Both *A Day in Liverpool* and *Liverpool Sounding* were commissioned by the city's public relations office, whereas the rest were produced by public institutions like the BBC (*Morning in the Streets*), the BFI (*Who Cares?*) or the NFTS (*Behind the Rent Strike*).

8   Tilston, in particular, has made a series of compilation films from footage taken by local filmmakers, such as *Liverpool, Echoes of the 1940s and 1950s* and *Liverpool: The Swinging Sixties* (1994), to name but those referred to the same period addressed by Davies in *Of Time and the City*.

9   This project was based at the University of Liverpool and funded by the Arts and Humanities Research Council from 2006 to 2010. Its main researchers were Julia Hallam, Richard Koeck, Robert Kronenburg, Les Roberts and Ryan Shand.

10   Nowadays, Liverpool is the most filmed city in the United Kingdom only after London, a status that confirms its condition of cinematic city in spite of the fact that it rarely plays itself: according to Hallam and Roberts, Liverpool has served as a stand-in for cities as different as Amsterdam, Cannes, Chicago, Dublin, Moscow, New York, Paris, Rome, St. Petersburg, Vienna, war-time Germany and also, of course, London (Hallam 2010b: 291; Roberts 2010: 190).

11   This quote belongs to chapter six, 'Hades', when Leopold Bloom attends Paddy Dignam's funeral at Glasnevin Cemetery. This is Joyce's exact wording: 'How many! All these here once walked round Dublin. Faithful departed. As you are now so once were we'

(1967: 95).

12   New Brighton is a seaside resort located at the north-eastern tip of the Wirral peninsula, across the Mersey estuary from Liverpool. 'In its heyday,' according to Les Roberts, 'New Brighton [was] a bustling and lively playground for day-tripping Liverpudlians, who in the summer months would arrive in their thousands by ferry from Pier Head on the other side of the River Mersey' (2010: 197).

13   The filmmaker himself has established this connection (see Yáñez Murillo 2008: 244).

14   Davies had already included this song in *Distant Voices, Still Lives*. Its original version was performed by Irene Dunne in the musical western *High, Wide and Handsome* (Rouben Mamoulian, 1937).

CHAPTER EIGHT

Self-Portrait as Self-Fiction

The border between fiction and non-fiction has evolved for decades by means of the continuous emergence of new techniques and technologies, each one considered more appropriate than its predecessors to represent reality. This vertiginous succession has followed the dynamics of a paradigm shift, replacing old styles with new ones in an apparently endless process: Grierson's reenactments, for example, ceased to be truthful when direct cinema developed its observational *mise-en-scène*, while this was in turn challenged and replaced by the participatory approach of *cinéma vérité*.

Throughout the last century, documentary film was filled with all kinds of codes of authenticity to guarantee its scientific truthfulness, resulting in 'the elaboration of a whole aesthetic of objectivity and the development of comprehensive technologies of truth capable of promoting what is right and what is wrong in the world, and by extension, what is "honest" and what is "manipulative" in documentary', as postmodern theorist and filmmaker Trinh T. Minh-ha has criticised (1993: 94). In view of the codifying of documentary film as a genre or style, she has argued that 'it no longer constitutes a mode of production or an attitude toward life, but proves to be only an element of aesthetics (or anti-aesthetics)' (1993: 99). Therefore, if documentary film is simply a matter of conventions, its visual features can be easily imitated, as many fake documentaries have demonstrated, from *The War Game* (Peter Watkins, 1966) to *The Blair Witch Project* (Daniel Myrick & Eduardo Sánchez, 1999) through *David Holzman's Diary* (Jim McBride, 1967), *Vérités et mensonges* (*F for Fake*, Orson Welles, 1973), *No Lies* (Mitchell Block, 1973), *Daughter Rite* (Michele Citron, 1979) or *This Is Spinal Tap* (Rob Reiner, 1984) to name just a few examples.

Fiction has always been present in one way or another within documentary film. Michael Renov talks about 'fictive elements' to refer to 'instances of style, structure, and expositional strategy that draw on pre-existent (fictional) constructs or schemata to establish meanings and effects for audiences' (2004: 22).

His short-list of these elements includes 'the construction of character as ideal type; the use of poetic language, narration, or musical accompaniment to heighten emotional impact or create suspense; the deployment of embedded narratives or dramatic arcs; and the exaggeration of camera angles, camera distance, or editing rhythms' (ibid.). The degree of development of these borrowings from fiction determines the position of any documentary in the non-fiction spectrum, which has been defined by Craig Hight as 'a continuum of fact-fiction forms that cross over generic boundaries' (2008: 208). That is to say that, contrary to what the discourse of sobriety usually maintains, there is no strict opposition between the two poles of this spectrum, but rather a subtle gradation which admits multiple combinations.

The use of fiction techniques in documentary film has increased exponentially after postmodern theorists argued that modernist attempts to find a truthful representation of reality were just an aesthetic choice among many others. Nowadays, found footage has become a useful tool to reflect on the film construction of reality, and reenactments are again considered a valid strategy to represent what the camera, for whatever reason, could not record. This return to Griersonian old practices does not meant a step back regarding the modernist search for the real, but rather a broadening of the available resources to continue with 'the search for the real within the fictional', as Catherine Russell has written (1999: 254). According to Antonio Weinrichter, the main goal of these practices is not exactly to bring a hidden reality to light, but to reveal its deep meaning through real elements that acquire a strong metaphorical sense (2010: 272). Consequently, defining the documentary at the end of the last century required, in Brian Winston's words, 'turning back to considerations of how materials could be subjected to "creative treatment" and yet not totally fictionalised' (1993: 56).

Regarding the limitations imposed by the discourse of sobriety, Renov has clearly argued that 'the documentary image functions in relation to both knowledge and desire, evidence and lure, with neither term exerting exclusive control' (2004: 101). Accordingly, the documentary gaze is 'constitutively multiform, embroiled with conscious motives and unconscious desires, driven by curiosity no more than by terror and fascination' (2004: 96). This claim to subjectivity indirectly supports the use of fiction techniques, provided that they serve to convey unconscious elements. In fact, avant-garde film had already paved the way for them by developing abstract forms that 'metaphorically represent states of mind and emotional estates' (Lane 2002: 13). These films renounced photographic realism to achieve what Bill Nichols has termed 'emotional realism', in which the audience still recognises a realistic dimension to the depicted experience because 'it is like other emotional experiences we have had: the emotion itself is familiar and genuinely felt' (2001: 93).

In the last few decades, the search for emotional realism has taken advantage of fiction techniques to explore intangible realities such as memories, feelings, perceptions and even fantasies, looking for a truthful way to represent both collective and individual imaginaries beyond the hazy line that separates fiction from non-fiction. Many autobiographical films, in particular, locate themselves on both sides of that line in order to 'seek a self which is often hidden behind a mask, disintegrated or recomposed', as Gregorio Martín Gutiérrez has pointed out (2010: 373). These hybrid works swing between 'the "life story", the search for a direction, an itinerary, one's roots, and a continuous fragmentation in which the self seems to flee or dissolve' (bid.). They are not fully faithful to the facts (when including facts) but rather to the feelings and emotions that lie behind them. Their main concern is thereby the inscription of the filmmaker's subjectivity in the film, even through a blatant blend of real events and personal fabrications that ultimately leads autobiographical approach into the domain of self-fiction.

The two case studies in this chapter, *Porto da Minha Infância* (*Porto of My Childhood*, Manoel de Oliveira, 2001) and *My Winnipeg* (Guy Maddin, 2007), are two urban self-portraits made from explicit self-fictions: on the one hand, Portuguese filmmaker de Oliveira mobilises all kind of means of representation to recall his childhood and youth memories in his hometown, Porto, from fictional sequences to archival footage; while on the other, Canadian director Maddin reaches the point of appropriating real found footage to fake it in reenactments shot by himself, turning his fantasies into an alternative history of Winnipeg. These films, however, are still documentaries because they depict, above all, the filmmakers' relation to their hometowns from the fictional logic of memory, exploring what should be named 'the creative fake of reality'. Thus, both Oliveira and Maddin use their imagination to document their memories, portraying not only what they actually remember – missing cityscapes, past events, fleeting emotions, etc. – but also the way they recall these memoryscapes as artists and inhabitants of those cities.

Porto of My Childhood: A Portrait of the Artist as an Old Man[1]

Manoel de Oliveira's extraordinary longevity (at the beginning of 2015, he was one hundred and six years old) has allowed him to develop a film career that spans from the silent era to the digital age. His lifetime has elapsed for almost the whole twentieth century and the beginning of the twenty-first, although his mentality can be traced back to the nineteenth century since he was born in 1908 in a conservative Catholic family of wealthy industrialists and agricultural landowners.

Considering these life circumstances, Galician critic Xurxo González argues that Oliveira's film style has established a link between different periods of film history, from certain movements related to modernity, such as the avant-gardes, neo-realism or the new waves, to the postmodern reinterpretations of older genres, such as costume drama or the historical film (2004: 35, 72).

His first work, the short documentary *Douro, Faina Fluvial* (*Working on the Douro River*, 1931), is a late urban symphony that displays many similarities to *Berlin: Symphony of a Great City* and *Entuziazm (Simfoniya Donbassa)* (*Enthusiasm: The Dombass Symphony*, Dziga Vertov, 1931). From the former, it takes the structure of 'a day in the city' and the interest in the inner rhythms of the modern metropolis; while it shares with the latter the idea of depicting an urban community through its daily work activities: coal mining in Vertov's documentary and dock work in Oliveira's. A decade later, Oliveira's first feature film, *Aniki Bóbó* (1942), anticipated many proposals of Italian Neorealism, such as location shooting, the use of non-professional actors and interest in underrepresented social groups, among which children especially stand out. Unfortunately, the film was not very successful at the time, despite the fact that the 1940s were the only period in which Portuguese cinema had a wide audience able to finance its own film industry. Its commercial failure forced Oliveira to remain inactive as filmmaker for many years, until the making of *O Pintor e a Cidade* (*The Artist and the City*, 1956), another short documentary about Porto that completes his modernist trilogy about everyday life on the banks of the Douro River. Given that these three films – *Working on the Douro River*, *Aniki Bóbó* and *The Artist and the City*– are all quoted in *Porto of My Childhood*, it seems opportune to briefly comment on their similarities and differences, paying particular attention to the last one.

The Artist and the City combines several ideas taken from *Working on the Douro River* with certain formal novelties – mainly, its experiments with colour – and a higher awareness regarding issues of representation. Its main leitmotifs are the movement of people in public spaces, everyday scenes and city landmarks, such as the Clérigos Church and Tower, the Porto City Hall or the Luís I Bridge, which had already been similarly filmed in *Working on the Douro River*. This iconography actually comes from previous representations of the city, mostly nineteenth-century paintings, which Oliveira includes in the film in order to acknowledge his debt to this visual tradition.

Once again, Oliveira uses the temporal structure of 'a day in the city' by following painter António Cruz through a full working day, in which urban life is depicted as the product of the triad formed by work, transportation and leisure time, while the residents of Porto are represented as an anonymous mass. Nevertheless, the painter's presence as implied narrator of the film establishes an individualised gaze at urban space that reveals the presence of certain people who stand out in the crowd, such as an elderly beggar and several policemen, brief glimpses of the poor and repressed Portuguese society under Salazar's dictatorship. Another difference regarding *Working on the Douro River* is that the film image of the city is mediated by its pictorial representation: Oliveira films the same places, views and frames painted by Cruz, thereby contributing to their production and consolidation as landmarks. Both artists strive to capture the real, but Oliveira also reveals the artifice of representation, as González has pointed out:

> He wants to establish a contrapuntal comparison between reality, understood as a motif, and artistic creation. This documentary was a first step … to present images framed within an aesthetic ritual, analysing the reality of the shadows, making clear the nature of the artifice and gathering information about the configuration of delusion and the peculiarities of perception. (2004: 57; my translation)

By showing the creative process behind António Cruz's paintings, *The Artist and the City* makes explicit its condition as reproduction of reality: in the final sequence, Oliveira edits a shot of the waterfront followed by increasingly more abstract watercolours that depict the same view. The film is thus consciously located within the tradition of reflexive documentary, even though it does not include any shot of the cinematic apparatus. Arguably, it even anticipated the reflection on the failure of both cinema and painting to achieve a faithful representation of reality that *El sol del membrillo* (*Dream of Light*, 1992) would further develop four decades later. The director of this film, Víctor Erice, has stated in a text on Oliveira's work that 'all we see is presented as theatre, which means that cinema, by assuming the idea of modernity, is faced with two alternatives: whether to film the spectacle of life or the spectacle of the stage' (2004: 30; my translation). Considering that *Aniki Bóbó* was Oliveira's clearest attempt to film the spectacle of life, *The Artist and the City* would be in turn his first film interested in the spectacle of theatre, that is, in the methods and devices devoted to depict – or rather, reenact – reality.

Surprisingly, Oliveira found more opportunities to make movies at the end of his life, when it was assumed that he would retire from filmmaking (see González 2004: 67). In the early 1970s, he obtained funding to make 'a "last" film' (Sales 2011: 111; my translation), which actually opened a series of four literary adaptations later known as the 'Tetralogy of Frustrated Loves': *O Passado e o Presente* (*Past and Present*, 1972), *Benilde ou a Virgem Mãe* (*Benilde or the Virgin Mother*,

1975), *Amor de Perdição* (*Doomed Love*, 1979) and *Francisca* (1981). Since then, Oliveira has worked at a furious pace, especially for his age, making practically a film a year. This period, which can be described as deeply postmodern, combines historical films about the discourses and narratives that underpin Portugal – *Non, ou a Vã Glória de Mandar* (*No, or the Vain Glory of Command*, 1990), *Palavra e Utopia* (*Word and Utopia*, 2000), *O Quinto Império – Ontem Como Hoje* (*The Fifth Empire*, 2005) – with titles that deal with more recent problems, such as the plight of the urban poor or the aged rural population – *A Caixa* (*The Box*, 1994) or *Viagem ao Princípio do Mundo* (*Voyage to the Beginning of the World*, 1997). The most remarkable feature of these films, as Xurxo González explains, is their tendency to integrate autobiographical accounts and personal statements within their narratives in order to leave proof of the filmmaker's existence for eternity:

> Oliveira gives value to the word, staging conversations that cover ellipses and allow him to integrate his observations about the world. Like a wise old man, the proximity of death enables him to tell exemplary stories and make utopian glosses about the fate of the world. His combative spirit was already relegated to the past: he is currently tired and faces life with detachment, theorising, questioning the relativity of things. His extremely long-lived condition serves him to act as a medium between life and afterlife. [...] The filmmaker expresses his nonconformity with the state of the world and the recent evolution of humanity by means of these disenchanted comments, with which he aims to fulfil a double duty: on the one hand, to be exemplary for the audience; and on the other, to redeem his own 'sins' in view of the proximity of the ultimate trance. (2012; my translation)

This desire for transcendence has led Portuguese filmmaker João Mário Grilo to state that 'Oliveira currently films for God' (2006: 129; my translation). Regardless of whether or not Oliveira feels like 'a divine instrument', as González suggests (2012; my translation), he is, at least, ontologically involved in his later works: since each new film he directs might be the last one, the temptation of expressing his last will is always present.[2] Memory has become one of the main subjects of his postmodern works, but he does not understand it as a stable collection of experiences that may be faithfully recovered. On the contrary, he uses it as an uncontrolled source of inspiration for exploring his self, his past and the historical imaginary of his country, reaching the point of faking it when necessary.

All these postmodern films share, according to González, the same elegiac look at people, customs and things that have been left behind by the passage of time (2012). Their mood has to do with what Portuguese call *saudade*, a complex emotional state, similar to the Turkish *hüzün* or the Romanian *dor*, which is not exactly the same as nostalgia, longing, melancholy or loneliness, but rather their deep awareness. The dictionary from the Royal Galician Academy, for instance, defines this term as 'an intimate feeling and mood caused by the longing for something absent that is being missed and that can take different aspects, from specific realities (a loved one, a friend, the motherland, the homeland...) to the absolute and mysterious transcendence' (García & González 1997: 1090; my translation). A clear example of *saudade* within Oliveira's work would be the following dialogue from *Voyage to the Beginning of the World*, pronounced by the filmmaker's fictional alter ego: '*You've embraced your aunt, body and soul,*' he says to a travelling companion who has just visited his father's home village, '*Me, even my childhood friends, my brother Casimiro and all my friends of that time, they are all gone. A long life is a gift from God, but it has its price.*' In this case, the real expression of *saudade* is the last sentence, because it goes beyond the nostalgia for the loved ones by referring to the intimate perception of this absence. Similarly, the initial statement of intent of *Porto of My Childhood* addresses the act of remembering from a 'saudosist' approach: '*To recall moments from a distant past is to travel out of time. Only each person's memory can do this. It is what I shall try to do.*' That is to say that Oliveira's intention, officially, is to recall, but he implicitly admits, with *saudade*, that he will probably not always succeed. Memory, therefore, is regarded as the raw material that fuelled his creativity, because all that he can no longer remember must be imagined through self-fiction. For Oliveira, this is not a problem when making an autobiographical documentary, since any film is always full of ghosts, as he has stated:

> Images on the screen are a spell of the camera, they are no more than ghosts of a reality that hides other ghosts, which accompany them in actual life. [...] Even when images look very realist, they are simply appearance, they are just cinema, whether they are part of a fiction or come from actual life. They are immaterial. They are still and always ghosts of something that there is no longer or that never was. (Oliveira in Zunzunegui 2004: 87, my translation)

In order to summon the ghost of his past, Oliveira resorts to different techniques and devices that ultimately give rise to a film palimpsest in which several visual materials coexist: archival footage from the first third of the twentieth century, images from *Working on the Douro River*, *Aniki Bóbó* and *The Artist and the City*, current views of Porto at the turn of the century, and finally fictional reenactments of meaningful episodes. Moreover, the soundtrack alternates a first-person commentary read by the filmmaker himself with passages of classical music and popular songs that strengthen the emotional dimension of the images, as in *Of Time and the City*. The set of all these strategies aims to represent the logic of memory, assuming that neither images nor stories are enough in themselves to recall the filmmaker's memoryscapes in their full complexity.

On the narrative level, *Porto of My Childhood* dates back to the 1920s and 1930s, when Oliveira was a young man in a city that faced a particularly unstable historical period. Two years after Oliveira's birth, in 1910, the Portuguese monarchy was overthrown by a military *coup d'état*; then, from 1910 to 1926, the First Portuguese Republic was undermined by the internal division of the Republican Party and the pressures exerted by several strikes and uprisings; and finally, in 1926, another military *coup d'état* led to António Salazar's corporatist-authoritarian dictatorship, which lasted forty-eight years, until the Carnation Revolution. In this period, Oliveira completed his high school education in a sort of exile in A Guarda, a town located right across the northwest border between Portugal and Galicia, where the Portuguese Jesuits settled temporarily after having been expelled from the country – in the first half of *Voyage to the Beginning of the World*, Oliveira's alter ego precisely recalls these years. Thereupon, in 1924, he decided not to go to college: in view of the well-off economic position of his family, he preferred to devote himself to his passions, which at the time were theatre, sports and bohemian life. In these circumstances, he soon became a moviegoer, and one day he had the chance to see *Berlin: Symphony of a Great City*. 'That film touched me,' he has repeated on several occasions, 'it was a proposal for which I felt qualified' (in Andrade 2002: 25; my translation). Cinema thus became his main interest, '*a passion that stole me from sport, just as the latter stole me from the bohemian life*', as he says in the commentary of *Porto of My Childhood*.

Like the previous case studies, this film also addresses the relation between the filmmaker and the city by associating memories and places: on the one hand, Oliveira's past emerges from current urban space; while on the other, his stories recreate a missing city. Indeed, *Porto of My Childhood* stands as a precursor for *Of Time and the City*: in addition to their most obvious similarities, such as being first-person autobiographical narratives or having been produced within the context of the European Capital of Culture, both films contrast old and contemporary cityscapes in order to criticise their transformations, using music to highlight the emotional perception of the process as well as to stimulate memories. Urban self-portraits, as noted above, are not as interested in recalling the past as in establishing a dialogue with it by means of the act of remembering, through which filmmakers simultaneously depict the past and present of their hometowns and, above all, their own self over time. The feedback between place and self is thus reciprocal: memories allow the film to time travel to the past of the place, while each new visit to these places grants access to increasingly deep layers of the self.

The main difference between *Porto of My Childhood* and *Of Time and the City* lies in the degree of transparency with which this mental mechanism is showed: Oliveira is much more explicit than Davies because he does not hesitate to distrust his own ability to remember. For this reason, *Porto of My Childhood* continuously tends towards self-fiction, staging Oliveira's memories through fictional reenactments played by professional actors, something that Davies already did at the beginning of his career: the English filmmaker separated self-fiction and documentary, devoting different films to each one, while the Portuguese director has combined them in several works, whether feature films (*Voyage to the Beginning of the World*) or documentaries (*Porto of My Childhood*). In the latter case, reenactments and archival footage have the same documentary value as evidences of the functioning of Oliveira's memory, a feature that recalls Tony Buba's fantasies in *Lightning Over Braddock*: in both self-portraits, the staged sequences are not outside reality but part of it, always considering that the product of our mental activity also belongs to reality.

These reenactments do not seek to reproduce the real appearance of Porto in the past, but just Oliveira's memoryscape. At times, and this is the most astonishing quality of these sequences, the characters help the filmmaker recall forgotten details of his own memories, as when his fictional doubles whisper certain words before he says them. This idea suggests that memories do not pass from the creator to his creations, but conversely: fiction seems to be what guides the filmmaker's account, instead of his past experiences giving rise to fiction. Furthermore, the actors who embody Oliveira in the documentary are precisely his grandsons, Jorge and Ricardo Trêpa, a casting choice based on their physical resemblance that indirectly reinforces the mastery of the present (fiction) over the past (memory).

From the documentary point of view, as Laura Rascaroli has explained, *Porto of My Childhood* cannot be considered a self-portrait of the artist as a young man because that character is only present in absence, whether described by the voiceover or replaced by doubles (2009: 175). Having no in-

Image 8.1: *Porto of My Childhood*, Oliveira himself playing the role of an actor on the stage

dexical evidence of its existence, the audience has to trust the narrator's words, which are actually one of the two indexical evidences of the existence of another different character: the artist as an old man. The other evidence is the personal appearance of Oliveira himself in the sequence that reenacts one of his frequent visits to the theatre at the time. This visual inscription is like a game of mirrors: old Oliveira – the real Oliveira – plays the role of an actor who embodies a thief on the stage, while his young double – Jorge Trêpa – is seeing the play from a box seat (Image 8.1). The latter image is practically identical to a shot from *Inquietude* (*Anxiety*, Manoel de Oliveira, 1998), in which the camera frames another box seat from a very similar position. Accordingly, if reenactments are inspired by previous feature films, the past automatically becomes a fiction of the present, in which Oliveira portrays himself as an old filmmaker who tries to remember his past through staged sequences. After all, much of the truthfulness of *Porto of My Childhood* relies on his director's testimony, and any testimony, as Bill Nichols has warned, always gives less priority to what happened in the past in a strict sense than to 'what we now think happened and what this might mean for us' (1993: 177).

This dialogue between past and present is developed in both temporal and spatial terms. For example, a usual strategy to insert the filmmaker's memories within historical time is the editing of fictional reenactments as reverse shots for authentic documents: in the sequence in which a man climbs to the top of the Clérigos Tower, the real footage of the event is punctuated by several high-angle shots of Oliveira's double looking up, giving the impression that the image of the man climbing the tower comes from the filmmaker's gaze. Other times, certain scenes of old bourgeois life are showed twice, like the after-dinner stroll in the Avenida das Tilias, which is first seen through archival footage and then reenacted in the same location. This detail reveals that Oliveira is always careful to match his memories with the real settings where they took place, as when he juxtaposes old images of his places of memory with shots of their current avatars on the urban surface: his favourite cake-shop, the Confeitaria Oliveira, was a clothing store in 2001; the Café Central, where he met his bohemian friends in the 1930s, had become a banking office; and the first movie theatre built in Porto, the Cinema High-Life, was transformed into the Cinema Batalha in 1947, a venue that unfortunately closed at the turn of the century. In all these psychogeographical comparisons, Oliveira's laconic voice usually states '*this is it today*'.

The only exception to this dynamic is the Café Majestic, which still remains open thanks to the beauty of its art deco interiors. In 1983, it was declared Building of Public Interest and then, in the 1990s, it was restored and reopened as a relic of the Belle Époque. There, Oliveira films the exact corner where he wrote the shooting plan for *Gigantes do Douro* (*Douro Giants*), a film that he could not make at the time because of censorship. This idea of returning to the crime scene already appeared in *Les hommes du port*, although in that film Alain Tanner went back to an empty office that bore almost no resemblance to the one he had known. On the contrary, Oliveira finds everything in place in the Majestic, but he does not seem particularly pleased about that. In this sequence, his voice keeps the same 'saudo-sist' tone as in the rest of the film, perhaps because the success in preserving this space makes more evident his own process of aging. For this reason, he emotion-ally feels more attached to missing places, like the old nightclubs, than to those that still stand.

The psychogeographical comparison that offers the key to the film is the rewriting of the first Portuguese moving picture: *Saída do Pessoal Operário da Fábrica Confiança* (*Workers Leaving the Confiança Factory*, Aurélio Paz dos Reis, 1896). *Porto of My Childhood* includes its whole footage (almost a minute in length) as well as its contemporary version, in which Oliveira recreates the original scene (Images 8.2 & 8.3). The old shirt factory located at No. 181 Rua de Santa Catarina curiously became the headquarters of Oporto 2001, European Capital of Culture at the turn of the century, one of the production companies of this documentary along with Madragoa Filmes, Gemini Films and the RTP, the Portuguese public television. Thus, by replacing the seamstresses who

Image 8.2 & 8.3 (top): *Workers Leaving the Confiança Factory*, the fist Portuguese moving picture, (bottom): *Porto of My Childhood*, rewriting of *Workers Leaving the Confiança Factory*

left their workplace in 1896 by other workers in 2001, including an actor who embodies the pioneer Aurélio Paz dos Reis, Oliveira combines up to four reading levels in the same shot: first, it documents the Rua de Santa Catarina in 2001; sec-ond, it reproduces a previous document of the same place; third, it partly reenacts its filming process; and finally, it makes real his own fantasies.

This tribute to Paz dos Reis suggests that cinema is an essential element to pre-serve the memory of the city and recall the filmmaker's memoryscape. The direct quotations from *Working on the Douro River, Aniki Bóbó* and *The Artist and the City* also contribute to giving the impression that Oliveira remembers the past of his hometown through the films that he shot there, a strategy that relates his urban self-portrait to the metafilm documentaries discussed in chapter nine. The sum of these four works set in Porto – *Working on the Douro River, Aniki Bóbó, The Artist and the City* and *Porto of My Childhood* – constitutes a tetralogy that shows the evolution of the cityscape and its representations through time, estab-lishing a visual history of the city from images belonging to different film periods and styles. This praise of cinema's ability to stimulate memory is nevertheless far from naïve, because the filmmaker admits the limitations of this device in the commentary. His frustration about the impossibility of remembering everything is, again, an expression of *saudade*:

> *Thanks to the cinema, we can see these bits over and over again. But only each person's memory can recall things that only we did live through. And is doing so not the best way of showing who we are? But many of my memories, in going back into the past, have been lost and today are entombed.*

Oliveira has assumed that cinema can only preserve tiny fragments of memory, which does not prevent him from filming to create new memories. In this sense, he has arrived at the same conclusion as Nicholas Ray in *Lightning Over Water* (Nicholas Ray & Wim Wenders, 1980), in which the American filmmaker stated, in a lecture at Vassar, that 'the closer one comes to an ending, the closer one moves to a rewriting that is a beginning' (in Scheibler 1993: 137). Reenactments in *Porto of My Childhood* are not only an attempt to recover past memories, but also a way of creating new ones for the future: the memory of making another film, and even the memory of the act of remembering, because we do not always remember our experiences directly, but rather through their later account.

The film ends with a carscape that resembles those recorded by Tanner from Genoa's elevated highway in *Les hommes du port*. This time, the camera is placed on a car that slowly traverses the Viaduto do Cais das Pedras, a small bypass over the Douro that runs about two hundred metres in parallel to the waterfront. Thanks to the curve of the bridge, the city is seen from the river for a few seconds, as if it were a boatscape instead of a carscape. Oliveira adopts this perspective to reproduce the view of the city that the old Portuguese navigators had before departing into the unknown. The end of this shot reinforces this idea by zooming into a tiled mural that represents a portrait of Prince Henry the Navigator, the patron who encouraged Portuguese exploration in Africa.[3]

The conclusion of *Porto of My Childhood* metaphorically relates, on the one hand, the mouth of the river with the end of Oliveira's autobiographical account, and on the other, overseas discoveries with his discovery of life through film: the closing shot precisely shows a lighthouse in the midst of the evening, a symbolic image that matches the infinite spaciousness of the horizon with the infinite possibilities of the film screen. This lighthouse in particular is the Farolim de Felgueiras, which had already appeared in the opening and closing shots of *Working on the Douro River*. Therefore, by looking for an ending to his urban self-portrait, Oliveira encounters the foundational image of his film career and rewrites it, establishing a cinematic eternal return that allows him to fulfil his purpose of travelling out of time: '*the city is being renewed*', he says, '*but no matter how much it is changed, it will always be the Porto of my childhood with a gold stream running at its feet.*'[4] Thanks to cinema, Oliveira's return to his beginnings implicitly entails a new beginning, which actually simply follows the example of his hometown: to update certain features in order to remain the same as ever, even when it is no longer possible to remain exactly the same.

My Winnipeg: The City as a Text to Be Decoded[5]

Guy Maddin's urban self-portrait resorts to self-fiction to convey his subjective perception of the slow decline of Winnipeg, historically one of the main industrial centres in Canada. This 'docu-fantasy', a term coined by Maddin himself, lacks the political commitment of *Roger & Me* or the social conscience of *Les hommes du port* and *Of Time and the City*, but it shares with *Lightning Over Braddock* and *Porto of My Childhood* their ability to explore imaginary cityscapes in order to depict the emotional experience of urban space. This choice seems quite appropriate to address the love/hate relationship that anyone establishes with their hometown, because it exposes the irrational ties that bind us to it. In the case of Winnipeg, this relationship also includes a supernatural dimension that certainly comes from Maddin's tendency towards fantasy, a clear transgression of the discourse of sobriety that nevertheless serves to provide the city with a whole urban mythology.

The Canadian filmmaker is best known for his insistence on recovering the aesthetics of silent film in postmodern times. Barry Keith Grant have summarised the contradictions of his style by describing it as 'so avant-garde that his movies look like they were made almost a hundred years ago' (Grant & Hillier 2009: 143). Maddin has no problem to imitate, copy, quote or simply plagiarise a wide range of styles, many of them already buried, including German Expressionism, Soviet montage, French surrealism, film noir, excessive melodramas, classical horror movies, trash cinema and even early musicals (see Beard 2010: 7).[6] Such a blend of referents usually leads to pastiche, but it has also allowed him to develop an unmistakable aesthetics based on excess, saturation and, above all, an impressive wealth of visual resources. Like other postmodern filmmakers, from Quentin Tarantino to Todd Haynes, Maddin understands the history of cinema as an inexhaustible source of inspiration from which he can focus on any technique or device to reuse it in a completely different context: thus, despite not having been trained in filmmaking,[7] he has been able to create a work that emerges from the cannibalisation of all the references that he has accumulated throughout his long and omnivorous career as a passionate moviegoer.

The isolation imposed by Winnipeg's geographical location and its severe climate – the city is located hundreds of miles away from any other major city, and it has below-zero temperatures for five months a year – has indirectly fuelled Maddin's film activity. He has explained that 'unlike big cities, where there are lots of things to do and warmer weather, we don't talk our best ideas out into the café night air. You're stuck inside, and there's nothing to do but actually doing your stuff' (in Darr 2008: 1). Thanks to these restrictions, Maddin has managed to shoot eight feature films and over twenty shorts before making his urban self-portrait, including a couple of self-fictions: *Cowards Bend the Knee*, which is also known as *The Blue Hands* (2003), and *Brand upon the Brain!* (2006). These two films, along with *My Winnipeg*, make up an autobiographical cycle called the 'Me Trilogy' that contains several repeated elements (see Halfyard 2007).

Firstly, the three films are silent parodies of family dramas starring a fictional double of the author, also named Guy Maddin, although he is played by different actors (Darcy Fehr in *Cowards Bend the Knee* and *My Winnipeg*, and Sullivan Brown and Erik Stephen Maahs in *Brand upon the Brain!*). Secondly, the trilogy presents the same types of parental figures: a domineering mother and an absent father. Indeed, *Cowards Bend the Knee* and *My Winnipeg* blend fact and fiction by reproducing the same dichotomy between female space, associated with the beauty salon owned by Maddin's real mother, and male space, identified with the place where Maddin's real father used to work as a volunteer for the local hockey team, the Winnipeg Arena. Lastly, these films always include references to traumatic events and sexual intrigues that date back to the childhood or adolescence of the characters. The set of all these features calls into question the autobiographical dimension of the 'Me Trilogy', since the content of these films does not rely on actual facts, but on Maddin's mindscapes. Consequently, *My Winnipeg* resorts to self-fiction in order to depict the filmmaker's inner world with the greatest possible depth.

The original idea of making a documentary on Winnipeg came from the president of the Documentary Channel in Canada, Michael Burns, who commissioned Maddin to direct it (see Beard 2010: 313). The main subject should have been the city itself, but the filmmaker quickly realised that, in order to show his Winnipeg, he needed to show himself first (see Halfyard 2007). For this reason, his urban self-portrait explores three superimposed layers: Winnipeg's local history, Maddin's family portrait and a series of surreal episodes that belong to the realm of imagination (see Lahera 2008). Accordingly, the narrative of the film constantly combines opposing elements: objectivity and subjectivity, reality and imagination, history and fake, memories and fantasies, etc., an endless list of binary oppositions in which we cannot distinguish what is true from what is invented.

Dave Saunders, however, maintains that *My Winnipeg* is 'more immersed in the "truth" of the city and its psychological effects than any by-the-book chronicle' (2010: 153), an idea that Grant had previously defended by stating that the film 'is probably closer to the way most people relate to their environment than the urban celebrations depicted in city symphony films' (2009: 144). Fake thereby works as a way to achieve an abstract or at least subjective truth, as explained by the filmmaker: 'The truth lies in the exaggeration. […] I can better control the truth when I know that nothing is literally true. I can be sure that something is true if I control the necessary device to represent a copy of the truth' (Maddin in Kovacsics 2011: 81; my translation). Thus, by means of this creative fake of reality, *My Winnipeg* suggests a model of relationship with our everyday environment in which subjective perception and personal inventions are valid tools to develop a cognitive map beyond pre-established representations.

Maddin's fabrications aspire to be plausible within the internal logic of the film, which tries to imitate the disjointed logic of memory. In order to achieve this purpose, the documentary deploys up to six different narrative devices: voiceover commentary, archival footage, Winnipeg's current images, Maddin's mental images, animation sequences and title cards. The first of these elements, the filmmaker's commentary, uses a poetic and repetitive tone to recall both memories and impressions of the past from an omniscient position, as well as to control the transitions from one story to another. Archival footage, in turn, corresponds to the images of the past, which usually show people having fun, especially outdoors: much of this footage are scenes of winter activities that recall actuality films such as *Ice-Yachting on the St. Lawrence* (Joseph Rosenthal, 1903) or *Skating for the World's Championship at Montreal* (Joseph Rosenthal, 1903). Maddin has ensured that this footage is authentic, although it is so short that he decided to increase it by filming fictional reenactments as if they were old actuality films (see Brooke 2008: 12; Darr 2008). Since it is not possible to distinguish which images are real and which are not at first sight, the audience has to choose between trusting their authenticity or assuming that any image of the past might be a fake. Any of these two possibilities challenges the conventional perception of archival footage, according to which we must decode old images as 'authentic signs of their times' (Nichols 1993: 177) unless the film gives us any reason to think otherwise. In this case, we have every reason to distrust, but the presence of some authentic images forces us to wonder to what extent this device is able to convey that subjective truth.

Meanwhile, Winnipeg's current images document the real cityscape, sometimes including traces of the filmmaker's inscription within the film, such as his shadow or his footprints. These images are the closest ones to the autobiographical approach: for example, in the sequence in which the filmmaker walks his dog at night, he himself holds the camera to personally capture the feeling of walking over snow. On the contrary, the mental images are always reenactments performed by actors and filmed in studio settings: the bulk of the sequences devoted to his family life clearly fit into this category. The most implausible events, such as the death of racehorses in the frozen river or the destruction of an amusement park due to a bison stampede, are visualised through Andy Smetanka's animation sequences, whose primitive style has been compared to Lotte Reiniger's since they both use the technique of silhouette animation (see Darr 2008; Beard 2010: 314). Finally, the title cards serve to introduce new sequences and, above all, to emphasise certain ideas that are already present both in the images and the commentary.

These narrative devices are not always associated with a single style in particular, given that they all share a hybrid visual texture that comes from the juxtaposition of eleven recording formats: Super-8mm film, 16mm film, Super-16mm film, analogue video, mini-DV video, HD video, cell phone, animation shot on video, animation shot on Super-8, several archival footage formats, and finally rear projections that were originally shot on video and later reshot on film (see Halfyard 2007; Beard 2010: 313). Such a variety of media helps to hide the texture differences between archival footage and staged sequences, resulting in an anachronistic aesthetic that seems to be out of time, to the point that Maddin's Winnipeg looks like a Central European city in the interwar period: the real cityscape thereby becomes an imaginary place composed of parts of other cities, other films and other representations, that is, an urban palimpsest shaped according to the filmmaker's visual referents.

This imaginary city is built through the counterfactual logic of 'what if?' Maddin explores all those denied futures that Winnipeg never developed, beginning with his own escape from there, a scene defined by William Beard as 'the film's narrative locus, to which it returns with great regularity throughout its entirety' (2010: 315). In that sequence, the main character – Maddin's fictional double – attempts again and again to leave Winnipeg by train, but he is trapped in a labyrinth (memory) from which he will only get out once the narrator (Maddin himself) relives all his past experiences there. This endless journey through the urban surface symbolises the act of remembering, as the commentary clearly implies: '*I just have to make my way through town, through everything I've ever seen and lived, everything I've loved and forgotten.*' Later on, as this purpose is not easy to fulfil, the narrator explicitly suggests filming his way out of Winnipeg, a self-conscious statement of intent that directly reveals the inner workings of the film.

The metaphor of the journey through time and space serves to delve into Winnipeg's local history and collective memory in search of those places and stories that better express its contradictory identity. The main criteria for choosing them has to do with their ability to summarise its idiosyncrasy which, according to Beard, seems to consist of everything that 'symptomatizes the place's sickness, forgottenness, isolation, inauthenticity, decay, pathology … just what makes it home, just what makes it lovable' (2010: 335). This negative perception of Winnipeg had already appeared in *The Saddest Music in the World* (2003), and it may be a consequence of the excessive expectations placed on the city when it was the staging point for the colonisation of western Canada (see Beard 2010: 336). In recent decades, Winnipeg's economy seems to have stalled in comparison with the prosperity of other western provinces of the country, such as British Columbia, Alberta or even the neighbouring Saskatchewan, whose gross domestic product currently surpasses Manitoba's.[8] This has led Winnipeggers to develop an inferiority complex towards their neighbours that has adversely affected their self-esteem.

The search for meaningful places and stories imitates the local tradition of 'buried treasures', an annual contest organised by the Canadian Pacific Railway in which, according to the filmmaker's account, Winnipeggers wandered around their city in search of hidden treasures. The prize for the winner was a one-way ticket on the next train out of town, but the idea of the contest was right the opposite: to strengthen the link between the city and its residents by encouraging their sense of belonging to the place, supposing that, as the commentary states, *'once someone had spent a full day looking this closely at his own hometown, he would never want to leave'*. This story provides another metaphor for the narrative device of the film: like his fellow citizens, Maddin also explores the cityscape in search of 'buried stories' that expose a mythical city hidden beneath the surface. Through this process, he rescues from oblivion quite a number of urban legends that ultimately restore Winnipeg's right to have its own mythology, a claim that appears in several interviews:

> Canadians … are a bit shy about mythologizing themselves and they feel the need to make their historical figures and historical events smaller than life rather than bigger than life. So I just thought, every other culture in the world, including the Inuit in Canada, are great at mythologizing, so let's just give Winnipeg its fair shake. (Maddin in Halfyard 2007)

In order to render visible certain episodes forgotten by official history, Maddin undertook the task of conducting an archaeological survey in public and private film archives. Nevertheless, the lack of enough stock footage compelled him to produce his own historical documents, a solution that had previously been successfully used in the documentary *History and Memory: For Akiko and Takashige* (Rea

Tajiri, 1992). From this perspective, *My Winnipeg* is almost a work of experimental archaeology, because it strives to create replicas of historical images through techniques similar to those used in the past. Moreover, the film understands the city as a set of layers of meaning that need to be decoded: the commentary explicitly describes Winnipeg as '*a city of palimpsest, of skins, of skins beneath skins*', a place, in short, whose identity is successively inscribed and reinscribed by the spatial practices of its inhabitants. This archaeological-semiotics approach expresses the alleged local clairvoyance, according to which '*Winnipeggers have always been skilled in reading past the surface and into the hidden depths of their city*'. This faculty allows the filmmaker to interpret the slightest detail as a euphemism for a much more sordid truth, establishing a permanent confusion between everyday anecdotes and historical events. For instance, he juxtaposes the Scandal of the Wolseley's Elm, a neighbourhood protest to avoid the felling of a tree in 1957, with the Winnipeg Revolutionary Strike of 1919, the first labour riot in North America after the Russian Revolution. For the discourse of sobriety, this comparison would be unacceptable, to say the least, but it actually makes sense within the logic of memory, in which everyday anecdotes and historical events share the same mental level.

The film systematically twists and trivialises any story about the city's past: the sequence about the Revolutionary Strike, to continue with the same example, ends by focusing on the very unlikely clash between armed nuns and lustful Bolsheviks, who supposedly would have fought to protect or rape the female students of Saint Mary's School. In this case, real data (the spot where the major clashes of the uprising took place) degenerate into an implausible episode (the sexual menace against the daughters of the local bourgeoisie). The same dynamic is repeated throughout the film: the male beauty contests held in the Paddle Wheel Club were the iceberg tip of a shameful political corruption scandal, the remains of the amusement park destroyed by the bison stampede served to build invisible shantytowns on the rooftops of downtown Winnipeg, and the tragic death of a group of racehorses during the first cold snap of 1926 gave rise to a macabre landscape that soon became a pleasant place for local couples (Image 8.4). Despite their exaggerated tendency to fabulation, most of these sequences are inspired by true stories – the story of the frozen racehorses comes from local archives (see Kovacsics 2011: 81) – although their truth value is much less important than their metaphorical ability to draw attention to the most controversial aspects of the city. Thus, the shantytowns on the rooftops would be a consequence of '*a law which keeps homeless out of sight*', while the transformation of the horse cemetery into a *locus amoenus* would symbolise the local gloomy character. '*We grow used to sadness,*' the narrator says in this sequence, '*simply, [we] incorporate it into our days.*'

The only time Maddin lies blatantly is when he seems to tell the truth: right after deciding to film his way out of Winnipeg, he announces that he is going to stage his childhood memories at his old family home, for which he admits having hired professional actors. According to this assertion, his closest relatives would be fictional doubles with the sole exception of his mother, who would play herself. The latter is utterly false, because the mother is none other than Ann Savage, the *femme fatale* of *Detour* (Edgar G. Ulmer, 1945), a professional

Image 8.4: *My Winnipeg*, a macabre landscape turned into a pleasant place for local couples

actress without any kinship with the filmmaker. Furthermore, it is not clear either that these reenactments were filmed on location rather than in a studio set. The reasoning suggested by the editing to convince the audience is so simple and effective that it might well be a fallacy: first, we are provided with authentic documents of the filmmaker's past, such as family pictures and home movies, that demonstrate that he did live at 800 Ellis Avenue; and thereupon we are told that he rented the house for one month in order to film the reenactments there. As there is no way to verify this information, we must take it for granted, but nothing guarantees its truthfulness, not even the fact that the house still stands today.

These red herrings about the construction of the film seek to erase the distinction between documentary footage and fictional reenactment. Such *mise en abyme* begins at the prologue, in which Anne Savage rehearses a scene that will be shown later: Maddin's voice prompts her lines from off-screen and the actress repeats them immediately afterwards, creating the effect of 'a reverse echo', as described by Denis Seguin (2008: 1). These images must be considered documentary footage, because they are a record of the actual shooting of the film, while the scene that is being rehearsed belongs in turn to the domain of fiction, because it loosely recreates a traumatic memory with a very high level of parody and affectation. Hence *My Winnipeg* arguably borrows certain features from the reflexive mode (the persistent references to the creative process) and especially from the performative one (the obsession with staging new versions of the past).

The first of these reenactments is the family reunion around the television set to watch their favourite programme, 'Ledge Man', a local soap opera which tells the same story every day since the filmmaker's birth year, 1956: an oversensitive man, played by Darcy Fehr, threatens to jump from a ledge and only his mother, played by Ann Savage, can convince him not to do it. Every day, the man goes out to the ledge, and every day the mother prevents him from jumping. Her eternal intervention as a saviour, as well as Savage's and Fehr's casting for the roles of mother and child, has been interpreted by Saunders as an allegory of the anchor, the chain or even the umbilical cord that keeps Maddin in Winnipeg:

> The parallels with Maddin's struggle to escape the clutches of his home-town, and his mother's apron strings, are abundant: Ledge Man's leap into the unknown world, the world outside Winnipeg, is constantly prevented by his mother's hectoring and infantilising; the Maddin surrogate ... is unable to get away, or to fulfil even the death drive for fear of matriarchal reprimand. [...] 'Archetypal episodes' from the psychoanalytic id become literal episodes of a still ongoing daily drama, the struggle and ultimate failure of its protagonist acted out on television for all to see and maybe to mock. (2010: 160)

Other reenactments refer to the tedious task of straightening the hall runner or to the mother's two main phobias: fear of birds and, above all, fear of being di-shevelled. These scenes reveal the existence of family tensions and traumas hidden

Image 8.5: *My Winnipeg*, a car accident as euphemism for something darker

beneath the banality of the everyday, meaning that Maddin pursues the same goal both in his family portrait and his urban self-portrait: to discover what lies below the surface. The sequence that Ann Savage rehearses in the film's prologue – a violent argument between mother and daughter due to a traffic accident – explains by itself the interpreta-tive dynamics of the film. One night, the daughter came home late after having hit and killed a deer with her car, but the mother identifies the traces of blood and fur on the bumper as unquestionable evidence of a sexual encounter (Image 8.5). '*No in-nocent girl stays out past ten with blood on her fender,*' she concludes after hav-ing mercilessly insulted her daughter. According to her interpretation, which is the filmmaker's, a car accident in Winnipeg has to mean something else, it has to be a euphemism for something darker, something that we are not always willing to admit because it may disclose the real reasons for our actions. That is to say that euphemisms provide access to thoughts, opinions, desires, experiences and even memories that belong to the realm of the unconscious, whether individual or collective. Therefore, by similarly addressing the secrets of his family and his hometown, Maddin balances both narratives and, what is more important, turns them into interdependent accounts.

At the beginning of the film, a brief review of Winnipeg's founding myth establishes a first connection between local history and the filmmaker's mind-scape. According to the official chronicle, the city was born from a fur trading post built on the confluence of the Assiniboine and the Red River of the North, a place located at the crossroads of many commercial routes that soon boomed as meeting point. Maddin visually compares this spot with a female pubis while he rhythmically recites the words '*the forks, the lap, the fur*', each one matched with its respective illustration. Their insistent repetition as if they were a spell suggests two mental associations: on the one hand, the city is related to the filmmaker's family through the connection between the river confluence and his mother's lap, which justifies the autobiographical approach of the film; and on the other, the city is associated with fantasy since it is introduced as a mythical crossroads, which explains, in turn, Maddin's choice of fake and self-fiction as narrative devices. The latter connection is based on a native legend about a second subterranean confluence located right underneath the two rivers, from which supernatural powers would emanate. If we believe the story of 'the Forks beneath the Forks', as the filmmaker does, Winnipeg's magical nature should be at the very foundation of any attempt to describe its identity and idiosyncrasy. From this viewpoint, Maddin's fabrications would then be a reflection of the collective unconscious of the city, which has been shaped by beliefs, traditions and myths similar to this legend.

The emphasis on this imaginary dimension inevitably overshadows the actual cityscape, leading to the replacement of the city-referent by a city-character. At first sight, Winnipeg's visual identity does not differ from the generic image of Midwestern cities: its skyline consists of a few pretentious skyscrapers that stand over a small downtown surrounded by an undifferentiated mass of identical neighbourhoods. Given this lack of personality, Maddin avoids most of Winnipeg's usual landmarks and historic sites to focus instead on what he calls a 'heartsick architecture', a term referring to those buildings, constructions and places that have not been able to fulfill their original purpose. The first example of this local peculiarity is the story of the Arlington Street Bridge, an iron viaduct that crosses the huge train yards of the city: according to the myth, this structure was manufactured by the Vulcan Iron Works of London at the beginning of the twentieth century in order to be subsequently brought to Egypt, where it was supposed to span the Nile. Unfortunately, '*a mistake in specs made the fit with that river impossible, and the bridge was sold at a bargain price to bargain-crazy Winnipeg*'. Again, this story is not entirely true, but it is not easy to know which data have been tampered with by the filmmaker. The following quotes try to solve the mystery, but even so they disagree regarding the origin of the bridge:

The bridge was in fact built by the Cleveland Bridge Works. It was commissioned for Egypt, but there was nothing wrong with the specs; rather,
no one took delivery. But it was indeed purchased at auction by the City
of Winnipeg for considerably less than it would have cost new. (Seguin
2008)

It has long been rumoured that the Arlington St. Bridge was originally
built to cross the Nile in Egypt and how it later ended up in Winnipeg. It
was indeed designed for Winnipeg as its width would not have spanned
the much wider Nile. That it was built in Birmingham, England, by the
Cleveland Iron Works, which also did bridges for places around the world,
probably lead to this speculation. (Siamandas 2007)

Despite its lack of historical accuracy, Maddin's version succeeds in conveying the
oppressive atmosphere of the place by humanising the bridge through a prosopopoeia: the narrator interprets the dilation of its iron structure in the cold winter
nights as a disconsolate moan, an expression of sorrow that would arise from the
longing for what should be its promised land, the Nile Valley. Accordingly, the reference to Egypt is essential to define the *genius loci* of this junkspace, even though
it has nothing to do with its true story. Far from being just a witty joke, the idea of
a heartsick architecture provides Winnipeg landmarks with an emotional biography, which sometimes also serves to denounce 'architectural tragedies' such as the
replacement of Eaton's by the MTS Centre or the demolition of the old Winnipeg
Arena (Images 8.6 & 8.9).

Regarding the first, Eaton's was the largest department store retailer in Canada
for decades, and its Winnipeg store, a red brick building that occupied an entire
city block on Portage Avenue at Donald Street, was once considered the most profitable department store in the world. However, the company's bankruptcy in 1999
led to the closure of the store and the sale of its plot, which was finally bought by
True North Sports & Entertainment in 2001. After a few brief episodes of token
resistance, the building was demolished in 2002 to make way for a new entertainment and sports venue: the ominous MTS Centre, an indoor arena built to bring a
NHL team back to the city after the traumatic relocation of the original Winnipeg
Jets to Phoenix in 1996.[9]

In order to summarise the process of replacing a building with another, Maddin
juxtaposes a few images of Eaton's demolition with a contemporary view of the
MTS Centre, all framed from the same camera position (Images 8.7 & 8.8). For
a few seconds, he even alters the visual style of the film by replacing its outdated
black-and-white textures by flat digital colours, an aesthetic choice that helps to

emphasise the estrangement effect caused by the new building in the cityscape. To make matters worse, the arena was initially too small for the NHL standards and it could not fulfil its purpose until 2011, when True North Sports & Entertainment bought the Atlanta Thrashers and moved them to Winnipeg.[10] Nevertheless, before that were to happen, Maddin found a malicious pun in the cityscape that expressed his contempt for the building better than any other poisonous joke: due to a temporary failure, the 'S' in the neon sign of the MTS Centre did not work when he filmed its façade, so the name of the arena could then be read as 'empty centre'.

The construction of this venue was used as a pretext for the demolition of the Winnipeg Arena, the local 'cathedral' of ice hockey during the second half of the twentieth century: it was built in 1955, a year before the filmmaker's birth, and pulled down nearly half a century later, in 2004, only three years before the making of *My Winnipeg*. Maddin's affection for this building, which had already appeared in *Cowards Bend the Knee*, comes from its familiar connotations, since his father used to work there when he was a child, as noted above. In another prosopopoeia, the filmmaker states that '*this building was my male parent*', and he subsequently projects the image of his father's face upon its ice rink. The arena is thereby identified as a source of male influence that counters and complements the female influence of his mother's beauty salon. Of course, this autobiographical reference immediately opens the door to self-fiction: the narrator claims to have been born and grown up in the locker room, where he would even have been breastfed. Consequently, he associates his childhood memories with the smell of breast milk, sweet and urine, '*a holy trinity of odours*', as he calls it, which inspires his personal farewell to the arena: he goes to its urinals and documents his 'last

Images 8.6 & 8.7: *My Winnipeg*, Eaton's heyday (top) and demolition (bottom)

Images 8.8 & 8.9: *My Winnipeg*, MTS Centre (top) and Winnipeg Arena (bottom)

pee' there, an act of self-expression described by Beard as 'infantile (reacting to negative stimulus with an excretory event) ... animal-like (marking the territory that is about to be destroyed), [and] memorial (ritually repeating an act already performed "a million times before")' (2010: 342).

This tribute to the Winnipeg Arena is again developed in terms of fantasy and testimony: first, Maddin resorts to the logic of 'what if' to dream of a hockey team called the Black Tuesdays, which would be formed by Manitoba's best players of all times; and then, he ends the sequence with an amazing shot of the failed demolition of the building in which a group of nostalgic supporters shout 'go, Jets, go!' off-screen. Being aware of the historical value of this image, the filmmaker repeats it up to three times to emphasise the heroic resistance of the Winnipeg Arena to be removed from the cityscape. One more time, the supernatural atmosphere of the film is reinforced by an unusual event which apparently fits the imaginary city better than the real one.

The end of *My Winnipeg* borrows a similar gimmick to that which closed *8½* (Federico Fellini, 1963): Maddin summons all the ghosts of the city, or at least all those who appear in the film, by means of a character called 'Citizen Girl'. This superheroine would be the imaginary pin-up girl of *The Winnipeg Citizen*, a collective newspaper published at the time of the Winnipeg Revolutionary Strike of 1919. According to the narrator, this *'concerned comrade'* would be the only one able to *'undo all the damage done during Winnipeg's first trip through time'*: with a simple wave of her hand, she might restore Eaton's and the Winnipeg Arena, bring the Jets back to the city, plant a new elm on Wolseley Avenue or refill the Paddle Wheel Club, among many other incredible feats. At best, Citizen Girl would become a new lap for Winnipeg, allowing Maddin to leave it at last because *'she would look after this city, my city, my Winnipeg'*. Her intervention is a shameless *deux ex machina* in which citizen awareness meets the filmmaker's wet dreams, one last example of the close alliance between politics and sex (or Marx and Freud) that shapes *My Winnipeg*.

Maddin's concern for the transformations of his hometown places the film in the wake of many other urban self-portraits. Like *Les hommes du port*, *Porto of My Childhood* and *Of Time and the City*, *My Winnipeg* is another visual eulogy for a missing city, whose architectural tragedies symbolise 'the long, gradual slide downhill of a city that had not so many decades earlier been so bustling and full of promise' (Beard 2010: 336). The Canadian filmmaker attempts to protect his places of memory by filming them, especially those threatened by obsolescence, because he is aware of their great memorial value. This is the reason why he portrays himself as the guardian of Winnipeg's ghosts and hidden stories, someone able to put the city back on the map again through films and fantasies, many of which, it must be said, only bear a slight resemblance to reality. In conclusion, both Manoel de Oliveira and Guy Maddin understand cinema in general and self-fiction in particular as a means to construct and express their respective identities and worldviews, in which there seems to be no separation between memory and imagination. *Porto of My Childhood* and *My Winnipeg* are thus closer to fiction than to documentary because they depict a cityscape that has definitely become a mindscape, as already happened in the case of autobiographical landscaping. Therefore, in this third type of urban self-portrait, the representation of the lived city requires the creation of its fictional double, which can only exist as a city-character on the screen.

NOTES

1   The Spanish version of this section has been published as a chapter in the volume *Imágenes conscientes* (see Villarmea Álvarez 2013).

2   His most recent films, however, do not even seem to have testamentary intentions: it is the case of *Singularidades de uma Rapariga Loura* (*Eccentricities of a Blonde-haired Girl*, 2009), *O Extranho Caso de Angélica* (*The Strange Case of Angelica*, 2010) and *O Gebo e a Sombra* (*Gebo and the Shadow*, 2012).

3   This mural is on the façade of the Mother Church of Massarelos.

4   In Portuguese, the name of the Douro sounds like '*rio d'ouro*', which literally means 'gold river'.

5   A shorter version of this section has been previously published in the Revue *LISA / LISA e-journal* (see Villarmea Álvarez 2014c).

6   William Beard notes that 'his taste for entertaining aesthetic failure' is also compatible with 'a deep admiration for genuine masters of the cinematic medium', such as Friedrich Wilhelm Murnau, Eric Von Stroheim, Josef Von Sternberg, Carl Theodor Dreyer, Luis Buñuel, Jean Renoir, Jean Vigo, Max Ophüls and Alfred Hitchcock, besides certain animation filmmakers close to Surrealism such as Jan Svankmajer or Stephen and Timothy Quay (2010: 7–8).

7   Maddin usually introduces himself as 'a "garage-band" filmmaker', that is, 'somebody who doesn't really have a technical ability to be a professional artist but might have something authentic and personal to say anyway' (Beard 2010: 5).

8   In 2012, Alberta's GDP amounted to 288,548 million Canadian dollars, British Columbia's to 208,961 million, Saskatchewan's to 58,581 million, and finally Manitoba's to 54,633 million. Source: Statistics Canada. Table 384-0038; http://www5.statcan.gc.ca/cansim/a26?lang=eng&id=3840038. Accessed 24 February 2014.

9   The National Hockey League (NHL) is the major ice hockey competition in North America.

10 The franchise was renamed as the Winnipeg Jets, borrowing the name of the city's former NHL team.

METAFILMIC
STRATEGIES

Film history can be regarded as a field of study open to researchers of different disciplines, but it is also an account, a historical narrative usually divided into four periods: silent (1890s–1920s), classical (1930s–1950s), modern (1960s–1970s) and postmodern (1980s–2010s). French sociologists Gilles Lipovetsky and Jean Serroy have renamed these stages as 'primitive modernity', 'classical modernity', 'emancipatory modernity' and 'hypermodernity' because they consider that cinema has always been a modern art, an expression of modernity (2009: 16–21). Furthermore, Lipovetsky has been fighting against the term 'postmodernity' for more than thirty years, repeating in book after book that it would be more suitable to talk about 'hypermodernity' (2009: 68). Leaving this terminological debate aside, Lipovetsky and Serroys's description of hypermodern cinema provides three useful categories to define its main features: 'excess-image', 'multiplex-image' and 'distance-image' (2009: 68–70). 'Distance-image' specifically addresses the rise of self-reference in film from the 1980s, a growing tendency in recent decades whereby filmmakers systematically quote, honour, parody, rewrite, reinterpret or simply recycle previous works:

> Cinema has become a classic 'continent' with its legendary history, models, references and founding works which may be unexpectedly revisited over and over again, following the example of other artistic fields. [...] Far from reflecting a creative void, recycling the past places cinema in a situation that allows its continuous reinvention: it is not a repetition or a retrogression, but a neo-modern logic that takes advantage of old resources in order to create new works. (Lipovetsky & Serroy 2009: 129, my translation)

The tradition of the compilation film, like that of collage or photomontage, is precisely based on the creative appropriation of previous materials. Many documentaries have been made from excerpts of other films since *Padenie dinastii Romanovykh* (*The Fall of the Romanov Dynasty*, Esfir Shub, 1927), but it did not become a common practice in fiction films until the time of hypermodernity. Some of its forerunners were early attempts at *détournement*, such as *What's up, Tiger Lily* (Woody Allen & Senkichi Taniguchi, 1966) or *La dialectique peut-elle casser des briques?* (*Can Dialectics Break Bricks?*, René Viénet & Kuang-chi Tu, 1973), in which Western directors borrowed the whole footage of Eastern films and dubbed them into English or French with a comic or political intention.[1] Later on, at the beginning of the 1980s, Alain Resnais went further by including brief excerpts from classical films in *Mon oncle d'Amerique* (*My American Uncle*, 1980) in order to comment on the story from outside the diegesis. The success of this device, which also appears differently in *Crimes and Misdemeanours* (Woody Allen, 1989), depends on the audience's complicity, inasmuch as the idea is that viewers recognise both the quote and its cultural meaning. Thus, Resnais and Allen invite the audience to decode these excerpts twice: first, as part of their films, and then as part of collective memory.

Most contemporary moviegoers have grown up with a TV set at home, especially in Western countries, a circumstance that determines our relation with the current mediascape: we are used to reading moving images from an early age, and we are so immersed in visual culture that we do not even notice its ubiquity wherever we go. This dominance of the visual has led many documentary makers to wonder about the meaning of images, regardless of their origin: an excerpt from a film may deserve as detailed analysis as the best-known historical document because both are ultimately vehicles of ideology. For this reason, current compilation films, to mention the most obvious case, have understood that 'thinking history', as Antonio Weinrichter states, 'involves rethinking the *representation* of history' (2010: 277). In this context, Catherine Russell, among others, has reminded us that 'all images become documentary images once their original contexts are stripped away' (1999: 271), an idea that has encouraged researchers and filmmakers from around the world to re-read any waste of visual culture as a product of a given society.

The first outcome of this global interest in reviewing film heritage has been the emergence of non-fiction works that cannibalise previous images and icons in order to interrogate them from an essayistic perspective. These documentaries have been labelled by Timothy Corrigan as 'refractive essay films', a term that establishes a linguistic link with the reflexive mode, although it actually refers to titles that go beyond its usual features and purposes:

Refractive essay films concentrate the representational regime of the essay-istic on the cinematic itself in order to distill and intensify the essayistic by directing it not, for instance, at portraits of human subjectivity or the spac-es of public life but at the aesthetics or, more exactly, the anti-aesthetics of representation that always hover about essay films as a filmic thinking of the world. Refractive suggests a kind of 'unmaking' of the work of art or the film or, as we will see, its failure or 'abjection'. Like the beam of light sent through a glass cube, refractive cinema breaks up and disperses the art or object it engages, splinters or deflects it in ways that leave the original work scattered and drifting across a world outside. Rather than the mi-metic idea of a mirror reflecting a world, these films set up a chain of mir-rors ... that disperses the image through a social space. Whether the object is other artistic media or other films, these films interrogate first and, most important, their own representational regime not so much to call attention to themselves in a more or less binary relationship but to call attention to the world as a multidimensional field where film must ultimately be thought [...] At the heart of many of these films – especially essay films about film – is then a critical reenactment of the cinematic representation itself as a way of reconceptualizing that process as an open-ended encounter with the world, as an act of criticism rather than commentary. (2011: 191)

Corrigan distinguishes two main categories within refractive cinema: the first would be composed of those films that 'reflect on art, literature, or other artis-tic practices as oblique engagements with cinematic practice', such as *Van Gogh* (Alain Resnais, 1948), *Vérités et mensonges (F for Fake)*, *L'hypothèse du tableau volé (Hypothesis on a Stolen Painting,* Raúl Ruiz, 1979), *Russian Ark* (Alexander Sokurov, 2002) or *Exit Through the Gift Shop* (Banksy, 2010) (2011: 182). The second category, in turn, specifically includes 'those films that engage in a more ostensibly direct relationship with another film or filmmaker', whether 'the tradi-tional films about the making of a film' – *Burden of Dreams* (Les Blank, 1982), *Hearts of Darkness: A Filmmaker's Apocalypse* (Fax Bahr, George Hickenlooper & Eleanor Coppola, 1991), *Lost in La Mancha* (Keith Fulton & Louis Pepe, 2002), etc. – or those films that aspire to enter theoretical or historiographical debates – *Tokyo-Ga* (Wim Wenders, 1985), *Histoire(s) du Cinema* (Jean-Luc Godard, 1988–98), *Une journée de Andrei Arsenevitch (One Day in the Life of Andrei Arsenevich,* Chris Marker, 1999), *De fem benspænd (The Five Obstructions,* Lars von Trier & Jørgen Leth, 2003) or *The Pervert's Guide to Cinema* (Sophie Fiennes & Slavoj Zizek, 2006) (ibid.). In the last case, filmmakers assume an in-between position which is simultaneously critical and creative: on the one hand, they locate themselves outside their object of study to interpret it from a personal perspective; while on the other (and unlike most film critics, historians and theorists) their discourse uses the same language that they are analysing. Accordingly, these film-makers are actually inside their object of study too, because they develop their argument through techniques and devices that somehow mirror those of their case studies.

A metafilm essay would then be a documentary on other films, filmmakers, genres or styles that expresses its main ideas visually, going beyond textual analy-sis to construct its discourse through audiovisual elements. These films consider that images are not simply reproductions or duplicates of the real, but new re-alities, partly because they are responsible for the configuration of our cognitive mapping: a key feature of hypermodern times is precisely the ability of images to condition and determine the perception of our everyday environment, as well as the perception of those places where we have never been. It does not even mat-ter who has produced those images: they may belong to a feature film, a docu-mentary, a TV programme, a commercial, a photographic report, an institutional campaign, a website or a YouTube video. In practice, they are interchangeable and almost anonymous, including ours, but never neutral: they always have an ideo-logical substrate that influences our worldview. Rather than giving rise to a paral-lel reality, the current omnipotence and omnipresence of images have established a set of mindscapes that have become an increasingly important part of our reality, as Arjun Appadurai and Michael Storper argued in the 1990s:

> The image, the imagined, the imaginary – these are all terms that direct us to something critical and new in global cultural processes: *the imagi-nation as a social practice.* No longer mere fantasy (opium for the masses whose real work is elsewhere), no longer simple escape (from a world de-fined principally by more concrete purposes and structures), no longer elite pastime (thus not relevant to the lives of ordinary people), and no longer mere contemplation (irrelevant for new forms of desire and subjec-tivity), the imagination has become an organized field of social practices, a form of work (in the sense of both labor and culturally organized prac-tice), and a form of negotiation between sites of agency (individuals) and globally defined fields of possibility. [...] The imagination is now central to all forms of agency, is itself a social fact, and is the key component of the new global order. (Appadurai 1996: 31)

Interpretations and constructed images of reality are now just as impor-tant as any 'real' material reality, because these interpretations and images are diffused and accepted and become the bases on which people act: they become real. (Storper 1997: 29)

In the same decade, these ideas were applied to urban studies by Edward Soja (1996), and their quick spread led Rob Lapsley to warn that 'it has become a cliché of contemporary writing that the city is constructed as much by images and representations as by the built environment, demographic shifts and patterns of capital investment' (1997: 187). Lapsley wrote this sentence in an essay included in the influential volume *The Cinematic City*, in which, a few pages later, James Hay defined this concept as 'a formation whose value to cities lies in the production of the past' (1997: 226). In addition to this primary function, cinematic cities are also replacing real ones as social constructs for their usual residents and occasional visitors, creating an aura of realness that goes beyond what real cities can actually offer, especially when their heyday has already gone. Both past and present are overshadowed by a timeless idea of what a city should be: for this reason, people who go to Hollywood Boulevard in search of film icons must stay within a few blocks, because if they walk too far east, they will find themselves in Thai Town. Wherever we go, nothing will be exactly as it is in films, but we have unconsciously assumed that mental image. Lipovetsky and Serroy consider that this process of replacement of real cities by cinematic clones is so advanced that 'many spheres of social life have ended up by imitating the film universe' (2009: 322; my translation). Metafilm essays would therefore be one more product derived from this triumph of the cinematic, although their in-between position, partly critical and partly creative, allows them to question this phenomenon.

Exploring the way in which the cinematic city has been created may seem a task for film fans, usually too obsessed with the accumulation of data, or film theorists, whose professional deformation forces them to seek some meaning in the data. Most filmmakers, however, combine these two approaches in their metafilm essays because they are, first and foremost, moviegoers who have their own subjective relationship with film history: for example, in *A Personal Journey with Martin Scorsese Through American Movies* (1995) and *Il mio viaggio in Italia* (*My Voyage to Italy*, 2001), Martin Scorsese speaks as much about cinema as about himself and his film tastes. Indeed, the choice of one film quote over another may often have more to do with personal issues than with the discourse needs. In this sense, the most abstract and intellectual metafilm essay – let us say, for instance, *Histoire(s) du Cinema* – always exposes the filmmaker's self regarding the issue (or the city) addressed in the film.

The final section of this book will analyse, in particular, the metafilmic strategies of two titles focused on the way Hollywood has historically represented the city of Los Angeles. The first, *The Decay of Fiction* (Pat O'Neill, 2002), is an avant-garde work that documents the last days of a symbolic place, the Ambassador Hotel, by means of a series of fictional reenactments inspired by film noir. The second, *Los Angeles Plays Itself* (Thom Andersen, 2003), is a metafilm essay composed of more than two hundred excerpts from other films that reflects on mainstream cinema's politics of representation. Both works explore the commonplaces of what Rafael Pizarro has termed 'the Hollywood Urban Imaginarium' (2005), challenging its visual monopoly from the margins of film industry. As we shall see below, the outcome of these two experiments is an ambiguous celebration of the cinematic city that cleverly warns against its systematic tendency towards fake and oblivion.

NOTE

1 *What's Up, Tiger Lily* is made from a Japanese spy film, *Kokusai himitsu keisatsu: Kagi no kagi* (*International Secret Police: Key of Keys*, Senkichi Taniguchi, 1965), while *Can Dialectics Break Bricks?* appropriates a Chinese martial arts film, *The Crush* (Kuang-chi Tu, 1972).

CHAPTER NINE

Inside Hollywood Film

Academic prose sometimes gives unexpected surprises to the reader, especially when its refined wording offers a glimpse of the writer's humanity. In this regard, the most remarkable feature of *America*, Jean Baudrillard's travelogue across the United States, is its shameless arrogance:

> Where the others spend their time in libraries, I spend mine in the deserts and on the roads. Where they draw their material from the history of ideas, I draw mine from what is happening now, from the life of the streets, the beauty of nature. This country is naive, so you have to be naive. Everything here still bears the marks of a primitive society: technologies, the media, total simulation (bio-, socio-, stereo-, video-) are developing in a wild state, in their original state. Insignificance exists on a grand scale and the desert remains the primal scene, even in the big cities. Inordinate space, a simplicity of language and character. [...] My hunting grounds are the deserts, the mountains, Los Angeles, the freeways, the Safeways, the ghost towns, or the downtowns, not lectures at the university. I know the deserts, their deserts, better than they do, since they turn their backs on their own space as the Greeks turned their backs on the sea, and I get to know more about the concrete, social life of America from the desert than I ever would from official or intellectual gatherings. (1988: 63)

Judging by these impressions, Baudrillard certainly had a good time on his American holidays. Such an exhibition of superiority does not seem the best way to understand a foreign country, but it must be recognised that Baudrillard managed quite well to synthesise the most obvious features of hyperreal America in a handful of aphorisms. Regarding urban experience, for example, he wrote one of the most quoted passages about the cinematic city:

The American city seems to have stepped right out of the movies. To grasp its secret, you should not, then, begin with the city and move inwards to the screen; you should begin with the screen and move outwards to the city. It is there that cinema does not assume an exceptional form, but simply invests the streets and the entire town with a mythical atmosphere. (1988: 56)

This idea has inspired almost as many researchers as city planners in the last twenty-five years. Nowadays, the model for reshaping urban space does not come from architectural theory anymore, but from film practice: the current political agenda is less concerned about the integral transformation of the built environment than about the aesthetic renewal of strategic locations. In fact, since the crisis of modernist approaches in urban planning, the city is no longer conceived as the sum of its parts, because it is much more profitable to break its unity and concentrate efforts and investments in isolated and limited spaces, downsizing the scope of action to the level of the film set. The city is thereby divided in increasingly smaller parts that gradually lose their connections to the point of becoming a scattered archipelago in which the old continuum is replaced by a sequential experience. This process seems to be especially advanced in Los Angeles due to its long tradition of urban ghettoisation, which operates at both ends of the socio-economic ladder, but also to the gradual appropriation of the cityscape by the film industry. For better or worse, the local government has definitely assumed the historical identification between Los Angeles and Hollywood, causing a reversal in their usual relationship: for decades, the image of the city was created inside studio lots, but since the 1980s, according to Tony Fitzmaurice, several parts of the city have begun to consciously mimic 'images from Hollywood's past in the name of urban renewal ... reshaping the physical fabric of the city itself into the simulation of a simulation' (2001: 21).

This is not exactly a novelty, given that the architectural heritage of Los Angeles has always been characterised by its eclecticism. In the 1920s, Grauman's Egyptian and Chinese Theaters were originally designed as fakes in which the ornamental elements of their façades did not correspond to their time and place. Half a century later, however, the same buildings reached the status of cultural monuments thanks to their condition as mythical venues for moviegoers and, above all, because they remained in place in a city with very few old buildings. In the 1960s, Kevin Lynch had already noticed that 'the fluidity of the environment and the absence of physical elements which anchor to the past are exciting and disturbing' (1960: 45), a perception that led him to diagnose a 'widespread, almost pathological, attachment to anything that had survived the upheaval' among the

Angelinos (1960: 42). Grauman's Egyptian and Chinese Theaters have benefited from these circumstances, insofar as they have passed from blatant simulations of exotic settings to authentic examples of the 1920s' fantastic architectures.

Following this logic, the postmodern revival of this style – the simulation of a simulation – should also be 'authentic' as a product of our time, in which the excess of hyper-awareness and the systematic abuse of quotes, tributes, plagiarism, remixes and mash-ups threaten to exhaust our creativity. A typical product of this kind of urban planning is the Hollywood and Highland Center, which has been described by Josh Stenger as 'a space wherein the gaze of the moviegoer, the shopper, and the tourist become interchangeable, where the spectacular overwhelms the mundane and where Hollywood-the-place can be rendered in stucco façades of Hollywood-the-cultural-myth' (2001: 69–70). In spots like this, Los Angeles becomes a city-spectacle as influenced by Hollywood as by Disneyland, a fantasy restricted to a few blocks where 'everything is tactile and visible, but it has been emptied of any deep meaning', as Carlos García Vázquez has said (2004: 79; my translation). Consequently, urban space undergoes a process of theming in which the spatialities and temporalities characteristic of leisure complexes have created a distorted perception of the city.

Once this point is reached, Baudrillard's theory about the precession of simulacra, based on the Borgesian metaphor of the map and the territory, finds its best expression: 'the territory no longer precedes the map, nor does it survive it. It is nevertheless the map that precedes the territory – precession of simulacra – that engenders the territory' (1994: 1). In Southern California, without going any further, the relation between the city and the territory is completely mediated by the cinematic, which would be the map that covers the territory, or rather the model that shapes what is supposed to be reality. Nevertheless, there have always been as many realities as observers, as the two films discussed below seem to suggest: first, *The Decay of Fiction* contrasts the material reality of the Ambassador Hotel ruins with the mental reality of its cinematic avatars; and then, *Los Angeles Plays Itself* looks for documentary revelations – that is, the real – in more than two hundred feature films – that is, the imaginary.

The Decay of Fiction: Ghosts of Film Noir

Pat O'Neill's creative personality is split into two different facets. On the one hand, he is an avant-garde filmmaker interested in exploring the filmic surface of multiplanar images; on the other, he is also an expert technician specialising in optical printing.[1] His career combines the production of more than twenty experimental works with the management of a successful special effects company,

Lookout Mountain Films, whose services have been required in mainstream films such as *Piranha* (Joe Dante, 1978), *Star Wars Episode V: The Empire Strikes Back* (Irvin Kershner, 1980), *Star Wars Episode VI: Return of the Jedi* (Richard Marquand, 1983), *Superman IV: The Quest for Peace* (Sidney J. Furie, 1987) and *The Game* (David Fincher, 1997). This blend of independent filmmaking and technical proficiency has earned him the nickname 'two-faced' (see De Bruyn 2004), although it is unclear who is Dr. Jekyll and who is Mr. Hyde: for decades, he has applied the findings of his experimental works to Hollywood features, using the income received from these jobs to finance new films and thus further his formal investigations.

David E. James has located O'Neill's artistic roots in four different traditions: Expressionism, Surrealism, abstract animation and structural film (2005: 439). His work, as Paul Arthur argues, 'operates in the gap between the hermetic and the demotic, between image-fragments whose significance remains obscure and iconography familiar enough be lodged in our cultural memorial banks' (2004: 67). Accordingly, his tendency to play with the usual narratives and archetypes of popular genres is quite remarkable: 'O'Neill's early films,' Arthur says, 'display the strongest affinities for sci-fi, the next group leans toward the western, while his latest projects explore formal and cultural resonances attached to film noir' (2004: 73). The western and film noir have shaped the imaginary of Los Angeles throughout the entire twentieth century, creating a cinematic city that is explicitly recalled in O'Neill's three feature films: *Water and Power* (1989), *Trouble in the Image* (1996) and *The Decay of Fiction* (2002). All of them, as James has pointed out, simultaneously address 'the medium of film, the history of the movies, and the geography in which the former became incarnate as the latter', exploring both the image and the landscape in search of clues that explain their historical interdependence in Southern California (2005: 439).

Water and Power, O'Neill best-known work, represents the urban experience through a kaleidoscopic editing of disjointed images. The film deals with the negative effects that Los Angeles's water policy has caused in the surrounding countryside, which has been exposed to accelerated desertification due to its systematic overexploitation for decades. Certain passages seem to have been inspired by the story of the Owens Valley – one of the main scenes of the California Water Wars in the 1910s and 1920s – but the narrative framework is so cryptic that it prevents any attempt at establishing a closed interpretation. Anyway, what is clear is that O'Neill reflects on the complementary nature of the California wilderness – the landscapes of the western – and the hidden places of the city – the usual setting of film noir. His way to visually match these spaces is to superimpose them in long dissolves that suggest their geological continuity, creating the impression that the city and the territory are actually embedded into one another. A similar effect is achieved thanks to the use of 'a specially designed computerized motion-control device that permitted O'Neill', as James has explained, 'to make very exact tracking and panning shots and to duplicate those motions exactly', thereby creating a visual palimpsest in which rural and urban landscapes are simultaneously shown through the same camera choreography (2005: 432). By means of these techniques, *Water and Power* raises the issue of the confusion between the map and the territory, or between the city and its representations, reaching the point of reducing Los Angeles to a series of western and film noir commonplaces. For this reason, the excerpts of *The Docks of New York* (Josef von Sternberg, 1928), *The Last Command* (Josef von Sternberg, 1928), *The Lady Confesses* (Sam Newfield, 1945) and *Detour* included in the film do not only serve to set a noir atmosphere, but rather to locate the audience in the domain of the simulacra.

The Decay of Fiction shares some features with *Water and Power*, such as its sense of place, the use of superimposed images and the abundance of film references. Its main novelties, however, are the spatial unity of the plot and the decision to organise most sequences around a few narrative strands. The setting of the film, the old Ambassador Hotel in Los Angeles, is its main subject and character, basically due to its nature as place of memory at a time in which it had already lost its functionality. In the following quote, Marsha Kinder offers a good summary of the accumulation of significant events that took place in the hotel during the seven decades that it was open, from 1921 to 1989:

> Built in 1920 on LA's 'Wilshire Corridor', the hotel helped redirect the city's urban sprawl from east to west, from downtown to the sea. Its glamorous Coconut Grove nightclub was the place where downtown power brokers first mingled with Hollywood stars, where Joan Crawford was discovered in a dance contest and Marilyn Monroe in a bathing-suit competition, and where many celebrities won their Oscar and Golden Globes. The hotel had permanent residents, like newscaster Walter Winchell, while others, like FBI chief J. Edgar Hoover visited every year. The hotel is now remembered primarily as the place where Robert Kennedy was assassinated while campaigning for the Democratic presidential nomination – a traumatic event that transformed the hotel's cultural capital and changed the course of American history. (2003: 356)

Paul Arthur has compared the hotel with 'the desert's urban double', because it is 'an oasis for the gathering of mythic as well as social significance' (2004: 75). Each guest has left there a tiny part of him or herself, contributing to both the physical erosion of the place and its preservation in the social imaginary. Hollywood, in turn, has used the Ambassador Hotel as location for many features, television programmes and music videos, such as *The Graduate* (Mike Nichols, 1967), *Pretty Woman* (Garry Marshall, 1990), *True Romance* (Tony Scott, 1993), *Fear and Loathing in Las Vegas* (Terry Gilliam, 1998), *Catch Me If You Can* (Steven Spielberg, 2002) and *Bobby* (Emilio Estevez, 2006), to name but a few. These titles have already documented the place – both the real and imaginary place, as Edward Soja would say – but *The Decay of Fiction* seeks to go further: this time, O'Neill looks for the *genius loci* of the hotel in both its physical ruins and the echoes of the narratives that took place there.

The first shot of the film is a time-lapse image of an empty and derelict room: the paint has flaked off, the windows are broken and the wind slowly moves the curtains. In a few seconds, the light changes from dawn to dusk, establishing the guiding metaphor for the film: the decline of the Ambassador Hotel is preferentially depicted at twilight, because that hour symbolises a liminal state between day and night, decay and dematerialisation, presence and absence, existence and non-existence. That is the time in which 'the ghosts of long-departed guests', as James has called them, can return to the hotel, which become the 'crime scene' for some and a place of memory for most (2005: 436). This memorial dimension has been highlighted by the filmmaker himself in his statements about the film:

> The film takes place in a building about to be destroyed, whose walls contain (by dint of association) a huge burden of memory: cultural and personal, conscious and unconscious. To make the film was to trap a few of its characters and some of their dialogue, casting them together within the confines of the site. The structure and its stories are decaying together, and each seems to be a metaphor for the other. (O'Neill in Rosenbaum 2003b)

Image 9.1: *The Decay of Fiction*, the translucent guests of the Ambassador Hotel

By means of his optical printer, O'Neill explores the formal possibilities of the visual palimpsest to bring life back to the building: first, he documented the appearance of its ruins at the turn of the century, filming them in colour, and then on these spaces he superimposed black-and-white images of a series of translucent figures that seem to have been endlessly repeating the same kind of dialogues and situations for half a century (Image 9.1). These characters, played by contemporary actors, represent the former inhabitants of the place, who come to life thanks to fictional stories that imitate the film noir narratives of the mid-to-late 1940s and early 1950s. The film, however, does not develop a linear plot, but several unfinished micro-narratives that form a collage of film references. In principle, everything seems familiar to the audience in spite of its artificial nature, although most sequences do not refer to any particular title, except for those that visually or aurally refer to *Detour*, *Possessed* (Curtis Bernhardt, 1947), *His Kind of Woman* (John Farrow, 1951), *Sudden Fear* (David Miller, 1952) or *The Big Combo* (Joseph H. Lewis, 1955), among other noirs. The main source materials for *The Decay of Fiction* are then snatches of 'half-remembered' and 'half-imagined' films, as James has described them (2005: 436), a particular mindscape evoked from the very title, as the filmmaker has revealed:

> I scribbled the words 'The Decay of Fiction' on the back of a notebook almost 40 years ago, tore it off and framed it 15 years later, and have wanted ever since to make a film to fit its ready-made description. To me it refers to the common condition of stories partly remembered, films partly seen, texts at the margins of memory, disappearing like a book left outside on the ground to decompose back into the earth. (O'Neill in Rosenbaum 2003b)

Inside this mindscape, the characters are always in trouble: both guests and staff are involved one way or another in suspicious activities, from coercion and betrayal to arguments and, who knows, perhaps murders. All of them are imbued with an aura of mystery and secrecy, and some have 'names, backstories, tangled relationships [and] even individual nightmares', as Arthur has noted (2004: 75). The *dramatis personae* includes the manager of the hotel, Jack, who seems to be the main character; a few guests who have their own narratives, like a couple of honeymooners or an elderly woman who lives in the hotel under the care of a nurse; the maids, waitresses, cooks, bellboys and the rest of the staff, who often serve as witness-narrators; the entertainers, torch singers and other performers of the Coconut Grove nightclub; some people who run their business in the hotel, such as a psychoanalyst or several prostitutes; and finally, as it could not be otherwise, the main couple of film noir, the crooks and the cops. These archetypes repeat situations seen a thousand times in classical films: a chase along a corridor, the search of a membership list, the removal of a body found in a room, etc. They embody the film imaginary associated with the place, an idea that had already appeared in other urban documentaries, such as *A Cidade de Cassiano* (*Cassiano's City*, Edgar Pêra, 1991) or *Shotgun Freeway: Drives Through Lost L.A* (Morgan Neville & Harry Pallenberg, 1995).

The first of these two films is a short documentary made for an exhibition about Cassiano Branco, Portugal's best-known modernist architect. Since one of his main works was a movie theatre, the Eden Cinema in Lisbon, experimental filmmaker Edgar Pêra decided to depict it in a staged sequence in which a man chases another from its art-deco lobby to its rooftop, thereby linking the building with its original purpose: to give life to all kinds of cinematic fantasies. Later on, the same idea was used by Morgan Neville and Harry Pallenberg in *Shotgun Freeway*, a talking-heads documentary about Los Angeles. Most of the film consists of on-location interviews with local personalities: for instance, Mike Davis speaks from the concrete channel of the Los Angeles River, Buck Henry in front of a dressing room mirror, and James Ellroy while pretending to burgle a house at night. Nevertheless, there is a leitmotif that fills the editing gaps: the presence of two fictional characters, a private eye and a *femme fatale* dressed in the fashion of the 1940s, who appear in different places of the city throughout the documentary. The private eye spends most of the footage taking pictures of certain places in which he later sees their current appearance, as if in a flash-forward, and the *femme fatale* behaves like a ghost that symbolises the spirit of the city. The ethnic dimension of the cast's choice (the man is played by an Anglo-Saxon actor, while the woman is embodied by a Latina actress) places these archetypes within Southern California history, according to which Anglo-Saxon settlers inherited Latino landlords' properties by marrying their daughters (see Davis 1990: 106–7). In this case, film references introduce a subtle reflection on the history of the territory, because they mirror the racial evolution of its population.

The metafilmic dimension of *The Decay of Fiction* also pervades the soundtrack, in which the voices of certain film noir stars (Kirk Douglas, Robert Mitchum, Joan Crawford, Dana Andrews, etc.) can be heard as if they were an EVP. Indeed, many invisible actions are represented through soundscapes that seem echoes of the past: the bell of the elevators, the sound of running water, a few telephone conversations in empty rooms, guffaws, shouts, passing cars... Even Bobby Kennedy's assassination is recalled through a radio broadcast while images show the empty Embassy Room, the place where he gave his last speech after winning the California Democratic primary election; this time, the translucent extras will only appear after the tragedy, playing the onlookers who saw how the politician's wounded body was evacuated on a stretcher.

Most sounds, as Jonathan Rosenbaum has pointed out, are 'pitched at the periphery of normal perception, so that even when they connote dramatic or violent action, they seem to be on the verge of evaporating' (2003b). The resulting effect contributes to the impression that the Ambassador Hotel is haunted by ghosts who are doomed to repeat familiar dialogues. To give an example, here is a transcription of the last conversation in the film, in which a couple splits up:

> Woman (*talking on the phone*): Hi, I'm checking out the room 1104. Yes.
> I'll be done in ten minutes.
> Man (*entering the frame*): Hey, hey, what's this?
> Woman (*to the man*): What it looks like … I have to go.
> Man (*trying to embrace her*): Come on, can we talk?
> Woman (*angry*): I think we've done enough talking and you have not said
> anything yet.
> Man (*trying to kiss her*): But … I love you!
> Woman (*sad*): Are you joking?
> Man (*offended*): Yeah, yeah … it's joke, just words.
> Woman (*laconic*): That's what I thought. Just words…

This kind of dialogue helps to create a particular tone and mood that condition the audience's perception of the place: after having inspired many film locations, the Ambassador Hotel finally became a real film location where everything echoes past events. In this sense, *The Decay of Fiction* follows the trail of two previous works that reflected on the issue of the eternal return: the short novel *La Invención de Morel* (Adolfo Bioy Casares, 1940) and the film *L'année dernière à Marienbad* (*Last Year at Marienbad*, Alain Resnais, 1961). In Bioy Casares's book, the narrator falls in love with a woman who is actually a spectre produced by a mysterious device, the same as other people that he meets on the island where he lives. All of them had been recorded long time ago by the invention that names the novel, which might be a futuristic form of holographic cinema. *Last Year at Marienbad*, in turn, presents a series of characters apparently trapped in a luxury hotel where a man approaches a woman and keeps trying to convince her that they have already met, something that is never clear if it really happened. Resnais and his screenwriter, Alain Robbe-Grillet, systematically explore all the possible developments of that situation to the point that the man's story becomes a premonition of what will finally happen, as well as a memory of what might have already happened.

Both *La Invención de Morel* and *Last Year at Marienbad*, as well as *The Shining* (Stanley Kubrick, 1980) and obviously *The Decay of Fiction*, are based on the idea of the endless repetition of previous events within a closed space, where the time of the story has first stopped and then prolonged until a present that is actually a variation of the past. In these places, according to Arthur, 'history has collapsed, time is definitely out of joint, and we can no longer parse substance from illusion' (2004: 74). Consequently, the Ambassador Hotel is depicted as 'a place of both narrative and analytic possibility', the main virtue that Charlotte Brunsdon attributes to cinematic empty spaces such as 'bombsites, demolition and building sites, parks, temporary car-parks, derelict warehouses and docks':

> These spaces are often the site of what we might call a 'hesitation' in the cinematic image, when it can be read either within the fictional world of the narrative, or as part of extra-filmic narratives about the history of the material city, or, more formally as a self-reflexive moment of urban landscape. (2010: 91)

In *The Decay of Fiction* the Ambassador Hotel admits these three levels of reading: regarding the first, it is the fictional setting of different individual stories that take advantage of what Kinder describes as 'the meta-narrative function of the inn as stopping place in picaresque fiction' (2003: 357); furthermore, it also plays itself as a vestige of another era, which coincides with what Gilles Lipovetsky and Jean Serroy call 'classical modernity' (2009: 17); and finally its ruins at the turn of the century work as a spatio-temporal landmark of the evolution of Los Angeles's cityscape. In this last sense, the abandoned building chronicles several stages in local history: its heyday, when Wilshire Boulevard provided a common ground for the meeting of Downtown, Hollywood and Westside residents; its decline, when the urban crisis of the 1970s and 1980s hit the city and especially this area; and its renewal, when the neighbourhood became 'the booming Koreatown', an expression coined by Korean American sociologist Eui-Young Yu (1992) after the 1992 riots, although that transformation arrived too late for the Ambassador Hotel.

Dirk De Bruyn has also interpreted the building as 'a metaphor for the camera itself (a monolithic camera obscura which O'Neill intermittently occupied and explored during the six years of the film's stop/start making)' (2004). This approach suggests that it is the hotel that ultimately creates its ghost and narratives, even when they are beyond real referents: for instance, the naked spectres who take part in an orgy towards the end of the film actually come from the filmmaker's unconscious, as James has noted (2005: 436), but even so they are summoned by the *genius loci* of the place. The way O'Neill understands the creative process opens the door to the expression of his own subjectivity: 'I like to work within the gaps between reality and story, to look at what is going on around the story, its context, and to make that a part of my conversation with the audience' (in Rosenbaum 2003b). The presence of 'my' in this statement reveals the perspective from which *The Decay of Fiction* was conceived: the film is a personal interpretation of the cultural significance of the Ambassador Hotel that uses film noir archetypes as references suggested by the place itself in order to establish a playful dialogue with the audience. This subjective dimension is reinforced by the inclusion in the footage of an imperceptible self-portrait of the filmmaker: 'in the middle of the film', James explains, 'we find him, sitting in one of these empty salons, typing, until his attention is drawn away by a ghostly woman' (2005: 438). Arthur has said that O'Neill usually appears in his films as a way of playing with the anonymity of avant-garde filmmakers (2004: 68), but this self-portrait in particular is also a voluntary inscription within the fictional world: the filmmaker depicts himself as a demiurge who has been haunted by the place, its ghosts and its 'huge burden of memory' (O'Neill in Rosenbaum 2003b).

In conclusion, *The Decay of Fiction* uses film references as mediums to return to the Ambassador Hotel's heyday just before its dematerialisation, thereby addressing both its past and present. This device brings to the foreground two related issues: the way 'old movies continue to circulate in consciousness' (Arthur 2004: 75), and the way they shape our current perception of urban space. Nowadays, that building is a missing landmark in Los Angeles – it was demolished between September 2005 and January 2006 – but it still stands in the local imaginary thanks to its film appearances. O'Neill's time-lapse shots captured the erosion of time on its ruins, sometimes establishing a visual contrast between its architecture and the downtown skyscrapers, which represent a city to which the hotel no longer belongs. Therefore, all those who want to visit this anachronistic place again will have to look for it in film heritage.

Los Angeles Plays Itself: A Critical Tour Through Cinematic LA

Thom Andersen belongs to the same generation and film milieu as James Benning and Pat O'Neill: they were born around 1940, became experimental filmmakers under the influence of structural film, and have taught at the California Institute of the Arts (CalArts) in recent decades.[2] Over the years, their prime interest has shifted from formal concerns to social issues, although Andersen's works have always kept a 'metafilmic self-consciousness associated with structural film' (James 2005: 420). According to Daniel Ribas, most of his films are explicitly focused on 'the way cinema alters our perception of reality' (2012: 89), especially three of his four features: *Eadweard Muybridge, Zoopraxographer* (1974), *Red Hollywood* (Thom Andersen & Noël Burch, 1996) and *Los Angeles Plays Itself*. After the last of these, Andersen's growing interest in urban space has led him to film his own city symphony, the short *Get Out of the Car* (2010), and a documentary on the work of Portuguese architect Eduardo Souto de Moura, *Reconverção* (*Reconversion*, 2012), made the year after he was awarded the Pritzker Architecture Prize. All these films combine a historical approach with a subjective sense of place, which ultimately locates Andersen's spatial and metafilmic reflections within the tradition of the essay film.

The analytical device of *Los Angeles Plays Itself* was previously tested in *Red Hollywood*, a work that was already composed of film quotes: it consists of a few interviews with some blacklisted screenwriters, such as Paul Jarrico, Ring Lardner Jr. and Abraham Polonsky, and hundreds of excerpts from fifty-three Hollywood features made by Communist militants and sympathisers in the 1930s and 1940s. Both this documentary and its published version, *Les Communistes de Hollywood: Autre chose que des martyrs* (Thom Andersen & Noël Burch, 1994), are guided by a didactic impulse that seeks to restore the blacklisted people's place in film history, but its commentary also draws attention to progressive topics that later disappeared from mainstream cinema, such as solidarity among workers, support for the underprivileged or the claim of gender equality.

Unfortunately, Andersen and Burch did not own the rights of the films that they quoted, so they had to make *Red Hollywood* as a private videotape and then distribute it clandestinely. For this reason, this work, like *Los Angeles Plays Itself*, still lacks an official edition that can be legally acquired: they are, and will probably be for many years, bootleg films because the studios are not willing to lend their films for a nominal fee.[3] Accordingly, the images included in these two works actually come from Andersen's personal videotape collection, from which he usually takes short clips to show in his film classes:

> The teaching in small classes that I do in graduate seminars is based on lectures with movie clips. I've been working that way for a long time, since VHS started, but certainly, at least since I started at CalArts in 1989/90. [*Los Angeles Plays Itself*] began as a similar project. A talk – not for the school, but for the public – with movie clips that could be presented. [...] It's a lot of work to cue in all the movies on VHS and prepare all the clips, so I thought of making just a little movie, so it would all be there. Whenever somebody was interested I could offer it to them. But it changed. It transcended those beginnings. It turned into something a little more than an illustrated lecture, although I'm sure there are those who regard it as such. (Andersen in Ribas 2012: 92)

The main idea of *Los Angeles Plays Itself* is to read feature films as indirect and unpremeditated documents of their time: '*If we can appreciate documentaries for their dramatic qualities,*' the narrator says in the prologue, '*perhaps we can appreciate fiction films for their documentary revelations.*' From this initial statement, Andersen claims the memorial value of those titles that preserve the real image of missing places, inasmuch as *'images of things that aren't there any more mean a lot to those of us who live in Los Angeles'*. Moreover, he highlights the significance of film locations themselves by arguing that *'in a city where only a few buildings are more than a hundred years old, where most traces of the city's history have been effaced, a place can become a historic landmark because it was once a movie location'*. The accuracy with which he locates old images in the cityscape is comparable to the geographical precision of Leon Smith's and John Bengston's guides of film locations (see Smith 1988, 1993; Bengston 1999, 2006, 2011). Nevertheless, *Los Angeles Plays Itself* is much more than a plain description of the way Hollywood has depicted the main landmarks of the city. Beyond this approach, Andersen attempts to link the setting of a film to its meaning in order to expose the power discourses that lie behind many titles, an idea that was later developed by Alain Silver and James Ursini in their book *L.A. Noir: The City as a Character* (2005). Consequently, as Michael Chanan has pointed out, 'Andersen shifts the way we look at these images, defamiliarising them by deconstructing the language of screen space which produced them' (2007: 77)

After five years of work, Andersen 'published' the results of his research in a film instead of a book, although he later curated a retrospective on the same issue for the Austrian Film Museum and the Vienna International Film Festival (see Andersen 2008). Despite the logical similarities in terms of content between the film's commentary and the introduction to the retrospective's catalogue, both texts differ in style and, above all, in their way of creating meaning: the introduction is much more academic and digressive, because it is a text to be read; while the commentary is based on a continuous dialogue with images that goes beyond the format of an illustrated lecture. Thus, Andersen sometimes introduces certain sequences, but most times the quoted films directly answer his words or vice versa, as in a screwball comedy. Indeed, in many passages of *Los Angeles Plays Itself*, there is more information in the images than in the commentary: a single shot can contain the title of the quoted film, the presence of a famous performer, the mood and iconography associated with a given time and genre, some detail that allows the audience to identify the film location, and a fictional action that provides the setting with a certain meaning. Taking this polysemy into account, the discourse of the film is produced by both the commentary and the selection and editing of images. In this regard, it is significant that Andersen did not sign his work by means of the usual expression 'directed by'. Instead, he chose to write in the opening credits 'text, research and production by Thom Andersen', thereby emphasising the differences between these three activities.

The working hypothesis of the film assumes that there may be more or less truthful representations, but most are actually misrepresentations, as implied by the last sentence of the prologue: '*We might wonder if the movies have ever really depicted Los Angeles.*' And what about *Los Angeles Plays Itself*? Are its meta-filmic strategies a truthful representation? In principle, its fragmented nature has something in common with the city: it is a film made of pieces that attempts to depict a city made of pieces. Zapping from one film to another seems, therefore, an appropriate technique to convey the multiple and disjointed experience of a place where Thai Town is just north of Little Armenia. One of the chapters of Soja's book *Postmodern Geographies: The Reassertion of Space in Critical Social Theory* is precisely entitled 'It All Comes Together in Los Angeles', because there the real city is able to mimic anywhere in the world, just like the cinematic city:

> One can find in Los Angeles not only the high technology industrial com-
> plexes of Silicon Valley and the erratic sunbelt economy of Houston, but
> also the far-reaching industrial decline and bankrupt urban neighbour-
> hoods of rust-belted Detroit or Cleveland. There is a Boston in Los Ange-
> les, a Lower Manhattan and a South Bronx, a São Paulo and a Singapore.
> There may be no other comparable urban region which presents so vividly
> such a composite assemblage and articulation of urban restructuring pro-
> cesses. Los Angeles seems to be conjugating the recent history of capitalist
> urbanization in virtually all its inflectional forms. (1989: 193)

Andersen certainly feels at home in this urban chaos: both Los Angeles (his home-town) and the movies (his job) are his natural element, his place in the world. Hence the double reading of *Los Angeles Plays Itself*: on the one hand, it is a film mapping of LA; and on the other hand, it is also a personal mapping of meaning-ful films and places. This double coding is established from the very beginning of the commentary: '*This is the city: Los Angeles, California. They make movies here. I live here. Sometimes I think that gives me the right to criticize the ways movies depict my city. I know it's not easy. The city is big. The image is small.*' The use of the first-person commentary will continue throughout the entire film, blending objective information and subjective opinions without privileging one el-ement over another. The outcome, as already happened in many other case studies in this book, is a film portrait of a lived city, although this time it is not a direct re-cord of the filmmaker's urban experience, but a compilation of his film experience of the city, that is, a mediated experience. The difference between Andersen and most viewers lies in his gaze toward urban space: while most of us have a foreign gaze toward Los Angeles – especially those who have ever been there – Andersen in turn has a native gaze, which allows him to recognise many film locations and link them to his memories of these places. This is the reason why he especially appreciates those films in which *'what we see is what was really there'*, as he says regarding *Kiss Me Deadly* (Robert Aldrich, 1955).

Contrary to what may seem, the narrator is not Andersen, but his friend and fellow filmmaker Encke King. Why did Andersen not use his own voice to read such a subjective text? For once, the reason has no serious ontological implications:

> Encke King is an old friend of mine. He was a student at CalArts a long time ago, when I was first teaching there. I've always liked his voice. He knows me pretty well. I thought he could do a good job of playing me. I don't like hearing the sound of my own voice. A lot of people are like that, maybe most. Especially when you're editing narration and have to listen to someone talk constantly. It would have been a drag to edit my own voice. (Andersen in Erickson 2004)

Despite the fact that King is identified as narrator in the opening credits, only those who personally know Andersen can notice this splitting in the voice of the documentary: we hear Andersen's words, but we do not hear him. Accordingly, *Los Angeles Plays Itself* can be regarded as a case of explicit presence of the author, because the filmmaker directly intervenes in the plot, although he does so by means of a stand-in. This option does not alter the subjective component of the commentary, and it even improves its metafilmic connections: King's diction, as well as Andersen's literary style, recalls the tone of hard-boiled fiction and film noir in a prime example of how documentaries internalise certain tropes of fiction. In fact, the way the commentary interrogates the images has been compared by David E. James with the hard-bitten attitude of private eyes such as Sam Spade, Philip Marlowe, Mike Hammer or Lew Archer (2005: 421).

Like most detective stories, *Los Angeles Plays Itself* strives to bring to light what is beneath the surface, which in this case is an elusive city: '*Los Angeles may be the most photographed city in the world, but it's one of the least photogenic,*' Andersen (actually King) says. '*It's not Paris or New York. In New York, everything is sharp and in-focus, as if seen through a wide-angle lens. In smoggy cities like Los Angeles, everything dissolves into the distance, and even stuff that's close-up seems far off.*' This description puts LA within the category of what Ackbar Abbas calls 'the exorbitant city', which is 'neither securely graspable nor fully representable' (2003: 145). Faced with the inability of cinema to depict his hometown, Andersen suggests some causes that lead his analysis toward the field of urban planning and local history:

Los Angeles is hard to get right, maybe because traditional public space has been largely occupied by the quasi-private space of moving vehicles. It's elusive, just beyond the reach of an image. It's not a city that spread outward from a centre as motorised transportation supplanted walking, but a series of villages that grew together, linked from the beginning by railways and then motor roads. The villages became neighbourhoods and their boundaries blurred, but they remain separate provinces, joined together primarily by mutual hostility and a mutual disdain for the city's historic centre.

In order to overcome these limitations, *Los Angeles Plays Itself* quotes up to 210 different films, as well as a TV series, *Dragnet* (Jack Webb, 1951–59 and 1967–70). Depending on the needs of the argument, the quotes can either be single shots or complete sequences: sometimes, the development of an idea may require a dozen quotes, while other times it needs longer excerpts. These are not the only visual materials of the film, of course: there are also a hundred original shots, two dozens of newspaper clippings, eight old pictures of missing places, a few shots of non-fiction footage taken from television, newsreels and other documentaries, and even an excerpt from Ricky Martin's music video *Vuelve* (Wayne Isham, 1998). Perhaps some statistics, such as the distribution of films by decade and genre, may be useful to understand what kind of cinematic city is depicted in *Los Angeles Plays Itself.*

Table 9.1: Film Quotes by Decades

Decade	Number of Films	Percentage
1910s	1	0.47%
1920s	1	0.47%
1930s	10	4.74%
1940s	26	12.32%
1950s	24	11.37%
1960s	15	7.11%
1970s	24	11.37%
1980s	44	20.85%
1990s	62	29.38%
2000s	4	1.90%

Source: My Own Elaboration

Table 9.2: Film Quotes by Genre

Genre	Number of Films	Percentage
Drama	38	18.01%
Thriller	31	14.69%
Crime	30	14.22%
Film Noir	30	14.22%
Action	21	9.95%
Sci-Fi	21	9.95%
Comedy	20	9.48%
Disaster	6	2.84%
Horror	4	1.90%
Musical	4	1.90%
Avant-Garde	2	0.95%
Documentary	2	0.95%
TV Series	1	0.47%
Porn	1	0.47%

Source: My Own Elaboration

Half of the quotes come from films made in the twenty-five years prior to the release of *Los Angeles Plays Itself*. This overrepresentation of the 1980s and 1990s is firstly due to the temporal proximity of these decades: postmodern films were easier to find in VHS at the beginning of the 2000s than silent, classical or modern titles, and they were also more recognisable for contemporary audiences. Furthermore, this preference for recent features also reflects the tendency of postmodern cinema to appropriate previous references, ideas and film locations as if they had never been filmed before. Regarding the other periods, classical film is mainly represented by film noirs, and modern film by both local neorealism and titles by foreign filmmakers in Los Angeles. Only silent film is almost completely absent, partly because these films were mostly made inside the studios.

There are some genres that are more represented than others, of course, although many are interrelated. The two main blocks correspond, firstly, to thrillers, crime film and film noir, and secondly, to action, science fiction, disaster and horror movies. Dramas and comedies are well represented, unlike the musical, whose presence is purely anecdotal. Finally, other genres are included simply as oddities, such as gay porn cinema, avant-garde film or even documentary film.

In this selection, the dominant genres broadly coincide with the five concepts developed by Erwan Higuinen and Olivier Joyard in the encyclopaedia *La ville au cinéma*'s entry about Los Angeles: they speak about '*ville noire*', '*ville studio*', '*ville d'exil*', '*ville d'action*' and '*ville sans centre*', terms that may be translated, respectively, as 'noir city', 'studio city', 'city of exile', 'city of action' and 'city without a centre' (2005: 449–57). Obviously, the noir city comes from film noir, the studio city from the films about the making of other films, the city of exile from the titles directed by foreign filmmakers in Los Angeles, the city of action from postmodern thrillers and action movies, and the city without a centre from the multi-protagonist films of the 1990s and 2000s.

Not all significant works of these genres are included in *Los Angeles Plays Itself*: a few notable absences are, for instance, *Singin' in the Rain* (Stanley Donen & Gene Kelly, 1952), *Beverly Hills Cop* (Martin Brest, 1984), *Pulp Fiction* (Quentin Tarantino, 1994), *Magnolia* (Paul Thomas Anderson, 1999) and *Mulholland Dr.* (David Lynch, 2001). The reasons for these oversights are multiple: Andersen decided not to include any film about the entertainment industry unless he could approach it from another perspective; he did not always find something new to say about certain titles; or simply he was not always inspired, as he himself has admitted (in Erickson 2004).[4] Considering these limitations, *Los Angeles Plays Itself* might include many more quotes, but then it would be redundant or lose its punch. The only films that Andersen has openly regretted not having had the opportunity to quote are some recent documentaries that grant visibility to people who seldom appear in Hollywood features, such as *Hoover Street Revival* (Sophie Fiennes, 2002), *Bastards of the Party* (Cle Shaheed Sloan, 2005), *Leimert Park: The Story of a Village in South Central Los Angeles* (Jeannette Lindsay, 2006), *South Main* (Kelly Parker, 2008) and *The Garden* (Scott Hamilton Kennedy, 2008), which he considers 'the best films about Los Angeles in the past ten years' (2008: 22).

The most frequently quoted title is *To Live and Die in L.A.* (William Friedkin, 1985), which appears up to seven times, but Andersen does not go into detail about it: he just uses it as example of something else, not as one of the works that explain the city. The films that receive most 'screen share' would rather be *Double Indemnity* (Billy Wilder, 1944), *Rebel Without a Cause* (Nicholas Ray, 1955), *Kiss Me Deadly*, *The Exiles* (Kent MacKenzie, 1961), *Chinatown* (Roman Polanski, 1974), *Blade Runner* (Ridley Scott, 1982), *Who Framed Roger Rabbit* (Robert Zemekis, 1988), *L.A. Confidential* (Curtis Hanson, 1997) and the TV series *Dragnet*. Their analyses are located in the second and third part of the film, once the commentary has replaced its initial architectural approach with a more sociological one.

Los Angeles Plays Itself is divided into a prologue and three chapters, which are respectively entitled 'the city as background', 'the city as character' and 'the city as subject'. The first presents Los Angeles as a scattered collection of film locations that not always represent the real city, but *the city with no name*, a stand-in for anywhere in the world. The second explains how that nameless city became Los Angeles thanks to certain noirs that developed an accurate sense of place, such as *Double Indemnity* or *Kiss Me Deadly*. Finally, the third is devoted to works that explore local history in search of those unfortunate events that spoiled the Southern California dream, from the construction of the Los Angeles Aqueduct that deprived the Owens Valley of its water resources (the back-story in *Chinatown*) to the Los Angeles Police Department (LAPD) corruption and paranoid style in the 1950s, which was unintentionally revealed by *Dragnet* and later reenacted in *L.A. Confidential*. These intersections between local history and fictional plots express a nostalgia for *'what might have been'* that Andersen describes as *'crocodile tears'*, because these stories replace the public history of the city with a secret one. This three-act structure leads Andersen's discourse from the particular to the general, from the urban surface to the city's unconscious and, above all, from the 'representations of space' to the 'representational spaces', to use Henri Lefebvre's terms (1991: 33, 38–9).

In Los Angeles, as Andersen argues in the first chapter, the making of a film leaves traces in both its urban layout and the memory of its residents: *'plaques and signs mark the sites of former movie studios'*, *'streets and parks are named for movie stars'*, and even *'some buildings that look functional are permanent movie sets'*. Through this dynamic, certain places have become civic monuments after having appeared in a successful film, which may provide them a fleeting fame and even ensure their preservation. Andersen uses visual enumerations to review the film career of well-known landmarks that not always play themselves, such as the Bradbury Building, Frank Lloyd Wright's Ennis House or Union Station, as well as those that do so, from the City Hall or the Griffith Planetarium to the four-level freeway interchange or the Hollywood Sign. The full list also includes ordinary spaces like *'Circus Liquor at Burbank and Vineland'* or *'Pink's Hot Dogs at La Brea and Melrose'*, which Andersen consciously puts on the same level as glamorous landmarks. The film is pervaded by this kind of joke, which actually challenge the most annoying and malignant lies of mainstream film: according to Andersen, *'to someone who knows Los Angeles only from movies, it might appear that everyone who has a job lives in the hills or at the beach. The dismal flatland between is the province of the lumpen proletariat.'* That is to say that Hollywood has systematically favoured the two urban ecologies that have historically been identified with the way of life of the most affluent residents of the city: 'Surfurbia' and the 'Foothills', as Reyner Banham named them in the early 1970s

(2009: 19–37, 77–91). On the contrary, the space inhabited by the majority of the population, the 'Plains of Id', is only visible as a bland and uniform backdrop in the carscapes filmed from Banham's four ecology: 'Autopia' (2009: 143–59, 195–204). Andersen accuses these commonplaces of cheapening the real city, giving as examples Hollywood's inability to talk about an environment other than its own, or its tendency to denigrate the local heritage of modernist residential architecture '*by casting many of these houses as the residences of movie villains*'.

Glamorous landmarks are what Lefebvre described as 'representations of space', but their images can give rise to 'representational spaces', especially when they have disappeared from the urban surface. In these cases, Andersen claims the memorial value of those films that recorded missing places at the time in which they still stood, because they allow the audience to return there, if only in fiction. Moreover, *Los Angeles Plays Itself* also shows the evolution of everyday spaces that have to be constantly rebuilt in order to adapt to changing patterns of consumption: '*The image of an obsolete gas station or grocery store,*' Andersen says, '*can evoke the same kind of nostalgia we feel for any commodity whose day has passed.*' Again, the filmmaker matches high and low culture, represented here by architectural heritage and ephemeral buildings, inasmuch as he considers that their differences dissolve once they have been incorporated into popular memory.

One of the most poignant passages of *Los Angeles Plays Itself* is the sequence devoted to Bunker Hill, in which the history of the neighbourhood is re-enacted through less than a dozen titles: *The Unfaithful* (Vincent Sherman, 1947), *Criss Cross* (Robert Siodmak, 1949), *Shockproof* (Douglas Sirk, 1949), *The Glenn Miller Story* (Anthony Mann, 1954), *Kiss Me Deadly*, *Indestructible Man* (Jack Pollexfen, 1956), *Bunker Hill 1956* (Kent MacKenzie, 1956), *The Exiles*, *The Omega Man* (Boris Sagal, 1971), *Night of the Comet* (Thom Eberhardt, 1984) and *Virtuosity*

Images 9.2 & 9.3: Bunker Hill in *Kiss Me Deadly* (top) and *The Exiles* (bottom)

(Brett Leonard, 1995) (Images 9.2 & 9.3). From these films, Andersen summarises its process of decline and subsequent renewal in four stages: the starting point is the late 1940s, when Bunker Hill represented '*a solid working-class neighborhood, a place where a guy could take his girl home to meet his mother*'; then, by the mid-1950s, it became '*a neighborhood of rooming houses where a man who knows too much might hole up or hide out'*. Later, between the 1960s and 1970s, its physical destruction was documented by the post-apocalyptic dystopia *The Omega Man*; and finally, from the 1980s, its rebirth as a financial and arts district looks like *'a simulated city'* where nothing is real. This narrative largely coincides with Mike Davis's account of the same process, which was precisely written during the making of *Los Angeles Plays Itself*:

> According to the 1940 Census, [Bunker Hill's] population increased almost twenty percent during the Depression as it provided the cheapest housing for downtown's casual workforce as well as for pensioners, disabled war veterans, Mexican and Filipino immigrants, and men whose identities were best kept in shadow. Its nearly two thousand dwellings ranged from oil prospectors' shacks and turn-of-the-century tourist hotels to the decayed but still magnificent Queen Anne and Westlake mansions of the city's circa-1880 elites. Successive Works Progress Administration and city housing commission reports chronicled its dilapidation (sixty percent of structures were considered 'dangerous'), arrest rates (eight times the city average), health problems (tuberculosis and syphilis), and drug culture (the epicenter of marijuana and cocaine use). Yet grim social statistics failed to capture the district's *favela-like* community spirit, its multiracial tolerance, or its closed-mouth unity against the police. [...] A few years after the release of *Kiss Me Deadly,* the wrecking balls and bulldozers began to systematically destroy the homes of ten thousand Bunker Hill residents. [...] A few Victorian landmarks, like Angel's Flight, were carted away as architectural nostalgia, but otherwise an extraordinary history was promptly razed to the dirt and the shell-shocked inhabitants, mostly old and indigent, pushed across the moat of the Harbor Freeway to die in the tenements of Crown Hill, Bunker Hill's threadbare twin sister. Irrigated by almost a billion dollars of diverted public taxes, bank towers, law offices, museums, and hotels eventually sprouted from its naked scars, and Bunker Hill was reincarnated as a glitzy command center of the booming Pacific Rim economy. Where hard men and their molls once plotted to rob banks, banks now plotted to rob the world. (2001: 36–7, 43)

The main difference between Andersen's and Davis's accounts is the quantity and density of information that they contain. Apparently, Davis offers more data – after all, he has twelve pages to do it – while Andersen synthesises the same ideas in five minutes and twenty seconds. But far from being superficial, the filmmaker's version offers something that the scholar's lacks: the possibility to see the place before, during and after its transformation. Andersen provides the audience with visual evidences of the process that later became the subject of further research: for example, his vindication of *The Exiles* helped to rediscover this film and inspired more detailed analyses of its social and spatial mapping of Bunker Hill (see Gray 2011). This feature, the only one directed by Kent MacKenzie, recorded the mood of the time, when the neighbourhood was already doomed to destruction, and revealed '*a place where reality is opaque, where different social orders coexist in the same space without touching each other*'. Bunker Hill in *The Exiles* is thereby a liminal space that can be perceived and experienced in different ways, depending on who is the observer and what is his or her relationship with the place. Consequently, a good way to depict its changing nature over the second half of the twentieth century is precisely, as Andersen does, to make an inventory of the wide variety of roles that it has played in film.

For progressive historians, the renewal of Bunker Hill symbolises the end of public space in LA, perhaps because it was one of the consequences of the conservative counter-offensive led by the *Los Angeles Times* in the early 1950s against Mayor Fletcher Bowron's low-rent public housing programme (see Davis 1990: 122–3). *Los Angeles Plays Itself* echoes this episode in its third part, exposing the way LAPD chief William H. Parker helped to discredit Frank Wilkinson, Los Angeles City Housing Authority spokesman, by leaking Intelligence Division files that accused him of being a Communist. Once Republican Norris Poulson was elected as new mayor in the 1953 municipal elections, the only public housing that was built was located far from Downtown, in Watts and East Los Angeles, which were respectively the historic ghetto and barrio (see Soja 2000: 134). Accordingly, instead of serving to create an inclusive and heterogeneous community in Chavez Ravine, north of Downtown, the new housing actually increased racial segregation and helped 'to kill the crowd', as Davis has stated (1990: 231). Thus, when Andersen describes the California Plaza as '*a simulated city*', he is complaining about 'the *evacuation* of the public realm', a prerequisite to achieve what Rem Koolhaas ironically termed 'the serenity of the Generic City' (Koolhaas & Mau 1995: 1251).

In the last third of the twentieth century, public space was drastically downsized in Los Angeles to make way for non-places such as urban motorways, shopping centres, parking lots or motels. Andersen finds the first signs of this process in *Un homme est mort* (*The Outside Man*, Jacques Deray, 1972), in which the main character – '*a Parisian hit man stranded in Los Angeles*' – has to wander around a city of unfriendly non-places in order to escape the trap set for him. This gradual hardening of the urban surface has been strongly criticised by Davis, who has identified its symptoms in both the real and, above all, the cinematic city:

Contemporary urban theory, whether debating the role of electronic technologies in precipitating 'postmodern space', or discussing the dispersion
of urban functions across poly-centered metropolitan 'galaxies', has been
strangely silent about the militarization of city life so grimly visible at the
street level. Hollywood's pop apocalypses and pulp science fiction have
been more realistic, and politically perceptive, in representing the programmed hardening of the urban surface in the wake of the social polar-
izations of the Reagan era. Images of carceral inner cities (*Escape from
New York, Running Man*), high-tech police death squads (*Blade Runner*),
sentient buildings (*Die Hard*), urban bantustans (*They Live*), Vietnam-
like street wars (*Colors*), and so on, only extrapolate from actually existing trends (1990: 223).[5]

Many of the films praised as truthful representations in *Los Angeles Plays Itself*,
from *The Exiles* to *The Outside Man*, were symptomatically directed by foreign
filmmakers. According to their attitude towards Los Angeles, Andersen describes
them as 'low tourist directors' or 'high tourist directors': the first group would be
formed by those who avoid or disdain the city, like Alfred Hitchcock or Woody
Allen, while the second would include all those who became fascinated by it,
namely, Michelangelo Antonioni, John Boorman, Jacques Demy, Jacques Deray,
Maya Deren, Alexander Hammid, Tony Richardson or Andy Warhol, among others. Through this distinction, Andersen seems to say that, in a global city like Los
Angeles, where there is a clear inflation of images, high tourist directors contribute to problematising its representation beyond the native perspective, because
they usually pay attention to places and details that locals underestimate, even
though they do not always understand what they are seeing. Arguably, then, the
more interwoven the foreign and native gazes are, the more complex the film representation of a city will be.

This may be one of the reasons why the best features about Los Angeles of the
1970s and 1980s, that is, *Chinatown* and *Blade Runner*, were precisely directed
by foreign filmmakers: Roman Polanski and Ridley Scott. In the third part of
Los Angeles Plays Itself, Andersen argues that *Chinatown* set a pattern that was
later continued by *Who Framed Roger Rabbit* and *L.A. Confidential*. All these
neo-noirs took the city as their main subject, but they wasted the opportunity to
express its collective memory by mythologising its past. On the one hand, their
narratives reveal the growing self-awareness of the city regarding its social problems: first, *Chinatown* criticises both its aggressive water policy and endemic land
speculation, although Andersen suggests that the film is actually a displaced vision
of the 1965 Watts Riots; then, *Who Framed Roger Rabbit* mourns the dismantling

of the two old public transport systems in the city – the Pacific Electric and the Los Angeles Railway – in order to support their successor, the Metro Rail, which was under construction in the late 1980s; and finally, *L.A. Confidential* bluntly shows police brutality and corruption in the 1950s as an indirect reflection of police work at the worst days of the gang wars of the 1980s and 1990s. On the other hand, the moral of these films does little more than teach that '*good intentions are futile*' and that '*it is better not to act, even better not to know*', as Andersen states in the film. The last line of *Chinatown* – '*Forget it, Jake, it's Chinatown*' – advises the audience to keep away from public affairs, as does the final resolution of *L.A. Confidential*. In both films, their respective scandals are not made public, and the characters have to accept their powerlessness. Undoubtedly, a happy ending would have been worse in artistic terms, but at least it would have encouraged citizens to develop a less resigned attitude towards the abuses of power.

In several texts and interviews, Andersen has explained that these kind of films try to convince people that 'politics is futile and meaningless' (in Ribas 2012: 92). Obviously, the decision not to talk about politics is always political, because it ultimately serves certain agendas. In this regard, Hollywood is anything but innocent, given that its films have been partly intended for spreading the American way of life all over the world: the smallest detail, as Andersen demonstrates in *Los Angeles Play Itself*, may be a vehicle of ideology. Then, how to counteract Hollywood's discourse? What are the features that offer an alternative representation of the city? Most filmmakers are trapped in the same contradiction: '*It's hard to make a personal film, based on your own experience, when you're absurdly overprivileged*,' Andersen says, '*you tend not to notice the less fortunate, and that's almost everybody*.' This is to say that Hollywood's problems in depicting LA, or anywhere else in the world, have to do with its own geographical and social position: if its productions repeat the same spatial clichés this is because Hollywood is too closed in on itself to look beyond its territory.

The main antidote against these misrepresentations would be, according to Andersen, the neorealist cinema that began with *The Exiles*. For this reason, the final segment of *Los Angeles Plays Itself* focuses on three titles that belong to the L.A. Rebellion film movement: *Killer of Sheep* (Charles Burnett, 1977), *Bush Mama* (Haile Gerima, 1979) and *Bless Their Little Hearts* (Billy Woodberry, 1984). These films address the plight of the African-American community in South Central Los Angeles in the late 1970s, when the industrial crisis hit the neighbourhood and caused the destruction of thousands of jobs in the area:

> Working-class Blacks in the flatlands – where nearly 40 per cent of families live below the poverty line – have faced relentless economic decline.

While city resources (to the tune of $2 billion) have been absorbed in financing the corporate renaissance of Downtown, Southcentral L.A. has been markedly disadvantaged even in receipt of anti-poverty assistance, 'coming in far behind West Los Angeles and the Valley in access to vital human services and job-training funds' (Curran 1989: 2). Black small businesses have withered for lack of credit or attention from the city, leaving behind only liquor stores and churches. Most tragically, the unionized branch-plant economy toward which working-class Blacks (and Chicanos) had always looked for decent jobs collapsed. As the Los Angeles economy in the 1970s was 'unplugged' from the American industrial heartland and rewired to East Asia, non-Anglo workers have borne the brunt of adaptation and sacrifice. The 1978–82 wave of factory closings in the wake of Japanese import penetration and recession, which shuttered ten of the twelve largest non-aerospace plants in Southern California and displaced 75,000 blue-collar workers, erased the ephemeral gains won by blue-collar Blacks between 1965 and 1975. Where local warehouses and factories did not succumb to Asian competition, they fled instead to new industrial parks in the South Bay, northern Orange County or the Inland Empire [...] An investigating committee of the California Legislature in 1982 confirmed the resulting economic destruction in Southcentral neighborhoods: unemployment rising by nearly 50 per cent since the early 1970s while community purchasing power fell by a third. (Davis 1990: 304–5)

The films of the L.A. Rebellion put a face to these statistics, conveying the deep despair of African-Americans in view of their worsening living conditions. In this period, many people experienced the industrial crisis as an existential crisis, like the characters of *Bush Mama* and *Bless Their Little Hearts*. Iain Chambers has observed that this declassed population has been inserted into discourses that do not help to improve its socio-economic situation: these people do not usually appear in films about their professional success – with the sole exception to date of Chris Gardner, whose rags-to-riches story was adapted in *The Pursuit of Happyness* (Gabriele Muccino, 2006) – but in narratives about ethnic issues, urban poverty, inner-city decay, industrial decline, drugs or organised crime (1990: 53). Faced with these discourses, independent black filmmakers, many of whom were foreigners in Los Angeles, responded by directing social melodramas focused on family matters, in which they show the everyday struggle to survive in this hostile environment.

Andersen highlights the *'spatialized, nonchronological time of meditation and memory'* of these films, a new cinematic time that seeks to fill the gaps of the visual history of African-Americans: *Killer of Sheep*, for example, seems '*suspended outside of time*' because its director, Charles Burnett, '*blended together the decades of his childhood, his youth and his adulthood*'. This formal configuration is quite the opposite from that of *Chinatown*, *Who Framed Roger Rabbit* and *L.A. Confidential*: instead of going back to the past to talk about the present, *Killer of Sheep* is set in a present which includes memories of the post-war years that had never been represented from the African-American standpoint. This approach raises the issue of who can represent whom. Can Hollywood represent the people from which it actually knows nothing? Can minorities represent anything else than themselves? Andersen avoids this controversy by emphasising the universality of these films: '*Independent black filmmakers showed that the real crisis of the black family is simply the crisis of the working class family, white or black, where family values are always at risk because the threat of unemployment is always present.*'

Los Angeles Plays Itself ends with a beautiful sequence shot taken from *Bless Their Little Hearts* in which the main character drives by what Andersen terms '*a reverse landmark*', the ruins of the old Goodyear Factory on South Central Avenue, the largest tire manufacturing plant in the Los Angeles area, whose closure in 1980 left thousands of unemployed black workers. In *Bless Their Little Hearts*, this carscape is located towards the middle of the film and symbolically expresses the protagonist's distress after having lost his job. In *Los Angeles Plays Itself*, on the contrary, it closes the film and bears up to four different meanings. First, it is a direct quote of *Bless Their Little Hearts*; second, it echoes its original meaning; third, it explicitly provides a final reflection on the transition from an industrial economy to a service one ('*once upon a time, visitors could take a guided tour and see how tires were made just as today they can take a studio tour and see how movies are made*'); and four, it implicitly vindicates those 'modes of film production opposed to the industry ... that grow from the working class itself', as David E. James has pointed out (2005: 422).

By appropriating these images, Andersen takes sides with a kind of cinema and a kind of city that has nothing to do with the Hollywood urban imaginarium. Therefore, *Los Angeles Plays Itself* goes beyond negative criticism against Hollywood's misrepresentations to reveal the existence of an alternative cinematic city hidden in the neorealist tradition. Andersen certainly provides something more than an illustrated lecture: he offers a model and a tool to think images, as well as an entrance to that alternative cinematic city. Thus, by subjectivising the perception of film heritage, metafilmic strategies create a third space that serves to both preservation and analytical purposes: while *The Decay of Fiction* explores the expressive possibilities of the filmic surface; *Los Angeles Plays Itself* teaches us, in turn, how to look beyond surfaces, whether urban or filmic, in order to understand what is going on right before our eyes, both in the city and on its infinite screens.

NOTES

1   According to Paul Arthur, 'the range of printing options recruited by O'Neill include stationary and traveling mattes, bi-packing, color modulation, looping, image enlargement and reduction, even subtitling' (2004: 69).
2   Pat O'Neill was born in Los Angeles in 1939, James Benning in Milwaukee in 1942, and Thom Andersen in Chicago in 1943.
3   After the premiere of *Get Out of the Car* in Madrid, Andersen said that he tried to negotiate a symbolic price with the studios for the rights of reproduction of the quoted films, but his petition was ignored. This Q&A was held in La Casa Encendida on 18 February 2010.
4   The first two reasons do not appear in Erickson's interview, but were mentioned in a personal interview with Andersen held in Los Angeles on March 20, 2010.
5   The complete references of the films quoted by Davis that had not previously appeared in the text are *Escape from New York* (John Carpenter, 1981), *The Running Man* (Paul Michael Glaser, 1987), *Die Hard* (John McTiernan, 1988), *They Live* (John Carpenter, 1988) and *Colors* (Dennis Hopper, 1988).

Cinema as Agent of Urban Change

The set of formal strategies analysed here have been highly influenced by contemporary discourses on urban change, from Edward Soja's real-and-imaginary geographies to Francesc Muñoz's urbanalisation, but they also influence our perception of urban space, inasmuch as they establish a certain kind of gaze at the city that can be adopted by their usual residents and occasional visitors. Moreover, all these strategies share a similar subjective gaze that aims to be closer to citizens than to the institutions or corporations responsible for recent major transformations. This means that contemporary non-fiction production, especially when approaching the essayistic and experimental domain, tends to develop a critical reading of the urban surface guided by the two following purposes. The first would be to gather, give shape and express the different insights of citizenship on urban change, in an attempt to make the audience identify with the film's discourse; while the second would be to invite those viewers who are initially indifferent or opposed to this critical discourse to become aware of the consequences of this process. Many non-fiction films are therefore agents of urban change, because they ultimately express and convey a critical perception of late-capitalist urban planning in order to draw the audience's attention to the policies that filmmakers want to challenge, question or even change. Accordingly, the politics of representation in current urban documentaries has evolved into a politics of place-making and sense-making, which simultaneously serves to delve into the past of cities and shape their future, as suggested by François Penz and Andong Lu:

> Such an exploration of the filmic spaces of the past may enable historians, architects and urbanists to better anticipate the city of the future. [...] The processes involved in cinematic urban archaeology exhume, unlock and preserve past memories. And, as an applied concept, it may have far-

reaching implications for planning and urban regeneration purposes as well as for heritage and conservation. (2011: 12)

The concept of cinematic urban archaeology has to do with Marc Ferro's claim that cinema may be 'source and agent of history' (1988: 14), given that an image, or, more accurately, a single framing, can contain the entire memory of a place, both for what it shows (its past or current image) and for what it suggests (its missing image). Cinematic spaces, however, not only refer to the past, but also to the present and future of the depicted places. They are much more than memories of a now-defunct city, that is, a city that only exists on the screen, a source for cinematic urban archaeology, since they shape and underpin our sense of place and our ideas about how urban space should be – that is, they are a source of inspiration for urban planning. As discussed throughout this book, most cinematic cityscapes are also collective memoryscapes that go back to a more or less idealised past, as well as individual mindscapes that offer new meanings for old spaces, thereby creating an imaginary city that complements the real one and even foresees its future developments. In this sense, both landscape films such as *London*, *Lost Book Found* and *Los* and urban self-portraits such as *Porto of My Childhood*, *My Winnipeg* and *Of Time and the City* are prime examples of works capable of depicting the city as the set of these three landscapes – cityscapes, memoryscapes and mindscapes – in order to simultaneously address its past, present and future.

Considering that the post-industrial crisis and the subsequent urban renewal have left indelible traces on the urban surface, it is no wonder that almost all the films analysed in this book raise the need for the work of mourning. No matter how much time has passed since the disappearance of a given place of memory (it may be several years and even decades, as in some landscape films and most urban self-portraits), everyone – the inhabitants of the depicted spaces, beginning with filmmakers themselves, but also the audience – eventually misses the places that have somehow shaped their personality. The work of mourning can be fed by feelings of nostalgia, melancholy or *saudade*, or simply by awareness about the passage of time, but in all cases it stimulates the filmmakers' creativity when paying tribute to places of memory, whether by embracing the usual topics of funeral discourse, such as *tempus fugit* and *memento mori*, as *Thames Film* and *Of Time and the City* do, or by developing more playful strategies, as in *London*, *My Winnipeg* or *The Decay of Fiction*, three works in which the boundary between city-referent and city-character is consciously blurred.

Two reasons that explain the growing importance of the work of mourning in contemporary urban documentary are the key role places of memory play in the process of identity building and the recent shift in social sciences and humanities from an objective paradigm to a subjective one, in which facts are no longer more important than feelings. In this context, the triad formed by cinematic cityscapes, memoryscapes and mindscapes allows filmmakers to express different subjectivities at once, thereby combining several perspectives (from the inside and the outside, from below and from above, etc.) in narratives that usually extend from the present to the past, even when they take place in an apparently synchronic present. The main advantage of this approach based on intersubjectivity is its ability to represent urban change as a shared experience, in which spatiality arises from the blend of three complementary gazes: first, the gaze of the inhabitants of the depicted space; second, the filmmaker's gaze; and third, the audience's gaze. Thus, for the residents of any city-referent, intersubjectivity serves to convey the perception of their own habitat to a wider audience; for filmmakers, this approach is basically a way of speaking about themselves through the experience of others; and for the audience, it is a way of thinking about themselves and their places of memory through film. This last idea is ultimately behind the use of metafilmic strategies in those works in which filmmakers build the cinematic city from their own condition as viewers, as Thom Andersen did in *Los Angeles Plays Itself*.

Let us briefly see how this identification process operates in the first case study, *One Way Boogie Woogie / 27 Years Later*. On the one hand, some Milwaukeeans, when recognising certain film locations, may experience feelings ranging from topophilia to topophobia towards these places, such as nostalgia, affection, astonishment, annoyance, displeasure or even disinterest, especially the people who appear in the images. On the other, the filmmaker, by selecting the film locations, is consciously or unconsciously establishing a personal mapping of the depicted area based on his own preferences, as he also does in the rest of his landscape films, beginning with *Los*. And last but not least, viewers may appropriate these locations in order to project their own feelings and emotions on them, regardless of whether they have ever been there or not. In fact, the ability of some film locations to become receptacles of certain moods and meanings can explain the recent rise of film tourism.

Without going any further, I have myself visited many film locations just because they appeared in my case studies: the Griffith Observatory in Los Angeles, from where James Benning filmed the city's skyline in *Los*; the Boundary Estate in Shoreditch, which is praised in *London*; the Staten Island ferry in New York City, from where Chantal Akerman filmed the last shot of *News from Home*; Everton Brow in Liverpool, where Bernard Fallon originally took the picture 'The Long Walk' that would be later included in *Of Time and the City*; and the mouth of the River Douro, where Manoel de Oliveira ended *Porto of My Childhood*. One way or another, I have travelled through time and space over the past six years thanks to cinema, and I hope to continue doing so in the future. In fact, this is one of the many reasons why we should thank cinema for documenting, preserving and recreating cityscapes, because these kind of city films allow us, first and foremost, to return to many places of memory over and over again.

Maps and Locations of *Los*

L1. Cascade, Los Angeles Aqueduct, Sylmar

L2. Billboard, Outdoor Systems, Inc., West Hollywood

L3. Housing Lots, Newhall Land & Farming Co., Stevenson Ranch

L4. Summer Rain, Golden State Freeway, Newhall Pass

L5. Joggers, San Vicente Boulevard, Santa Monica

L6. Container Ship, Matson Navigation Co., San Pedro

L7. Men's Central Jail, Los Angeles County, Los Angeles

L8. Bi-level Street, Grand Avenue, Los Angeles

L9. Crystal Cathedral, Robert H. Schuller Ministries, Garden Grove

L10. Airplanes Landing, Los Angeles International Airport, Los Angeles

L11. Steam Plant, City of Burbank, Burbank

L12. Los Angeles River, Flood Control District, Maywood

L13. Auto Demolition, PYP Auto Wrecking, Anaheim

L14. Soccer, Hansen Dam Park, Pacoima

L15. Intersection, Henry Ford Avenue, Terminal Island

L16. Business People, Arco Plaza, Los Angeles

L17. Los Angeles Skyline, Griffith Observatory, Los Feliz

L18. Oil Refinery, Ultramar Corporation, Wilmington

L19. School Bus Stop, San Martínez Road, Val Verde

L20. Gardener, Parriot Residence, Encino

L21. Mini-Mall, Koreatown

L22. Police, Democratic National Convention, Los Angeles

L23. Oil Well, Stocker Resources, Inc., Baldwin Hills

L24. Ground Crew, Dodger Stadium, Chavez Ravine

L25. Waste Disposal Plant, Crown Disposal, Inc., Sunland

L26. Wetlands, Department of Fish & Games, Bolsa Chica

L27. Steel Workers, M. A. Mortenson Co., Inc., Los Angeles

L28. Cattle, Shamrock Meats, Inc., Vernon

L29. Memorial Graveyard, National Cementery, Westwood

L30. Commuter Train, Metrolink, San Fernando

L31. Community Gardens, 41st Street, Los Angeles

L32. Brush Fire, Pechanga Indian Reservation, Temecula

L33. Earth Movers, C. A. Rasmussen, Inc., Castaic Junction

L34. Homeless People, 6th Street, Los Angeles

L35. Pacific Ocean, Puerco Beach, Malibu

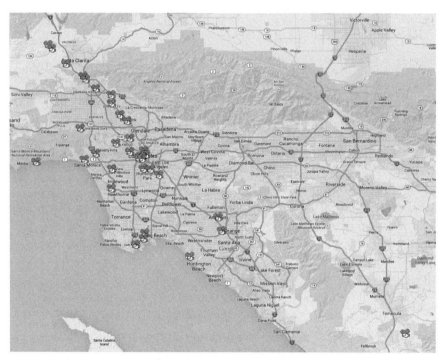

Map 2: *Los*, film locations (Map Available in http://g.co/maps/ct97j)

Bibliography

Abbas, Ackbar (2003) 'Cinema, the City, and the Cinematic', in Linda Krause and Patrice Petro (eds) *Global Cities: Cinema, Architecture, and Urbanism in a Digital Age*. New Brunswick, NJ: Rutgers University Press, 142–56.

Aldarondo, Ricardo (2008) 'Songs for a lifetime', in Quim Casas (ed.) *Terence Davies: The Sounds of Memory*. Donostia: Festival Internacional de Cine de Donostia-San Sebastián/Filmoteca Vasca, 200–5.

AlSayyad, Nezar (2006) *Cinematic Urbanism. A History of the Modern from Reel to Real*. New York, NY, and London, UK: Routledge.

Althabe, Gérard and Jean-Louis Comolli (1994) *Regards sur la ville*. Paris: Centre Georges Pompidou.

Andersen, Thom (2008) 'Los Angeles: A City on Film. An Introduction', in Astrid Ofner and Claudia Siefen (eds) *Los Angeles: A City on Film*. Vienna: Vienna International Film Festival, 11–23.

Andersen, Thom and Noël Burch (1994) *Les Communistes de Hollywood: Autre chose que des martyrs*. Paris: Presses de la Sorbonne Nouvelle.

Anderson, John (2012) 'A Steel Town's Chronicler and Conscience. Tony Buba: The Bard of Braddock, at Anthology Film Archives', *New York Times*, 1 June 2012; http://www.nytimes.com/2012/06/03/movies/tony-buba-the-bard-of-braddock-at-anthology-film-archive.html?_r=1&. Accessed 29 October 2012.

Anderson, Perry (1992) *English Questions*. London: Verso.

Andrade, Sergio C. (2002) 'O Porto é a Minha Casa', in Sergio C. Andrade (ed.). *O Porto na História do Cinema*. Porto: Porto Editora.

Andreu, Marta (2009) 'Cuando la producción se inscribe en la realidad filmada', in Imaculada Sánchez and Marta Díaz (eds) *Doc 21. Panorama del reciente cine documental en España*. Girona: Luces de Gálibo: 144–55

Andrew, Dudley (2006) 'An Atlas of World Cinema', in Stephanie Dennison and Song Hwee Lim (eds) *Remapping World Cinema: Identity, Culture and Politics in Film*. London: Walflower Press, 19–29.

Ang, Ien (1992) 'Hegemony-in-Trouble: Nostalgia and the Ideology of the Impossible in European Cinema', in Duncan Petrie (ed.) *Screening Europe: Imaging and Identity in Contemporary European Cinema*. London: British Film Institute: 21–30.

Appadurai, Arjun (1996) *Modernity at Large: Cultural Dimensions of Globalization*.

Minneapolis, MN: University of Minnesota Press.

Arthur, Paul (1993) 'Jargons of Authenticity (Three American Moments)', in Michael Renov (ed.) *Theorizing Documentary*. New York, NY: Routledge, 108–34.

____ (2003) 'Essay Questions: From Alain Resnais to Michael Moore', *Film Comment*, 39, 1, 58–62.

____ (2004) 'Permanent Transit: The Films of Pat O'Neill', in Julie Lazar (ed.) *Pat O'Neill: Views from Lookout Mountain*. Santa Monica, CA: Santa Monica Museum of Art, 66–75.

____ (2010) '"Everything Is Personal": Michael Moore and the Documentary Essay', in Matthew H. Bernstein (ed.) *Michael Moore: Filmmaker, Newsmaker, Cultural Icon*. Ann Arbor, MI: University of Michigan Press, 105–23.

Aufderheide, Pat (1989) 'Lightning Over Braddock', *The Washington Post*, 27 March; http://www.washingtonpost.com/wp-srv/style/longterm/movies/videos/lightnin-goverbraddocknraufderheide_a09e95.htm. Accessed 29 October 2012.

Augé, Marc (1995) *Non-Places: Introduction to an Anthropology of Supermodernity*. London/New York, NY: Verso.

Ault, Julie (2007) 'Using the Earth as Map of Himself', in Barbara Pichler and Claudia Slanar (eds) *James Benning*. Vienna: Austrian Film Museum, 88–112.

Banham, Reyner (1971) *Los Angeles: The Architecture of Four Ecologies*. Berkeley, CA: University of California Press.

Barber, Stephen (2002) *Projected Cities: Cinema and Urban Space*. London: Reaktion.

Barker, Jennifer M (1999) 'The feminine side of New York: travelogue, autobiography and architecture in *News from Home*', in Gwendolyn A. Foster (ed.) *Identity and Memory: The Films of Chantal Akerman*. Trowbridge: Flicks Books, 41–58.

Barnouw, Eric (1993) *Documentary: A History of the Non-Fiction Film*. Oxford: Oxford University Press.

Barrios, Guillermo (1997) *Ciudades de película*. Caracas: Eventus.

Baschiera, Stefano and Laura Rascaroli (2005) 'Glasgow, Liverpool, Manchester', in Thierry Jousse and Thierry Paquot (dir.) *La ville au cinéma. Encyclopédie*. Paris: Cahiers du cinéma, 389–94.

Baudrillard, Jean (1994) *Simulacra and Simulation*. Ann Arbor, MI: University of Michigan Press.

____ (1988) *America*. London: Verso.

Bauman, Zygmunt (2000) *Liquid Modernity*. Cambridge: Polity Press.

Beard, William (2010) *Into the Past: The Cinema of Guy Maddin*. Toronto: University of Toronto Press.

Bell, Daniel (1973) *The Coming of Post-Industrial Society: A Venture in Social Forecasting*. New York, NY: Basic Books.

Bellour, Raymond (1989) *Eye for I: Video Self-Portraits*. New York, NY: Independent Curators Inc.

Bengston, John (1999) *Silent Echoes: Discovering Early Hollywood Through the*

Films of Buster Keaton. Santa Monica, CA: Santa Monica Press.

___ (2006) *Silent Traces: Discovering Early Hollywood Through the Films of Charlie Chaplin*. Santa Monica, CA: Santa Monica Press.

___ (2011) *Silent Visions: Discovering Early Hollywood and New York Through the Films of Harold Lloyd*. Santa Monica, CA: Santa Monica Press.

Benjamin, Walter ([1927–40] 1999) *The Arcades Project*. Cambridge, MA: Belknap Press.

Bergstrom, Janet (2004) 'News from Home', in Claudine Paquot (ed.) *Chantal Akerman. Autoportrait en Cinéaste*. Paris: Cahiers du cinéma/Centre Georges Pompidou, 181.

Bernstein, Matthew H (1998) 'Documentaphobia and Mixed Modes', in Barry Keith Grant and Jeanette Sloniowski (eds) *Documenting the Documentary: Close Readings of Documentary Film and Video*. Detroit, MI: Wayne State University Press, 397–415.

___ (ed.) (2010) *Michael Moore: Filmmaker, Newsmaker, Cultural Icon*. Ann Arbor, MI: University of Michigan Press.

Bioy Casares, Adolfo (1940) *La Invención de Morel*. Buenos Aires: Editorial Losada.

Boyer, Marie-Christine (1992) 'Cities for Sale: Merchandising History at South Street Seaport', in Michalel Sorkin (ed.) *Variations on a Theme Park: The New American City and the End of Public Space*. New York, NY: Hill and Wang, 181–204.

Bradshaw, Nick (2013) 'James Benning', *Sight & Sound*, 23, 10, 46–50.

Brooke, Michael (2008) 'Home on the range', *Sight & Sound*, 18, 7, 12.

Bruno, Giuliana (2002) *Atlas of Emotion: Journeys in Art, Architecture and Film*. New York: Verso.

Brunsdon, Charlotte (2007) *London in Cinema: The Cinematic City Since 1945*. London: British Film Institute.

___ (2010) 'Towards a History of Empty Spaces', in Richard Koeck and Les Roberts (eds) *The City and the Moving Image: Urban Projections*. New York, NY: Palgrave Macmillan, 91–103.

Bruss, Elizabeth (1980) 'Eye for I: Making and Unmaking Autobiography in Film', in James Olney (ed.) *Autobiography: Essays Theoretical and Critical*. Princeton, NJ: Princeton University Press, 296–320.

Bruzzi, Stella (2006) *New Documentary*. 2nd edn. London: Routledge.

Bulgakowa, Oksana (2013) 'La fábrica cinematográfica de los gestos: Imágenes y memoria del cuerpo en la era de la globalización', in Fran Benavente and Glòria Salvadó Corretger (eds) *Poéticas del gesto en el cine europeo contemporáneo*. Barcelona: Prodimag, 251–86.

Burch, Noël (1990) *Life to Those Shadows*. Berkeley, CA: University of California Press.

Cairns, Graham (2007) *La visión espacial del cine. El arquitecto detrás de la cámara*. Madrid: Abada editores.

Careri, Francesco (2002) *Walkscapes: Walking as an Aesthetic Practice*. Barcelona:

Editorial Gustavo Gili.

Casas, Quim (ed.) (2008) *Terence Davies: The Sounds of Memory*. Donostia: Festival Internacional de Cine de Donostia-San Sebastián/Filmoteca Vasca.

Castells, Manuel (1989) *The Informational City: Information Technology, Economic Restructuring, and the Urban Regional Process*. Oxford/Cambridge, MA: Basil Blackwell.

Castro, Teresa (2010) 'Mapping the City through Film: From "Topophilia" to Urban Mapscapes', in Richard Koeck and Les Roberts (eds) *The City and the Moving Image: Urban Projections*. New York, NY: Palgrave Macmillan, 144–55.

Català, Josep María (2005) 'Film-ensayo y vanguardia', in Casimiro Torreiro and Josetxo Cerdán (eds) *Documental y vanguardia*. Madrid: Ediciones Cátedra, 109–58.

_____ (2010) 'View from the Bridge: New routes for the documentary', in Antonio Weinrichter (ed.) *Doc: Documentarism in the 21st Century*. Donostia-San Sebastián: Festival Internacional de Cine de Donostia-San Sebastián/Filmoteca Vasca, 278–91.

Català, Josep María and Josetxo Cerdán (2007/8) 'Después de lo real. Pensar las formas del documental, hoy', *Archivos de la Filmoteca. Revista de Estudios Históricos sobre la Imagen* 57/58, 1, 6–25.

Caughey, John and LaRee Caughey (1977) *Los Angeles - Biography of a City*. Berkeley, CA: University of California Press.

Cerdán, Josetxo and Gonzalo de Pedro (2009) 'Between Flow and Balance: An Interview with Jem Cohen', in Josetxo Cerdán, Gonzalo de Pedro and Ana Herrera (eds) *Signal Fires: The Cinema of Jem Cohen*. Pamplona: Gobierno de Navarra, INAAC, 28–77.

Cerdán, Josetxo, Gonzalo de Pedro and Ana Herrera (eds) (2009) *Signal Fires: The Cinema of Jem Cohen*. Pamplona: Gobierno de Navarra, INAAC.

Chambers, Iain (1990) *Border Dialogues: Journeys in Postmodernity*. London: Routledge.

_____ (1997) 'Maps, Movies, Musics and Memory', in David B. Clarke (ed.) *The Cinematic City*. New York, NY: Routledge, 230–40.

Chanan, Michael (2007) *The Politics of Documentary*. London: British Film Institute.

_____ (2012) 'The Role of History in the Individual: Working Notes for a Film', in Alisa Lebow (ed.) *The Cinema of Me: The Self and Subjectivity in First Person Documentary*. London/New York, NY: Wallflower Press, 15–32.

Chandler, Raymond (1949) *The Little Sisters*. Boston, MA: Houghton Mifflin Harcourt.

Chion, Michel (1994) *Audio-Vision: Sound on Screen*. New York, NY: Columbia University Press.

Clarke, David B. (ed.) (1997) *The Cinematic City*. New York, NY: Routledge.

Cohen, Daniel (1998) *The Wealth of the World and the Poverty of Nations*. Cambridge,

MA: MIT Press.

Cohen, Jem (2009a) 'Letter to Myself', in Josetxo Cerdán, Gonzalo de Pedro and Ana Herrera (eds) *Signal Fires: The Cinema of Jem Cohen*. Pamplona: Gobierno de Navarra, INAAC, 14–19.

____ ([2005] 2009b) 'An Open Letter from Jem Cohen to the Films and Arts Community', in Josetxo Cerdán, Gonzalo de Pedro and Ana Herrera (eds) *Signal Fires: The Cinema of Jem Cohen*. Pamplona: Gobierno de Navarra, INAAC, 104–9.

Comolli, Jean-Louis (2005) 'Documentaire', in Thierry Jousse and Thierry Paquot (dir.) *La ville au cinéma. Encyclopédie*. Paris: Cahiers du cinéma, 137–47.

Conolly, Jez (2011) 'Thames Tales: Stories by the Riverside', in Neil Mitchell (ed.) *World Film Locations: London*. Bristol: Intellect, 130–1.

Corrigan, Timothy (2011) *The Essay Film: From Montaigne, After Marker*. Oxford: Oxford University Press.

Costa e Silva, Manuel (ed.) (1994) *Lisboa a 24 imagens*. Lisboa: Caminho.

Coverley, Merlin (2010) *Psychogeography*. Harpenden: Pocket Essentials.

Crowdus, Gary (1990) 'Reflections on *Roger & Me*: Michael Moore and his Critics', *Cineaste*, 17, 4, 30.

Curran, Ron (1989) 'Malign Neglect: The Roots of an Urban War Zone', *L.A. Weekly*, 30 December to 5 January, 2.

Darke, Chris (2010) 'Robinson in Ruins', *Sight & Sound*, 20, 12, 74–6.

Darr, Brian (2008) 'Guy Maddin: «I Had This Haunted Childhood»', *Green Cinema*, 8 August; http://www.greencine.com/central/guymaddin/mywinnipeg. Accessed 8 June 2011.

Dave, Paul (2000) 'Representations of capitalism, history and nation in the work of Patrick Keiller', in Justone Ashby and Andrew Higson (eds) *British Cinema, Past and Present*. London: Routledge.

____ (2006) *Visions of England: Class and Culture in Contemporary Cinema*. Oxford: Berg.

Davis, Mike (1990) *City of Quartz: Excavating the Future in Los Angeles*. London/ New York, NY: Verso.

____ (2001) 'Bunker Hill: Hollywood's Dark Shadow', in Mark Shiel and Tony Fitzmaurice (eds) *Cinema and the City: Film and Urban Societies in Global Context*. Oxford: Blackwell, 33–45.

____ (2002) *Dead Cities and Other Tales*. New York, NY: The New Press.

De Bruyn, Dirk (2004) 'The Decay of Fiction', *Senses of Cinema*, 31, 22 April; http:// www.sensesofcinema.com/2004/cteq/decay_of_fiction/. Accessed 13 December 2011.

De Certeau, Michel (1984) *The Practice of Everyday Life*. Berkeley, CA: University of California Press.

De Lucas, Gonzalo (2008) 'Túnel de luz', *Cahiers du cinéma. España*, 15, 84–5.

De Pedro, Gozalo (2010) '*Everybody's Doing It*: Or How Digital Finished Off the Documentary (Thank You, Sir)', in Antonio Weinrichter (ed.) *Doc: Documentarism in the 21st Century*. Donostia-San Sebastián: Festival Internacional de Cine de Donostia-San Sebastián/Filmoteca Vasca, 396–409.

De Quincey, Thomas (1821) 'Confessions of an English Opium Eater', *London Magazine*, 4, 21/22, 293–312, 353–79.

Debord, Guy (1981a [1955]) 'Introduction to a Critique of Urban Geography', in Ken Knabb (ed.) *Situationist International Anthology*. Berkeley, CA: Bureau of Public Secrets, 5–7.

____ (1981b [1956]) 'Theory of the Dérive', in Ken Knabb (ed.) *Situationist International Anthology*. Berkeley, CA: Bureau of Public Secrets, 50–3.

____ (1990) *Comments on the Society of the Spectacle*. London: Verso.

Defoe, Daniel. 1719. *Robinson Crusoe*. London: W. Taylor.

____ 1722. *A Journal of the Plague Year*. London: E. Nutt.

Deleuze, Guilles (1989) *Cinema 2. The Time-Image*. Minneapolis, MN: University of Minnesota Press.

Delgado, Manuel (2007) *La ciudad mentirosa. Fraude y miseria del 'Modelo Barcelona'*. Madrid: Libros de la Catarata.

Dimendberg, Edward (2004) *Film Noir and the Spaces of Modernity*. Cambridge, MA: Harvard University Press.

Dimitriu, Christian (1993) *Alain Tanner*. Madrid: Ediciones Cátedra.

Durkheim, Emile ([1912] 1965). *The Elementary Forms of the Religious Life*. New York, NY: Free Press.

Eliot, T. S. (1935) 1943. 'Burnt Norton', in *Four Quartets*. San Diego, CA: Harcourt.

Erice, Víctor (2004) 'Manoel de Oliveira', in Folgar de la Calle, José María, Xurxo González and Jaime Pena (eds) *Manoel de Oliveira*. Santiago de Compostela: Universidade de Santiago de Compostela, 27–32.

Erickson, Steve (2004) 'The Reality of Film; Thom Anderson on *Los Angeles Plays Itself*', *indiewire*, 27 July; http://www.indiewire.com/article/the_reality_of_film_thom_anderson_on_los_angeles_plays_itself. Accessed 4 June 2013.

Everett, Wendy (2004) *Terence Davies*. Manchester: Manchester University Press.

Everett, Wendy and Axel Goodbody (eds) (2005) *Revisiting Space: Space and Place in European Cinema*. Bern: Peter Land.

Fallon, Bernard (2009) 'Between Beauty and Truth', in Terence Davies, *Of Time and the City* [DVD]. London: British Film Institute.

Ferro, Marc (1988) *Cinema and History*. Detroit, MI: Wayne State University Press.

Fisher, Mark (2010) 'English Pastoral', *Sight & Sound*, 20, 11, 22–4.

Fitzmaurice, Tony (2001) 'Film and Urban Societies in a Global Context', in Mark Shiel and Tony Fitzmaurice (eds) *Cinema and the City: Film and Urban Societies in Global Context*. Oxford: Blackwell, 19–30.

Floyd, Nigel (1988) 'A Pebble in the Pool & Ships like Magic', *Monthly Film Bulletin*, 657, 295–6.

Folgar de la Calle, José María, Xurxo González and Jaime Pena (eds) (2004) *Manoel de Oliveira*. Santiago de Compostela: Universidade de Santiago de Compostela.

Font, Domènec (2002) *Paisajes de la Modernidad. Cine europeo 1960–1980*. Barcelona: Ediciones Paidós.

Foucault, Michel (1984) *The History of Sexuality, Vol. 3. The Care of the Self*. New York, NY: Random House.

_____ (1988) 'Technologies of the Self', in Luther H. Martin, Huck Gutman and Patrick H. Hutton (eds) *Technologies of the Self: A Seminar with Michel Foucault*. Cambridge, MA: MIT Press, 16–49.

Galdini, Rossana (2005) 'Urban Regeneration Process: The Case of Genoa, an Example of Integrated Urban Development Approach', Paper presented at the 45th Congress of the European Regional Science Association, Vrije Universiteit Amsterdam, 23-27 August: http://www-sre.wu-wien.ac.at/ersa/ersaconfs/ersa05/papers/426.pdf. Accessed 3 December 2012.

Gandy, Matthew (2009) 'Of Time and the City', in Terence Davies, *Of Time and the City* [DVD]. London: British Film Institute.

García, Constantino and Manuel González González (eds) (1997) *Diccionario da Real Academia Galega*. A Coruña/Vigo: Real Academia Galega/Edicións Xerais/Editorial Galaxia.

García López, Sonia (2009) 'All That is Solid Melts into Air', in Josetxo Cerdán, Gonzalo de Pedro and Ana Herrera (eds) *Signal Fires: The Cinema of Jem Cohen*. Pamplona: Gobierno de Navarra, INAAC, 84–103.

García Vázquez, Carlos (2004) *Ciudad Hojaldre. Visiones urbanas del siglo XXI*. Barcelona: Editorial Gustavo Gili.

_____ (2011) *Antípolis. El desvanecimiento de lo urbano en el Cinturón del Sol*. Barcelona: Editorial Gustavo Gili.

Gaughan, Martin (2003) 'Ruttmann's Berlin: Filming in a 'Hollow Space'', in Mark Shiel and Tony Fitzmaurice (eds) *Cinema and the City: Film and Urban Societies in Global Context*. Oxford: Blackwell, 41–57.

Gebhard, David and Robert Winter (1977) *The Guide to Architecture in Los Angeles and Southern California*. Santa Barbara, CA: Peregrine Smith.

Gilbey, Ryan (2008) 'The Mersey Sound', *Sight & Sound*, 18, 11, 45–6.

Gold, John R. and Stephen V. Ward (1997) 'Of Plans and Planners: Documentary Film and the Challenge of the Urban Future, 1935–52', in David B. Clarke (ed.) *The Cinematic City*. New York, NY: Routledge, 59–82.

González, Xurxo (2004) 'As paisaxes do tempo en Manoel de Oliveira', in Folgar de la Calle, José María, Xurxo González and Jaime Pena (eds) *Manoel de Oliveira*. Santiago de Compostela: Universidade de Santiago de Compostela, 33–77.

_____ (2012) 'O Sebastianismo de Manoel de Oliveira', *Acto de Primavera*, 11 December; http://actodeprimavera.blogaliza.org/2012/12/11/el-sebastianismo-de-manoel-de-oliveira/. Accessed 17 December 2012.

González Zymla, Herbert (2011) 'El encuentro de los tres vivos y los tres muertos', *Revista Digital de Iconografía Medieval*, 3, 6, 51–82.

Gorostiza, Jorge (2011) 'Edificios reinterpretados', *Cahiers du cinéma. España*, 45, xviii–xix.

Grant, Barry Keith and Jim Hillier (2009) *100 Documentary Films*. London: Palgrave Macmillan.

Gray, David (2011) 'The *Exiles*, Angels Flight and Downtown Los Angeles' Commemorative Spaces: A Walking Tour', Paper presented on 12 March at the SCMS Conference held in New Orleans.

Grilo, João Mário (2006) *O cinema da não-ilusão. Historias para o cinema português*. Lisboa: Livros Horizonte.

Halberstam, David (1979) *The Powers that Be*. New York, NY: Knopf.

Halfyard, Kurt (2007) 'Guy Maddin talks *My Winnipeg*, self-mythologizing, psychological honesty, and even *The Host*', *Twitch*, 2 October 2; http://twitchfilm. net/interviews/2007/10/guy-maddin-talks-up-my-winnipeg-self-mythologizing-pyschological-honesty-an.php. Accessed 8 June 2011.

Hall, Stuart (1989) 'Cultural Identity and Cinematic Representation', *Framework*, 36, 68–81.

Hallam, Julia (2010a) '"City of Change and Challenge": The Cine-Societies' Response to the Redevelopment of Liverpool in the 1960s', in Richard Koeck and Les Roberts (eds) *The City and the Moving Image: Urban Projections*. New York, NY: Palgrave Macmillan, 69–87.

____ (2010b) 'Film, space and place: researching a city in film', *New Review of Film and Television Studies*, 8, 3, 277–96.

Halter, Ed (2009) 'Through the Mirror of Lost Time', in Josetxo Cerdán, Gonzalo de Pedro and Ana Herrera (eds) *Signal Fires: The Cinema of Jem Cohen*. Pamplona: Gobierno de Navarra, INAAC, 224–7.

Harrison, Bennett (1988) *The Great U-Turn: Corporate Restructuring and the Polarizing of America*. New York, NY: Basic Books.

Harvey, David (1989) *The Condition of Postmodernity*. Oxford/Cambridge, MA: Basil Blackwell.

Hay, James (1997) 'Piecing Together What Remains of the Cinematic City', in David B. Clarke (ed.) *The Cinematic City*. New York, NY: Routledge, 209–29.

Hewison, Robert (1987) *The Heritage Industry: Britain in a Climate of Decline*. London: Methuen.

Hight, Craig (2008) 'Mockumentary: A Call to Play', in Thomas Austin and Wilma De Jong (eds) *Rethinking Documentary: New Perspectives, New Practices*. Maidenhead: Open University Press, 204–16.

Higuinen, Erwan and Olivier Joyard (2005) 'Los Ángeles', in Thierry Jousse and Thierry Paquot (dir.) *La ville au cinéma. Encyclopédie*. Paris: Cahiers du cinéma. 449–57.

Hueso, Ángel Luis (1998) *El cine y el siglo XX*. Barcelona: Editorial Ariel.

Iglesias, Eulàlia (2008) 'Of *Time and the City*. Return to Liverpool', in Quim Casas (ed.) *Terence Davies: The Sounds of Memory*. Donostia: Festival Internacional de Cine de Donostia-San Sebastián/Filmoteca Vasca, 279–83.

Ingersoll, Richard (2006) *Sprawltown*. New York, NY: Princeton Architectural Press.

Jacobson, Harlan (1989) 'Michael & Me', *Film Comment*, 25, 6, 16–26.

James, David E. (2005) *The Most Typical Avant-garde: History and Geography of Minor Cinemas in Los Angeles*. Berkeley, CA: University of California Press.

Jameson, Fredric (1991) *Postmodernism, or, the Cultural Logic of Late Capitalism*. Durham, NC: Duke University Press.

Jelavich, Peter (2001) 'The City Vanishes: Piel Jutzi's Berlin Alexanderplatz', in Mark Shiel and Tony Fitzmaurice (eds) *Cinema and the City: Film and Urban Societies in Global Context*. Oxford: Blackwell, 58–79.

Jordan, Jennifer (2003) 'Collective Memory and Locality in Global Cities', in Linda Krause and Patrice Petro (eds) *Global Cities: Cinema, Architecture, and Urbanism in a Digital Age*. New Brunswick, NJ: Rutgers University Press, 31–48.

Jousse, Thierry and Thierry Paquot (dir.) (2005) *La ville au cinéma. Encyclopédie.* Paris: Cahiers du cinéma.

Joyce, James ([1922] 1967) *Ulysses*. London: The Bodley Head.

Kael, Pauline (1990) 'The Current Cinema: Melodrama / Cartoon / Mess', *New Yorker*, 8 January, 90–3.

Keiller, Patrick (1994) 'The Visible Surface', *Sight & Sound*, 4, 11, 35.

Kellner, Douglas (2010) 'Michael Moore and the Aesthetic and Politics of Contemporary Documentary Film', in Matthew H. Bernstein (ed.) *Michael Moore: Filmmaker, Newsmaker, Cultural Icon*. Ann Arbor, MI: University of Michigan Press, 79–104.

Kinder, Marsha (2003) 'Tracing the Decay of Fiction: Encounters with a Film by Pat O'Neill', in Jeffrey Shaw and Peter Weibel (eds) *Future Cinema: The Cinematic Imaginary after Film*. Cambridge, MA: MIT Press, 356–57.

Knabb, Ken (ed.) (1981) *Situationist International Anthology*. Berkeley, CA: Bureau of Public Secrets.

Koeck, Richard (2010) 'Cine-Montage: The Spatial Editing of Cities', in Richard Koeck and Les Roberts (eds) *The City and the Moving Image: Urban Projections*. New York, NY: Palgrave Macmillan, 208–21.

Koeck, Richard and Les Roberts (eds) (2010) *The City and the Moving Image: Urban Projections*. New York, NY: Palgrave Macmillan.

Koolhaas, Rem (2002) 'Junkspace', *October*, 100, 175–90.

Koolhaas, Rem and Bruce Mau (1995) *S, M, L, XL*. New York, NY/Rotterdam: Monacelli Press/010.

Koresky, Michael (2009) 'A Belgian in New York', in Jason Altman and Heather Shaw (prod.) *The New York Films: La Chambre, Hotel Monterrey & News from Home* [DVD]. New York, NY: Criterion Collection.

Kovacsics, Violeta (2011) 'Entrevista Guy Maddin. La lógica de los sueños', *Cahiers du cinéma. España*, 46, 80–1.

Krause, Linda and Patrice Petro (eds) (2003) *Global Cities: Cinema, Architecture, and*

Urbanism in a Digital Age. New Brunswick, NJ: Rutgers University Press.

Lagny, Michèle (1992) *De l'Histoire du Cinéma. Méthode historique et historie du cinéma*. Paris: Armand Colin Éditeur.

Lahera, Covadonga G. (2008) 'My Winnipeg. El cineasta que surgió del frío', *Blogs & Docs*, 3 April; http://www.blogsandocs.com/?p=103. Accessed 8 June 2011.

Landsberg, Allison (2004) *Prosthetic Memory: The Transformation of American Remembrance in the Age of Mass Culture*. New York, NY: Columbia University Press.

Lane, Jim (2002) *The Autobiographical Documentary in America*. Madison, WI: University of Wisconsin Press.

Lapsley, Rob (1997) 'Mainly in Cities and at Night: Some Notes on Cities and Film', in David B. Clarke (ed.) *The Cinematic City*. New York, NY: Routledge, 186–208.

Lasch, Christopher (1979) *The Culture of Narcissism: American Life in an Age of Diminishing Expectations*. New York, NY: W. W. Norton.

Lebas, Elizabeth (2007) 'Glasgow's Progress: The Films of Glasgow Corporation 1938–1978', *Film Studies*, 10, 34–53.

Lebow, Alisa (ed.) (2012) *The Cinema of Me: The Self and Subjectivity in First Person Documentary*. London/New York, NY: Wallflower Press.

Lefebvre, Henri (1991) *The Production of Space*. Oxford/Cambridge, MA: Basil Blackwell.

Lejeune, Philippe (1989) *On Autobiography*. Minneapolis, MN: University of Minnesota Press.

____ (2008) 'Cine y autobiografía, problemas de vocabulario', in Gregorio Martín Gutiérrez (ed.) *Cineastas frente al espejo*. Madrid: T&B Editores, 13–26.

Lerup, Lars (2000) *After the City*. Cambridge, MA: MIT Press.

Lipovetsky, Gilles (1986) *La era del vacío. Ensayos sobre el individualismo contemporáneo*. Barcelona: Editorial Anagrama.

Lipovetsky, Gilles and Jean Serroy (2009) *La pantalla global. Cultura mediática y cine en la era hipermoderna*. Barcelona: Editorial Anagrama.

Longstreet, Stephen (1977) *All Star Cast: An Anecdotal History of Los Angeles*. New York, NY: Thomas Y. Crowell.

Lynch, Kevin (1960) *The Image of the City*. Cambridge, MA: MIT Press.

Lynch, Kevin and Michael Southworth (1990) *Wasting Away, An Exploration of Waste: What It Is, How it Happens, Why We Fear It, How to Do It Well*. San Francisco, CA: Sierra Club Books.

MacDonald, Scott (1992) *A Critical Cinema 2. Interviews with Independent Filmmakers*. Berkeley, CA: University of California Press.

____ (2006) *A Critical Cinema 5. Interviews with Independent Filmmakers*. Berkeley, CA: University of California Press.

Machen, Arthur (1924) *The London Adventure, or the Art of Wandering*. London: Martin Secker.

Margulies, Ivone (1996) *Chantal Akerman's Hyperrealist Everyday*. Durham, NC:

Duke University Press.

Martin, Adrian (2010) 'The Documentary Temptation', in Antonio Weinrichter (ed.) *Doc: Documentarism in the 21st Century*. Donostia-San Sebastián: Festival Internacional de Cine de Donostia-San Sebastián/Filmoteca Vasca, 377–88.

Martín Gutiérrez, Gregorio (2010) 'Filming One's Own Shadow', in Antonio Weinrichter (ed.) *Doc: Documentarism in the 21st Century*. Donostia-San Sebastián: Festival Internacional de Cine de Donostia-San Sebastián/Filmoteca Vasca, 370–7.

Marx, Leo (1964) *The Machine in the Garden: Technology and the Pastoral Ideal in America*. New York, NY: Oxford University Press.

Mazierska, Ewa and Laura Rascaroli (2003) *From Moscow to Madrid: Postmodern Cities, European Cinema*. London: I.B. Tauris.

McArthur, Colin (1997) 'Chinese Boxes and Russian Dolls: Tracking the Elusive Cinematic City', in David B. Clarke (ed.) *The Cinematic City*. New York, NY: Routledge, 19–45.

McWilliams, Carey (1946) *Southern California: An Island on the Land*. Salt Lake City, UT: Gibbs Smith.

Mennel, Barbara (2008) *Cities and Cinema*. New York, NY: Routledge.

Minh-ha, Trinh T. (1993) 'The Totalizing Quest of Meaning', in Michael Renov (ed.) *Theorizing Documentary*. New York, NY: Routledge, 90–107.

Muñoz, Francesc (2010) *Urbanalización, Paisajes comunes, lugares globales*. Barcelona: Editorial Gustavo Gili.

Muñoz Fernández, Horacio (2011) 'Eses mestres que nos gustaría ter. Pedagoxía da imaxe: Straub-Huillet / Benning / Godard', *A Cuarta Parede*, 7, December 10; http://www.acuartaparede.com/pedagoxia-straub-huillet-benning-godard/. Accessed 16 October 2013.

____ (2013) 'Sobre a obra paisaxística de Lois Patiño', *A Cuarta Parede*, 17, 18 September; http://www.acuartaparede.com/obra-paisaxistica-lois-patino/. Accessed 24 October 2013.

Nancy, Jean-Luc (2000) *Being Singular Plural*. Stanford, CA: Stanford University Press.

Nichols, Bill (1991) *Representing Reality*. Bloomington, IN: Indiana University Press.

____ (1993) "Getting to Know You…': Knowledge, Power, and the Body', in Michael Renov (ed.) *Theorizing Documentary*. New York, NY: Routledge, 174–91.

____ (2001) *Introduction to Documentary*. Bloomington, IN: Indiana Univerity Press.

Niney, François (dir.) (1994) *Visions urbaines: villes d'Europe a l'ecran*. Paris: Centre Georges Pompidou.

Nora, Pierre (ed.) (1996) *Realms of Memory: Rethinking the French Past*. New York, NY: Columbia University Press.

Ocampo Failla, Pablo (2002) *Periferias: La Heterotopia del No-Lugar*. Santiago de

Chile: Ediciones A + C.

Oroz, Elena and Iván G. Ambruñeiras (2010) 'The Politics of Reality: The Reconfiguration of Public Space and Historical Territory through Contemporary North American Documentary', in Antonio Weinrichter (ed.) *Doc: Documentarism in the 21st Century*. Donostia-San Sebastián: Festival Internacional de Cine de Donostia-San Sebastián/Filmoteca Vasca, 321–36.

Ortega, María Luisa (2007) *Espejos rotos. Aproximaciones al documental norteamericano contemporáneo*. Madrid: Ocho y Medio.

Orvell, Miles ([1995] 2010) 'Documentary Film and the Power of Interrogation: *American Dream* and *Roger & Me*', in Matthew H. Bernstein (ed.) *Michael Moore: Filmmaker, Newsmaker, Cultural Icon*. Ann Arbor, MI: University of Michigan Press, 127–40.

Orwell, George (1948) *Nineteen Eighty-Four*. London: Secker and Warburg.

Pennant, Thomas (1801) *A Journey from London to the Isle of Wight*. London: Edward Harding.

Penz, François and Andong Lu (eds) (2011) *Urban Cinematics: Understanding Urban Phenomena Through the Moving Image*. Bristol: Intellect.

Pichler, Barbara (2007) 'An Iconography of the Midwest. *8 ½ X 11* (1974) to *Grand Opera* (1979)', in Barbara Pichler and Claudia Slanar (eds) *James Benning*. Vienna: Austrian Film Museum, 21–45.

Pichler, Barbara and Claudia Slanar (eds) (2007) *James Benning*. Vienna: Austrian Film Museum.

Pizarro, Rafael (2005) *Suburbanization of the Mind: The Hollywood Urban Imaginarium and the Rise of American Suburbia in the Colombian Caribbean*. Los Angeles, CA: University of Southern California.

Plant, Sadie (1992) *The Most Radical Gesture: Situationist International in a Postmodern Age*. London: Routledge.

Plantinga, Carl (1997) *Rhetoric and Representation in Nonfiction Film*. Cambridge: Cambridge University Press.

Plath, Nils (2007) 'On Future Arrivals of Container Drivers. Five Brief Comments on One Image from James Benning's *California Trilogy*, expanded', in Barbara Pichler and Claudia Slanar (eds) *James Benning*. Vienna: Austrian Film Museum, 193–209.

Pope, Albert (1996) *Ladders*. Houston, TX: Princenton Architectural Press.

Quintana, Àngel (2010) 'An Oasis in the Middle of the Desert: Non-fiction and Creation in Spanish Cinema', in Antonio Weinrichter (ed.) *Doc: Documentarism in the 21st Century*. Donostia-San Sebastián: Festival Internacional de Cine de Donostia-San Sebastián/Filmoteca Vasca, 291–305.

Rascaroli, Laura (2009) *The Personal Camera: Subjective Cinema and Essay Film*. London/New York, NY: Wallflower Press.

Rattingan, Terence (1952) *The Deep Blue Sea*. London: Hamish Hamilton.

Renov, Michael (ed.) (1993) *Theorizing Documentary*. New York, NY: Routledge.

____ (2004) *The Subject of Documentary*. Minneapolis, MN: University of Minnesota Press.

Reviriego, Carlos (2008) 'Entrevista con Terence Davies. Combates de la memoria', *Cahiers du cinéma. España*, 15, 80–3.

Reviriego, Carlos and Jara Yáñez (2008) 'Entrevista Jem Cohen. El 'punk' como tradición', *Cahiers du cinéma. España*, Special Issue, 5, 17–18.

Ribas, Daniel (2012) 'Thom Andersen. Uma lição de história / A history lesson', in Daniel Ribas and Mário Micaelo (eds.) *Puro Cinema: Curtas Vila do Conde, 20 Anos Depois*. Vila do Conde: Curtas Metragens CRL, 88–95

Rizzo, Sergio (2010) 'The Left's Biggest Star: Michael Moore as Commercial Author', in Matthew H. Bernstein (ed.) *Michael Moore: Filmmaker, Newsmaker, Cultural Icon*. Ann Arbor, MI: University of Michigan Press, 27–50.

Roberts, Les (2010) 'Projecting Place: Location Mapping, Consumption, and Cinematographic Tourism', in Richard Koeck and Les Roberts (eds) *The City and the Moving Image: Urban Projections*. New York, NY: Palgrave Macmillan, 183–204.

Robinson, Ian (2010) 'Searching for the City: Cinema and the Critique of Urban Space in the Films of Keiller, Cohen and Steinmetz and Chanan', in Richard Koeck and Les Roberts (eds) *The City and the Moving Image: Urban Projections*. New York, NY: Palgrave Macmillan, 114–24.

Rochberg-Halton, Eugene (1986) *Meaning and Modernity: Social Theory in the Pragmatic Attitude*. Chicago, IL: University of Chicago Press.

Rodríguez Ortega, Vicente (2012) *La ciudad global en el cine contemporáneo. Una perspectiva transnacional*. Santander: Shangrila Textos Aparte.

Romney, Jonathan (2010) 'In Search of Lost Time', *Sight & Sound*, 20, 2), 43–4.

Rosenbaum, Jonathan (2003a) 'Discovering Yasuzo Masumura: Reflections on Work in Progress', in Jonathan Rosenbaum and Adrian Martin (eds) *Movie Mutations: The Changing Face of World Cinephilia*. London: British Film Institute, 61–73.

____ (2003b) 'Ghost of Hollywood', *Chicago Reader*, 30 May; <http://www.jona-thanrosenbaum.com/?p=6140>. Accessed 20 April 2013.

Rosenstone, Robert A. (1995) *Visions of the Past: The Challenge of Film to Our Idea of History*. Cambridge, MA: Harvard University Press.

Rotzler, Willy (1961) *Die Begegnung der drei Lebenden und der drei Toten*. Winterthur: P. G. Keller.

Russell, Catherine (1999) *Experimental Ethnography: The Work of Film in the Age of Video*. Durham, NC: Duke University Press.

Russell, Patrick (2007) *100 British Documentaries*. London: British Film Institute.

Sales, Michelle (2011) *Em busca de um novo cinema português*. Covilhã: Livros Labcom.

Sand, Shlomo (2005) *El siglo XX en pantalla - Cien años a través del cine*. Barcelona: Crítica.

Sandeno, Robin M. (1997) *The Legend of the Three Living and the Three Dead: The*

Development of the Macabre in Late Medieval England. Corvallis, OR: Oregon State University.

Sanders, James (2001) *Celluloid Skyline: New York and the Movies*. London: Bloomsbury.

Sandusky, Sharon (1992) 'The Archeology of Redemption: Toward Archival Film', *Millennium Film Journal*, 26, 2–25.

Sassen, Saskia (1991) *The Global City: New York, London, Tokyo*. Princeton, NJ: Princeton University Press.

____ (2007) *A Sociology of Globalization*. New York, NY: W. W. Norton.

Saunders, Dave (2010) *Documentary*. London: Routledge.

Scheibler, Susan (1993) 'Constantly Performing the Documentary: The Seductive Promise of *Lightning Over Water*', in Michael Renov (ed.) *Theorizing Documentary*. New York, NY: Routledge, 135–50

Seguin, Denis (2008) 'Winnipeg mon amour. *Guy Maddin's hometown homage*', *The Walrus*, 5, 1; http://www.walrusmagazine.com/articles/2008.02-film-guy-maddin-my-winnipeg. Accessed 3 March 2013.

Shand, Ryan (2010) 'Visions of Community: The Postwar Housing Problem in Sponsored and Amateur Films', in Richard Koeck and Les Roberts (eds) *The City and the Moving Image: Urban Projections*. New York, NY: Palgrave Macmillan, 50–68.

Shaw, Deborah (2013) 'Deconstructing and reconstructing transnational cinema', in Stephanie Dennison (ed.) *Interrogating the Transnational in Hispanic Film*. Woodbridge: Tamesis, 47–65.

Shiel, Mark (2001) 'Cinema and the City in History and Theory', in Mark Shiel and Tony Fitzmaurice (eds) *Cinema and the City: Film and Urban Societies in Global Context*. Oxford: Blackwell, 1–18.

Shiel, Mark and Tony Fitzmaurice (eds) (2001) *Cinema and the City: Film and Urban Societies in Global Context*. Oxford: Blackwell.

____ (2003) *Screening the City*. London: Verso.

Siamandas, George (2007) 'Winnipeg's Historic Bridges', The Winnipeg Time Machine, 5 February; http://winnipegtimemachine.blogspot.com.es/2007/02/winnipegs-historic-bridges.html. Accessed 5 March 2013.

Silver, Alain and James Ursini (2005) *L.A. Noir: The City as a Character*. Santa Monica, CA: Santa Monica Press.

Simmel, Georg (1971 [1903]) 'The Metropolis and Mental Life', in Donald N. Levine (ed.) *Georg Simmel on Sociability and Social Forms*. Chicago, IL: Chicago University Press.

Sitney, P. Adams. (2000 [1969]) 'Structural Film', in P. Adams Sitney (ed.) *The Film Culture Reader*. New York, NY: Cooper Square Press, 326–48.

Sjöberg, Patrick (2011) 'I Am Here, or, The Art of Getting Lost: Patrick Keiller and the New City Symphony', in François Penz and Andong Lu (eds) *Urban Cinematics: Understanding Urban Phenomena Through the Moving Image*. Bristol: Intellect,

43–51.

Slanar, Claudia (2007) 'Landscape, History and Romantic Allusions. El Valley Centro (1999) to RR (2007)', in Barbara Pichler and Claudia Slanar (eds) *James Benning*. Vienna: Austrian Film Museum, 169–80.

Smith, Leon (1988) *Following the Comedy Trail: A Guide to Laurel and Hardy and Our Gang Film Locations*. Lewes: Pomegranate Press.

____ (1993) *Hollywood Goes on Location*. Lewes: Pomegranate Press.

Soja, Edward (1989) *Postmodern Geographies: The Reassertion of Space in Critical Social Theory*. London/New York, NY: Verso.

____ (1996) *Thirdspace: Journeys to Los Ángeles and Other Real-and-Imagined Places*. Oxford: Basil Blackwell.

____ (2000) *Postmetropolis: Critical Studies of Cities and Regions*. Oxford: Basil Blackwell.

Solomons, Gabriel (ed.) (2011) *World Film Locations: Los Angeles*. Bristol: Intellect.

Sorkin, Michael (ed.) (1992) *Variations on a Theme Park: The New American City and the End of Public Space*. New York, NY: Hill and Wang.

Sorlin, Pierre (1980) *The Film in History: Restaging the Past*. Oxford: Basil Blackwell.

____ (1991) *European Cinemas, European Societies*. London: Routledge.

____ (2005) 'Urban Space in European Cinema', in Wendy Everett and Axel Goodbody (eds) *Revisiting Space: Space and Place in European Cinema*. Bern: Peter Land, 25–36.

Stenger, Josh (2001) 'Return to Oz: The Hollywood Redevelopment Project, or Film History as Urban Renewal', in Mark Shiel and Tony Fitzmaurice (eds) *Cinema and the City: Film and Urban Societies in Global Context*. Oxford: Blackwell, 59–72.

Stevenson, Robert Louis (1886) *The Strange Case of Dr Jekyll and Mr Hyde*. London: Longmans, Green & Co.

Stewart, Justin (2012) 'Director in Residence: The Films of Tony Buba at Anthology Film Archives', *Film Comment*, 6 June 2012; http://filmcomment.com/entry/director-in-residence-the-films-of-tony-buba-at-anthology-film-archives. Accessed 29 October 2012.

Storper, Michael (1997) *The Regional World: Territorial Development in a Global Economy*. London: Routledge.

Strathausen, Carsten (2003) 'Uncanny Spaces: The City in Ruttmann and Vertov', in Mark Shiel and Tony Fitzmaurice (eds) *Cinema and the City: Film and Urban Societies in Global Context*. Oxford: Blackwell, 15–40.

Studlar, Gaylyn (2010) 'Class, Gender, Race and Masculine Masquerade in the Documentaries of Michael Moore', in Matthew H. Bernstein (ed.) *Michael Moore: Filmmaker, Newsmaker, Cultural Icon*. Ann Arbor, MI: University of Michigan Press, 51–76.

Toole, John Kennedy (1989) *The Neon Bible*. New York, NY: Grove Press.

Touraine, Alain (1969) *The Post-Industrial Society, Tomorrow's Social History:*

Classes, Conflicts and Culture in the Programmed Society. New York, NY: Random House.

Traquino, Marta (2010) *A construção do lugar pela arte contemporânea*. Ribeirão: Editorial Humus.

Tzara, Tristan ([1924] 2011) *Seven Dada Manifestos and Lampisteries*. Richmond: Oneworld Classics.

Villarmea Álvarez, Iván (2006) 'O cinema de Jacques Tati e o proceso de urbanización na Franza de posguerra (1945–1973)', *Murguía: Revista Galega de Historia*, 11, 105–25.

____ (2008) 'Saudades chabolistas. A imaxe da periferia marxinal francesa en *Le gone du Châaba*', in J. Evans Pim, B. Kristensen and O. Crespo Argibay (eds) *Entre os outros e nós. Estudos literarios e culturais*. Santiago de Compostela/A Coruña: Fundación Araguaney/Universidad Internacional Menéndez Pelayo, 97–122.

____ (2009) 'La imagen de la periferia marginal de Barcelona en *Los Tarantos*', in J. Pérez Perucha, F. J. Gómez Tarín and A. Rubio Alcover (eds) *Olas rotas. El cine español de los sesenta y las rupturas de la modernidad*. Madrid: Ediciones del Imán, AEHC, 255–71.

____ (2010a) 'Representaciones cinematográficas de la Barcelona marginal: del poblado del Somorrostro en *Los Tarantos* a la renovación del Raval en *De Nens* y *En construcción*', in M. Doppelbauer and K. Sartingen (eds) *De la zarzuela al cine. Los medios de comunicación populares y su traducción de la voz marginal*. Munich: Martin Meidenbauer Verlagbuchhandlung, 139–58.

____ (2010b) 'Urban Transformations in China through the Cinema of the Sixth Generation', *Zhongguo Yanjiu. Revista de Estudos Chineses*, 6, 169–200.

____ (2013) 'El autorretrato urbano de Manoel de Oliveira: *Porto da Minha Infância*', in Marta Álvarez (ed.) *Imágenes conscientes*. Binges: Éditions Orbis Tertius: 181–97.

____ (2014a) 'El hallazgo de una nueva ficción documental. La Trilogía de Fontainhas de Pedro Costa', in H. Muñoz Fernández and I. Villarmea Álvarez (eds) *Jugar con la memoria. El cine portugués en el siglo XXI*. Santander: Shangrila, 20–49.

____ (2014b) 'El paisajismo observacional de James Benning. La representación de Los Ángeles en *Los* (2000)', *Fotocinema: Scientific Journal of Cinema & Photography*, 9, 35–63.

____ (2014c) 'Cinema as Testimony and Discourse for History: Film Cityscapes in Autobiographical Documentaries', *Revue LISA/LISA e-journal*, 7, 1; http://lisa. revues.org/5579. Accessed 17 July 2014.

____ (2014d) 'Urban Self-Portraits and Places of Memory: The Case of Terence Davies's *Of Time and the City*', in A. López-Varela Azcárate (ed.) *Cityscapes: World Cities and Their Cultural Industries*. Champaign, IL: Common Ground, 40–53.

Virilio, Paul ([1984] 1997) 'The Overexposed City', in Neil Leach (ed.) *Rethinking Architecture: A Reader in Cultural Theory*. London: Routledge, 381–90.

Walpole, Horace (1764) *The Castle of Otranto*. London: William Bathoe.

Walsh, Maria (2004) 'Intervals of Inner Flight: Chantal Akerman's *News from Home*', *Screen*, 45, 3, 190–205.

Wasielewski, Amanda (2009) 'Psychogeographic Mapping Through Film: Chantal Akerman's *News from Home* and Patrick Keiller's *London*'; http://www.amandawasielewski.com/writing/2008%20-%20PAPER1-PsychogeographicFilm.pdf. Accessed 6 December 2013.

Watkins, Alfred ([1925] 1970) *The Old Straight Track*. London: Abacus.

Webber, Andrew and Emma Wilson (eds) (2008) *Cities in Transition: The Moving Image and the Modern Metropolis*. London/New York, NY: Wallflower Press.

Weihsmann, Helmut (1997) 'The City in Twilight: Charting the Genre of the 'City Film' 1990–1930', in François Penz and Maureen Thomas (eds) *Cinema and Arquitecture*. London: British Film Institute, 8–27.

Weinrichter, Antonio (2004) *Desvíos de lo Real. El Cine de No Ficción*. Madrid: T&B Editores.

_____ (2007) 'Festivales, museos y otras orillas del audiovisual. Notas sobre el estado de salud del documental y la ficción', in Domènec Font and Carlos Losilla (eds) *Derivas del cine europeo contemporáneo*. Valencia: Institut Valencia de Cinematografia, 69–79.

_____ (2008) '*Distant Voices, Still Lives*. Times of a Return', in Quim Casas (ed.) *Terence Davies: The Sounds of Memory*. Donostia: Festival Internacional de Cine de Donostia-San Sebastián/Filmoteca Vasca, 253–9.

_____ (ed.) (2010) *Doc: Documentarism in the 21st Century*. Donostia-San Sebastián: Festival Internacional de Cine de Donostia-San Sebastián/Filmoteca Vasca.

Wharton, Edith (1905) *The House of Mirth*. New York, NY: Charles Scribner's Sons.

Wilkerson, Travis (2007) 'Incomplete Notes on the Character of the New Cinema', *Kino!*; http://www.e-kino.si/2007/no-1/blazinice/incomplete-notes-on-the-character-of-the-new-cinema (accessed 11 July 2013).

Winston, Brian (1993) 'The Documentary Film as Scientific Inscription', in Michael Renov (ed.) *Theorizing Documentary*. New York, NY: Routledge, 37–57.

Wrigley, Richard (ed.) (2008) *Cinematic Rome*. Leicester: Troubadour.

Yáñez Murillo, Manuel (2008) 'Interview with Terence Davies', in Quim Casas (ed.) *Terence Davies: The Sounds of Memory*. Donostia: Festival Internacional de Cine de Donostia-San Sebastián/Filmoteca Vasca, 220–47.

_____ (2009) 'Mirar y escuchar. Entrevista James Benning', *Cahiers du cinéma. España*, 22, 80–1.

Yates, Robert (1994) 'London', *Sight & Sound*, 4, 6, 54–5.

Yu, Eui-Young (1992) 'We Saw Our Dreams Burned for No Reason', *Los Angeles Times*, 5 March; http://articles.latimes.com/1992-05-05/local/me-1255_1_hardwork. Accessed 29 May 2013.

Z., Julie (2012) 'Rase-dock et cherche-mémoire: Tanner et les hommes du port de Gênes', *Article 11*, 6, 25 April; http://www.article11.info/?Rase-dock-et-cherche-memoire. Accessed 29 November 2012.

Zunzunegui, Santos (2004) 'Non reconciliado. Manoel de Oliveira no labirinto do cinematógrafo', in Folgar de la Calle, José María, Xurxo González and Jaime Pena (eds) *Manoel de Oliveira*. Santiago de Compostela: Universidade de Santiago de Compostela, 79–90.

Zyrd, Michael (2003) 'Found-footage film as discursive metahistory: Craig Baldwin's *Tribulation 99*', *The Moving Image*, 3, 2, 40–61.

Index